The Spectacular Favela

CALIFORNIA SERIES IN PUBLIC ANTHROPOLOGY

The California Series in Public Anthropology emphasizes the anthropologist's role as an engaged intellectual. It continues anthropology's commitment to being an ethnographic witness, to describing, in human terms, how life is lived beyond the borders of many readers' experiences. But it also adds a commitment, through ethnography, to reframing the terms of public debate—transforming received, accepted understandings of social issues with new insights, new framings.

Series Editor: Robert Borofsky (Hawaii Pacific University)

Contributing Editors: Philippe Bourgois (University of Pennsylvania), Paul Farmer (Partners In Health), Alex Hinton (Rutgers University), Carolyn Nordstrom (University of Notre Dame), and Nancy Scheper-Hughes (UC Berkeley)

University of California Press Editor: Naomi Schneider

The Spectacular Favela

VIOLENCE IN MODERN BRAZIL

Erika Robb Larkins

UNIVERSITY OF CALIFORNIA PRESS

University of California Press, one of the most distinguished university presses in the United States, enriches lives around the world by advancing scholarship in the humanities, social sciences, and natural sciences. Its activities are supported by the UC Press Foundation and by philanthropic contributions from individuals and institutions. For more information, visit www.ucpress.edu.

University of California Press
Oakland, California

Library of Congress Cataloging-in-Publication Data

Robb Larkins, Erika, 1977– author.
    The spectacular favela : violence in modern Brazil / Erika Robb Larkins.
        pages   cm. — (California series in public anthropology ; 32)
        Includes bibliographical references and index.
    ISBN 978-0-520-28276-6 (cloth : alk. paper) — ISBN 978-0-520-28277-3 (pbk. : alk. paper) — ISBN 978-0-520-95869-2 (ebook)
    1. Violence—Social aspects—Brazil—Rio de Janeiro.   2. Rocinha (Rio de Janeiro, Brazil)—Social conditions.   3. Violence—Economic aspects—Brazil—Rio de Janeiro.   4. Rocinha (Rio de Janeiro, Brazil)—Economic conditions.   I. Title.   II. Series: California series in public anthropology ; 32.
    HN290.R5R63 2015
    303.60981—dc23

                                    2015003806

Manufactured in the United States of America

24   23   22   21   20   19   18   17   16   15
10   9   8   7   6   5   4   3   2   1

In keeping with a commitment to support environmentally responsible and sustainable printing practices, UC Press has printed this book on Natures Natural, a fiber that contains 30% post-consumer waste and meets the minimum requirements of ANSI/NISO Z39.48–1992 (R 1997) (*Permanence of Paper*).

To Michael, without whom none of this would be possible

Contents

Acknowledgments

A book is never the work of a single person, and I would like to acknowledge those who have helped make this project possible. I owe a great deal to the residents of Rocinha. Preserving their anonymity prevents me from naming them in full. D, R, TL, I, W, S, J, J, I, B, H, F, I, O, R, R, and P all contributed in major ways, graciously sharing their time with me. Each welcomed me into their home and openly talked about hard subjects with a levity and humility that continues to inspire me. I am also appreciative for the assistance of several tour owners who allowed me to accompany their tours.

The initial research for this book was funded by a National Science Foundation Doctoral Dissertation Improvement Grant, a Public Humanities Fellowship from the Center for the Humanities at the University of Wisconsin, a Scott Kloeck Jenson Fellowship, a research grant from the University of Wisconsin's Division of International Studies, and a Tinker-Nave short-term research grant from the Center for Latin American, Caribbean, and Iberian Studies Program at the University of Wisconsin. At the University of Oklahoma (OU), research support has come from the Research Council Faculty Investment Program, a Research Council Junior Faculty Fellowship, and a College of International Studies

Faculty Research Fellowship and Support Grant. The Social Science Research Council's Drugs, Security, and Democracy (SSRC-DSD) Fellowship supported the final stages of research and writing. I am especially appreciative of the feedback from my SSRC-DSD peers and mentors, in particular, Taniele Rui, Arthur Trindade, and Joana Vargas. Desmond Arias has been a source of ongoing support and feedback.

This work has benefited from the insight of many colleagues, mentors, and friends. Emiko Ohnuki-Tierney has been an inspiring mentor. Larry Nesper and Jo Ellen Fair provided useful critiques and encouragement. Special gratitude goes to Jim Sweet. Sverker Finnström and Carolyn Nordstrom were rays of light at a crucial moment.

Thank you to Alessandro Angelini, Sarah Besky, Chelsea Chapman, Krista Coulson, Sangeeta Desai, Kristen Dowell, Sarah Grant, Robin Grier, Miriam Gross, Lisa Jackson, Katie Lindstrom, Dan Mains, Olivia McCarty, Amanda Minks, Alex Nading, Jerusha Ogden, Alise Osis, Sara Osten, Emily Rook-Koepsel, Mitchell Smith, Paul Sneed, Justin Strock, Danielle Theriault, Theresa Whitehead, and Kent Wisniewski, all of whom have provided helpful input, laughter, and an important sense of perspective at different points along the way. I am particularly grateful to Tricia Olsen and John Fowler for afternoons at Arpoador and to Noah Theriault for his amazing ability to find the right word.

This book would have been far less readable without the assistance of my fabulous OU faculty writing group: Dan Emery, Lisa Foster, Sarah Ellis, Ellen Rubenstein, Ronnie Grinberg, and Andreana Pritchard. The encouragement of Kimberly Marshall has kept me sane and productive. Students Nick Aguilera, Kelli Silver, and Paul Vieth also provided assistance.

At the University of California Press, I am particularly grateful to Naomi Schneider, Ally Power, Rose Vekony, and Sheila Berg. Thank you also to Janet Keller for reading an early draft of the manuscript and to the anonymous reviewers for their constructive criticism. Any and all of the book's shortcomings are, of course, my own.

I acknowledge the journal *Law and Social Inquiry*, the American Bar Foundation, and Wiley Blackwell for allowing the reproduction of short excerpts of my previously published article "Performances of Police Legitimacy in Rio's Hyper-Favela" that appear in chapter 2.

I gratefully acknowledge the support of the Robb, Larkins, and Lebowitz families. My mother, Anna, introduced me to Brazil. She supported me always, nurtured my sense of adventure, and taught me "happy history." Thank you, *mamãe*, for raising me to believe that we should not only be outraged at the injustices of the world, but that we should do something to change them.

My children were born during the research and writing of this book, and much of it was typed with one hand while I held a baby in the other. Denali Rio and Annabel Gladys, thank you for sharing your young lives with the gestation of this project and for inspiring me to dream of a different Rio, and of a different favela.

Three of the people who were most central to the realization of this book did not live to see it in print. My mentor and graduate adviser Neil Whitehead entered the spirit world as I completed the first draft. A source of never-ending intellectual stimulation, I could not have asked for a better guide. Neil, you are alive in the conversations I have with you as I write.

My two closest friends and collaborators in Rocinha, D and L, both died young, not from bullets, but from treatable illnesses. They died poor and in pain, with substandard medical care. I am angry that it had to end this way. I miss them terribly.

Finally, to Michael. Thank you for sharing in the joys and sorrows of the favela, for all the sacrifices it took to arrive here, and for making my life so full and happy.

. . . . .

The author's proceeds from the sale of this book will be donated to Rocinha NGOs.

Introduction

November 2008. I was in the kitchen making breakfast when I heard the sound of Peter's voice from below the window. Peter was a twenty-something Brazilian American who volunteered at one of the nonprofit organizations where I worked and who rented the apartment downstairs.[1] I poked my head out and looked up and down the narrow alley of the favela.[2] Peter stood below the window, hands gesturing rapidly, trying to explain something to Chucky, one of the narco-soldiers who regularly patrolled the neighborhood in the favela of Rocinha where I had been living and conducting fieldwork.

The heavily armed traffickers who controlled my neighborhood were mostly polite guys. They would say "Good morning" and "Good evening" to me in the street like any other favela resident. If I made eye contact when I passed them, sometimes they would want to chat, or check out whatever song I had playing on my iPod, or practice their English on me. Then there were guys like Chucky. Taking his nickname from the murderous doll of 1980s American horror movie fame, Chucky was intimidating. His eyes were usually just a bit too glazed and bloodshot, his voice a little too raspy, and he took his job very seriously. So when Chucky started yelling "Liar!" at Peter and jabbing him in the chest with his M16 for punctuation, I knew there was trouble.

The weekly *baile funk* had taken place the night before, and Chucky had clearly not been to bed yet.[3] He wore a black Kevlar vest that read "Polícia Civil" (Civil Police) across the back in yellow letters. Lots of traffickers wore these, especially when there were rumors of impending police invasions. They were probably purchased from a police uniform store in the *centro* or maybe from police themselves. Chucky was shirtless under the heavy vest. It was late summer, and even in the morning it was already hot. His shorts had a garish neon pattern of naked ladies printed on them, and on his feet he wore a pair of Havaianas, the now-chic rubber sandals exported worldwide. An enormous gold medallion that spelled out C-H-U-C-K-Y in block letters hung from his neck, its diamonds catching the sunlight.

As soon as Chucky started yelling, the alley became strangely quiet, as though someone had pressed the mute button on what was usually a cacophony of sounds—children laughing and yelling, the latest Christian rock hit, the bass-pumping rhythm of funk, or the sound of the pressure cooker with lunch's beans cooking. The alley itself, where people usually sat outside on their stoops talking and where kids kicked soccer balls up and down the stairs, had emptied. Neighbors fled the street to watch the unfolding spectacle from the safety of their windowsills or doorways.

Though Peter had lived in the house for several months and the neighbors certainly knew him, no one came out to intervene. They knew better than to get involved. So it was just me, descending the stairs, then entering the street, apologizing profusely to Chucky, saying that Peter had surely not intended any disrespect (for whatever he had done; it wasn't clear yet) and suggesting that we all walk down to the *boca de fumo* (neighborhood drug-selling spot; lit., "mouth of smoke"), where cooler and more powerful heads would probably prevail. I knew that they were not likely to shoot a foreign woman. Popular belief held that if anything happened to someone like me the U.S. military would bomb the favela into oblivion—and I was more than happy to affirm this myth if it meant an extra layer of safety.

Afterward, competing versions of what had happened circulated in the gossip mill that always exhaustively covered such events in the favela. Details aside, what was clear was that Peter had taken some unauthorized video footage in the neighborhood. A friend from the States was in town and had his eye on a certain souvenir—a video of the inner alleyways of

Peter's favela neighborhood that would show his American friends just how crazy and cool his trip to Rio had been. Back home, the spectacular favela sequence in the wildly popular video game *Modern Warfare 2* had introduced a new audience to the favela and its traffickers. Evidence of one's own foray into trafficker territory was an edgy and status-conferring souvenir.

In our neighborhood of Rocinha, however, photography was more or less prohibited since the *dono do morro* (favela drug boss; lit., "owner of the hill") lived a few doors up from our apartment building. The scores of armed narco-soldiers who provided him with protection patrolled the area at all hours of the day and night and were constantly on the lookout for risks to his security. Photographs or, worse yet, video could provide the police with important information for their endless but ineffective pursuit of the boss, who was then among the most wanted men in Rio. Peter knew this just as well as I did. In fact, the "no photography" rule was one of the first things that our landlord routinely mentioned to the foreigners to whom he rented his apartments in order to supplement his family's modest income. With increased tourist interest in the favela—and with the proliferation of foreign nonprofit organizations and their sets of young volunteers—he had no shortage of renters.

Regardless of the danger, Peter acquiesced to his friend's desire and had taken a motorcycle taxi up the hill and down our alley, hanging off the back with his video camera outstretched to capture the chaotic favela landscape. Chucky had seen the camera when he passed by and had given chase. Realizing he was going to be in trouble, Peter had hidden the camera in his backpack, and when I first heard the argument he was trying to tell Chucky that there was no camera, that Chucky must have been seeing things. After all, it was the latest high-definition model, and Peter didn't want to give it up. It was a pretty stupid move, everyone later agreed. Did he want to die over a camera, even a fancy one that probably cost as much as a typical resident's yearly income?

Chucky wasn't willing to accept my apologies, but he was willing to walk down to the boca. The boca manager, who was called Rambo, acted his part as the de facto police chief and told Chucky to go and get some sleep. Faced with Rambo's chilly professionalism and intimidating arsenal of shiny new guns, Peter took the camera out of his backpack sheepishly, an act that made Chucky furious since it confirmed that he had been lied to. Again, he began to scream "Liar!" at the top of his lungs, as he did for weeks afterward every time he walked by the apartment where we lived. Rambo checked the image, deleted it, and sent Peter home with a warning that left him wobbly in the knees.

Peter and his friend spent a few hours laying low inside his apartment, after which he packed a suitcase and went off on a weeklong vacation to Buzios, the nicest and most expensive beach resort town in the region. The neighbors and I stayed behind, wondering whether Chucky would indeed cool it, cringing every time he walked by hurling insults at our front gate.

A few months later, I saw Chucky again. This time it was in the newspaper, which featured pictures of his lifeless body and shiny medallions. He was killed during a police invasion in the favela. Residents said that Chucky had been caught smoking crack, and since the drug boss had prohibited its use in the favela, he had to be punished. After all, he was getting more erratic and aggressive, behavior that could undermine resident tolerance of the narco-regime and potentially attract unwanted police attention. In order to get rid of the problem, the dono allegedly told the police where Chucky lived. During the next police invasion, he was left as a sacrifice to appease the cops, the spectacle of his corpse a prize for the legions of photographers who habitually chronicled police actions in the favela. Chucky was one of twenty-six traffickers who died during my first year of residence in Rocinha.[4]

This ethnographic anecdote, drawn from my 2008–10 fieldwork, captures many of the dynamics of violence and power I studied: trafficker governance, spectacular violence, the commodification of the trafficker image by foreigners, and the mediation of this fascination through souvenir images or sensational news reporting. When talking about violence, favela residents frequently sat back, sighed, and said, "É complicado." "It's complicated." The complexity to which they refer lies precisely in these overlapping and intertwined forms of violence. Traffickers like Chucky, who control extremely lucrative cocaine, marijuana, and weapons markets, act as the de facto government in the favela. Police appear only sporadically, and policing is far more brutal and oppressive than it is effective in improving security or protecting citizens. Given the absence of a more ample and fully developed state presence, traffickers maintain their own version of law and order, legitimating their authority through flashy displays of weapons and wealth (particularly potent symbols in the overall context of poverty in the favela) and by imitating the detached competence of an imagined state bureaucracy.

While violence is most overtly present as armed conflict, the favela population also suffers as a result of asymmetrical configurations of capital that constitute and perpetuate inequality. The overwhelming majority of residents experience what scholars call "structural violence," the unequal structures of society that prevent some people from meeting their basic human needs—for food, shelter, safety, health care, happiness, or a chance for a better life (Scheper-Hughes 1993; Scheper-Hughes and Bourgois 2004; Farmer 2004).

Historically, just as today, the favela constitutes an essential (if poor) labor force that enables the functioning of the rest of the city.[5] Yet despite the central contribution of favela residents as honest workers, entire communities have been reduced to places of criminality and trafficking in the wider cultural imaginary.[6] Rio's former governor Sergio Cabral, discussing the high birthrates in Rocinha, even referred to the community as a "factory that makes criminals" (Freire 2007). The power of such "dehumanizing imaginations" (Rozema 2011) both legitimates police violence against favela residents and, in the eyes of the public, justifies the inferior place of favela residents in the social and class hierarchy.

Class asymmetries are not just local or even national in nature. Rocinha is the site of a booming market in favela tours, during which foreigners observe favela life. Tourist interest and the pervasive presence of visitors like Peter and his friend attest to the imbrication of local crime and poverty with the desire for experiences of the favela on the part of more affluent members of the global North (including foreign anthropologists, a point I take up shortly and in the conclusion). Thus favela violence not only consumes the bodies of traffickers and cops in a profit-driven "war" on drugs while keeping the poor marginalized; it has also become a commercially viable by-product of an ongoing capitalist enterprise.

This book offers an ethnographic account of how entangled forms of violence, spectacle, and commodification become essential forces shaping everyday social relations in Rocinha, the most (in)famous favela in Latin America. Long considered one of the most violent favelas in Rio, Rocinha is also well known for its size: it is one of the largest favelas in Brazil. Given these factors and its location between two of the wealthiest neighborhoods in Rio, the community occupies a unique place in the public eye and is a particularly evocative site from which to observe the spectacular nature of drug war violence.

HISTORIES OF VIOLENCE

The story of favela violence in Rio doesn't begin with Chucky but rather with his ancestors stepping off a boat from Africa at the start of the transatlantic slave trade. Brazilian society, from its inception, was built on inequality between the Portuguese planter class that wielded economic and political power and the enslaved blacks whose labor constructed the emerging nation (Schwartz 1986; Skidmore 1999). The ideologies and practices of these formative colonial years have had lasting effects on Brazilian society. In a practical sense, they established a pattern of land and property ownership privileging a minority elite over the masses. In an ideological sense, they introduced long-lasting racial and class hierarchies that continue to inform prejudice and marginalization in Brazilian society today (Alves 2014; Fry 2000, 2005–6; Telles 2006; Sheriff 2001; Skidmore 1974; Needell 1995; Vargas 2004; Winant 1992; Perry 2013).[7] Colonial rule, during which dominance over slaves was maintained through a culture of terror centered on public punishment, also established a pattern whereby violence and spectacle would become central to the emergence and evolution of Brazilian society and its class and racial relationships.

When Brazil abolished slavery in 1888, it was the last country in the world to do so. Many newly emancipated Africans and their descendants moved to cities like Rio in search of work and a better life.[8] In the early decades of the twentieth century, Rio's urban population more than tripled in size (Fischer 2008: 17). New arrivals found little available housing and eventually settled in the hillside areas above the city center.[9] These areas came to be called favelas after one such squatter community was established on land given to soldiers returning from the Canudos War (1893–97). The freed men and women who settled there were eventually joined by waves of migrants from the country's interior, fleeing rural

Figure 1. Osvaldo Cruz, Rio's public health minister (1903–9) pictured here "sanitizing" the favela, represented by a grotesque head. A diseased underclass, visually represented in this image, required forcible sanitation and vaccination. This imagined threat of physical contagion has since merged with a social contagion of criminality epitomized by the figure of the narco-trafficker. Image from *Oswaldo Cruz: Monumenta Histórica*, Brasiliensia documenta 6 (São Paulo, 1971), 1:CLXXXVIII.

poverty in search of opportunity.[10] Together, former slaves and their descendants and other rural migrants formed a new urban working class, which (literally) constructed the bourgeoning metropolis.

From its inception, the favela was imagined as a hindrance to the development of the otherwise modern, "marvelous" city (see Fischer 2014: 9–67). Early incarnations of what would come to be known as the "favela problem" were centered on the bodies of residents, imagined to be diseased (fig. 1),[11] and on the unruly architecture of the informal settlements.

As the Brazilian elite strove to create a modern city in the image of Paris, urban development "was given force through the ambitious use of legal instruments such as building codes, zoning restrictions, and sanitary regulations—that would showcase Rio's beauty and sophistication and leave no crevices of unregulated growth" (Fischer 2008: 17).[12] Favelas, as informal, urban interstices beyond governmental control, were on the receiving end of state repression. In a few cases, they were tolerated because they provided labor for much of the city's service industry and housed the domestic workers of the elite.[13] More frequently, however, communities were torn down, their residents left homeless or forcibly relocated to Rio's outskirts.[14]

If one thinks of favela violence not so much as a series of events but as a kind of ongoing social project, Brazil's military dictatorship (1964–85) also changed the shape of the "favela problem" in important ways. Favela residents, who were largely considered by the junta to be apolitical, were not the primary target of right-wing generals and their death squads (Green 2003; Skidmore 1988).[15] Still, the routinization of everyday state violence against the civilian population during this period came to have important consequences for later favela policy.

In its campaigns against alleged "subversives," the military dictatorship depended on an ideology that Giorgio Agamben calls "the state of exception." For Agamben, the state of exception is a condition under which normal principles of law and order are superseded by exceptional acts or displays of force in the name of protecting citizens. The desire for a continental Brazilian modernity that produced the antifavela campaigns of the early years of the republic gave way to the military regime's exception-based abuses leveraged against supposed subversives.[16] Subversives were painted as enemies of the state. Their humanity thus degraded, they became a kind of nonperson stripped of citizenship, a condition Agamben calls "bare life" (1998: 11). As designated enemies of the military regime, it was far easier for the state to "legitimately" execute or disappear them.

Exception as a paradigm of government did not die out with the end of the dictatorship.[17] Rather, the state of exception continued, fueled by urgency on various, constantly shifting fronts. In the twilight of the dictatorship, oppressive tactics deployed in the war against political subversives were superimposed on the fight against organized crime (Pinheiro 1991; Huggins 1991). Even as Brazil's abertura, or return to democracy, brought a climate of hope to the favela (Gay 2009; Pandolfi and Grynszpan 2003), another state of exception was being created and disseminated.

Under this new state of exception, Rio de Janeiro was imagined as a "divided city," comprising two (supposedly) different places: the formal city and the favela (Arias 2006: 3–14; Penglase 2009).[18] Traffickers were reenvisioned not merely as common criminals, but as enemy combatants at war with the state, the aspiring leaders of supposedly parallel polities based in the city's favelas.[19] Residents became either staunch supporters of the narco-state or powerless, terrified bystanders. The government's response was to ramp up the practice of violent policing. As periodic police incursions into trafficker territory generated additional conflict, the process created a feedback loop reifying the exceptional favela as the natural dwelling place of violent enemies of state and society. This has produced what Vargas and Alves (2010: 613) describe as a highly racialized "relational citizenship" or "non-citizenship."

Despite the many flaws in this narrative of the war against the drug traffic in Rio, many of which I address in this book, this rendition of the state of exception has been absolutely central to the growth of favela violence. As such, all favela residents inhabit a form of bare life and are subject to routine violence both in physical form from police and, perhaps more significantly, in structural form. With favelas marked as enemy territory, the state is recused from providing quality essential services (sanitation, health care, education to its most marginalized populations, even if this group makes up more than one quarter of the population of the city as a whole. Thus, rather than being exceptional, violence has become a normal and accepted element of favela life.

The more time I spent in Rocinha, the clearer these dynamics of exclusion and exception became. For most of the residents I knew, the goal was most certainly not to be part of an imagined parallel trafficker state. Nor was it to form another society external to the larger Brazilian one. People longed to enter the economic, political, and cultural mainstream, even if that mainstream was built on ideologies that excluded them (see Holston 2008). Neither did the traffickers I spoke with, the supposed leaders of this allegedly parallel entity, wish to overthrow the system. Rather, they sought to use the sale of illegal drugs to buy the consumer goods they envisioned as necessary to enter a larger Brazil beyond the favela.[20] Thus, while in its initial tenuous moments of inception the narco-traffic might have possessed a sort of revolutionary spark, traffickers now are a product of current neoliberal times, where free market consumption is itself a political ideology.[21]

Today we can see yet another variety of the state of exception at work in Rio, brought on by the World Cup (2014) and the Olympic Games (2016) hosted by the city. What I call the "Olympic exception" demonstrates how states of exception can also be tied to global image making as Brazil prepares to enter the world stage. The favela is again a target. A new spectacle of favela integration and social progress masks the fact that poor communities are once again being torn down and residents pushed to the outskirts. Zoning and building laws are being rewritten, gentrification has become a weapon of removal, informal economies are being formalized and residents taxed. Thus, as the Olympic exception shows, bare life does not always result in torture or death but can authorize all sorts of other activities as well.

What all of this suggests is that the favela and the state remain locked in a symbiotic, interdependent relationship, wherein the ongoing threat of the favela is used to justify exceptional action that meets certain government development goals. Traffickers, meanwhile, continue to cite government failures to adequately improve the lives of residents, particularly in the security realm, as evidence for why they are the better choice for favela governance.

CULTURES OF VIOLENCE

The symbiosis of the state-favela relationship reveals something important about the nature of violence more generally. Intuitively, we often think of violence as the breakdown or absence of reason, deconstructive and destroying. Conversely, much recent work in anthropology has challenged this commonsense notion, demonstrating instead that violence is not a lack of order but itself an important force in the constitution of social institutions and cultural codes (Whitehead 2004; Bourgois 1995; Scheper-Hughes and Bourgois 2004; Ferguson and Whitehead 1992; Comaroff and Comaroff 2006; Sluka 1999; Whitehead and Finnström et al. 2013; Goldstein 2004, 2012).[22] Here I argue that violence is locally constituted and meaningful. This approach necessitates an ethnography of favela violence that unpacks and delineates the features of this violence through the lens of those who experience it by asking about the setting in which it occurs (the where) and its temporal properties (the when).

As other scholars have noted, the "when" of war has undergone a global shift, moving from something with a clear start and finish to a more drawn out, temporally disjunctive affair (Nordstrom 2004; Whitehead and Finnström 2013; Masco 2014).[23] The state of exception in the favela, in historical or contemporary form, does not produce continuous violent clashes. For example, in Rocinha, police and traffickers (or traffickers vs. other traffickers, as the case may be) do not actively engage with one another on every single day of the year. There are long gaps between actual confrontations. Despite the intermittent character of surges in armed confrontations between the state and the narco-regime, the time in between is replete with waiting, never knowing when armed violence is coming. The terror of these spaces of waiting, even as the fear they hold is often normalized by residents, must also be taken as part of the experience of violence. In its discontinuous and "low-intensity" incarnation, war has become, to quote Michael Hardt and Antonio Negri, a "permanent social relation" (2004: 14).[24]

The permanence of war in Rio's favelas takes the form of ongoing militarization.[25] Militarization renders favela war both quotidian and commodifiable. It is organized violence expressed in the form of commodities, both tangible and representational. As favela violence has become increasingly intertwined with commodification, it has expanded the conceptual scope of the conflict. The battlegrounds of Rocinha's war extend beyond the brick and mortar of the favela, beyond the frontier where favela meets formal city. They are also located along the pathways forged by the commodities that fuel the conflict such as cocaine, guns, and Kevlar. They are present in the gated condominiums protected by private security guards and in the bullet-proof cars, to name just a few of the by-products of the larger economy of fear in the urban Brazilian cityscape (Caldeira 2001). Insecurity is a permanent feature of life that is addressed or shored up by militarization. In this context, security regimes such as gated condominiums or shopping mall armed guards are unremarkable features of a militarized cityscape (Graham 2010) for a population that is all too worried about being robbed, assaulted, or hit by a stray bullet.

War is further embodied in numerous commodity forms beyond those directly deployed by armed actors (Nordstrom 2004; Allen 2013; Price 2013; Masco 2014). As even virtual spaces of infotainment and leisure are increasingly militarized, one finds that "violence circulates through all of us, as news, movies, games, photos, fashion and even smartphone applications" (Whitehead and Finnström 2013: 7). Indeed, images of Rocinha's war zone are found in locally and globally produced games, toys, and fashion and consumed both within national borders and internationally. The "experience" of war as it is sold to tourists, or represented in ethnographies such as this one, also contributes to the formation of Rocinha's virtual and disembodied war zone. War in the favela has an economic value, one that includes but is not limited to the media and experiential consumer products that trafficker and police violence generates.

Thus, the social relationships that arise from ongoing favela violence have a direct relationship with the market economy. Favela violence, like many other instances of violence globally, maintains productive inequalities necessary to the livelihood of the capitalist system (Hoffman 2011). Here, Marx's writing on the relationship between violence and capital is instructive. What he calls the original accumulation of capital, the initial process of expropriating resources that established capitalist class relations, was only possible through the use of force, particularly during the colonial period.[26] In Brazil, as elsewhere, there is a strong historical link between capitalism and violence, whether armed, structural, or institutional. The brutality of the plantation system enabled a flourishing colonial economy. The authoritarian military regime, while torturing and disappearing citizens, fostered a period of unprecedented economic growth (Haggard 1990: 161–88; Evans 1995; Filho 2010). The pattern is repeated yet again as the mega-event preparation involves tearing down and removing poor communities in order to build FIFA stadiums and Olympic venues.

Contemporary favela violence is directly informed by the ongoing connection between force and capital. David Harvey (2009) expands Marx's ideas about original or primitive accumulation in his writings on "accumulation by dispossession." In his formulation, capitalism, particularly in the age of neoliberalism, always needs a new market, a new group of consumers, something new to privatize and sell.[27] Accumulation by dispossession is at work in the favela in a number of ways: from the ever-expanding contours of the drug market to the branding of the favela and its violence as a commodity for sale to tourists to recent policies that seek to increase favela residents' consumptive capacities.[28] Therefore, while the weapons and material of war in the favela are used in deadly battles between violent actors, they also demarcate the policing of a social order and are the visible tokens of the spectacular order of violence. Automatic weapons do not merely fire rounds of ammunition and armored cars do not merely protect occupants. The presence of these items in plain sight are at once a spectacular form of consumption for their owners, a sign of the social order for residents, and props in the representation of the violent favela for audiences well beyond its borders.[29]

SPECTACLES OF VIOLENCE

Nuances in the nature of favela violence and its links to commodification tend to be masked by its spectacular form. Armed violence in Rocinha is not quiet or silent but performative.[30] Different actors perform violent acts in such a way as to ensure they reach broader audiences; they author violent spectacles. Because performative violence is so spectacular, it diverts attention from the social relationships that enable such violence in the first place. As Guy Debord's (1983) foundational work indicates, spectacles of violence (or of any kind) visually dazzle, occluding the processes that underlie their performance.

Debord's notion of the "society of the spectacle," along with his contemporaries' notions of the "pseudo-image"(Boorstin 1961) and "simulacrum" (Baudrillard 1994), describes forms of commodity production and consumption especially characteristic of late capitalism. According to these authors, the spectacle draws the eye to the dramatic and stunning, legitimating certain forms of political and economic power that create and reinforce social hierarchies. In Rocinha, spectacles of favela violence naturalize war while occluding the fact that present realities are intertwined with historical, economic, and cultural conditions. Any ethnographic exploration of life in the favela, therefore, needs to peel back the layers of spectacle to defetishize the social processes that produce violence, as well

Figure 2. The architectural spectacle of Rocinha from above.
Photograph by Rafaella Cardoso Fotografia.

as to be attentive to the local meanings of violence and the forms of production it takes.

Spectacle in Rocinha occurs across multiple scales and registers. As figure 2 shows, the favela itself, by virtue of its size and scale, is a kind of architectural spectacle. The favela-as-danger-zone represents another level of spectacle constituted largely through mass (and increasingly social) media. Stories about favela crime dominate local and national news coverage in Brazil.[31] A recent quantitative study that examined the frequency of stories about violence in the two main daily newspapers in Rio found that on any given day over 37 percent of the stories published focused on crime (Paiva and Ramos 2005). A large number of popular talk shows such as *Cidade alerta* and Wagner Montes's *Balanço geral* add to the exhaustive coverage. Endless mediated images create the hyperreal, "a real without an origin or reality" (Baudrillard 1994: 1), made up of empty signs, or simulacra, strung together to make a narrative that takes on a life of its own. The prevalence of violent spectacle and its circulation in the media thereby contribute to the formation of a "hyperfavela," where the favela as it is constituted through media is read as reality. The spectacle is not recognized for the construction it is.

The spectacle of the violent favela is also discursively constructed on a more minute level—by *cariocas* (as Rio residents are called) in everyday conversations on the bus, at the beach, or in the bakery. The "talk of crime," as Caldeira has so aptly described quotidian crime-related conversations among São Paulo residents, conflates poverty with criminality. She explains that such talk "feeds a circle in which fear is both dealt with and reproduced, and violence is both counteracted and magnified" (2001: 19). As I observed it, crime discourse is not just the purview of the middle and upper classes but is a key feature of favela sociality as well. Residents might engage in this kind of talk about their own place of residence in times of crisis, but they also habitually discuss favelas other than the one they live in. The *other* favela—over there on the margin of the city, populated by *other* kinds of people and *other* kinds of traffickers—becomes the foil against which one's own favela existence is cast. The talk of crime, whether on the intimate or the mass scale, dehumanizes residents and contributes to "the militarization of urban marginality" (Wacquant 2008: 58).

If the favela is *the* site of violence in the Brazilian cultural imaginary, state spectacle is required to subdue its alleged threat. Again, symbiosis between the favela and the state appears. On the most overt level, the actors in state spectacle are the police who are *"invadindo," "limpando,"* and *"pacificando"* the favela (to use their language).[32] Through performances of power, police invasions give shape to the state, capturing its essence in boots on the ground, armored tanks, and helicopters patrolling the sky. Leading the charge, symbolically if not always literally, is BOPE, the Batalhão de Operações Policiais Especiais (Elite Special Forces). Founded in 1973, BOPE is the direct descendant of the military police death squads deployed against subversives during the dictatorship. Famous for their penchant for extreme violence, they kill with utter impunity and are widely celebrated for their success in raiding favelas and "leaving bodies on the ground," as the lyrics of their squad anthem proclaim.[33]

For their part, favela traffickers employ spectacle through the enactment of highly visible, public performances of violence and power, ranging from the gruesome punishment of those who violate their "laws" to the ritualized flaunting of economic vitality through flamboyant displays of gold, designer clothing, and cash. Trafficker spectacle is repurposed as it is mediated. Media fetishization of trafficker wealth eclipses the fact that the true profit from the illegal drug trade is not in the hands of favela drug lords. The true *bandidos*, as I once heard former Brazilian president Luiz Inácio Lula da Silva suggest to a round of deafening applause from his rapt favela audience, are white-collar criminals who do not live in the excluded space of the favela but luxuriate in their beachfront condominiums. Yet the illegal behaviors of these non-favela-based profiteers are not only tolerated in Brazilian society, but mystified by the continued focus on the "favela problem."

COMMODIFICATION OF VIOLENCE

Through interlocking performances of power on the part of traffickers and the state, spectacular favela violence is implicated in wider political and economic projects that support the business of war and maintain the favela as a place for the enactment of state violence. While commodification is inherent to the form of the spectacle, favela violence is literally for sale. It is produced as a commodity for consumption in both embodied and disembodied forms.

Brazil has always had a cool and exotic global image. Rio de Janeiro in particular, the cradle of samba and replete with unparalleled natural beauty, represents the imagined features of the Brazilian nation to the world. Rio's romantic image was propagated in early media representations such as *Flying Down to Rio* (1933) and *Black Orpheus* (1959), in the soft harmonies of "The Girl from Ipanema," and via stage personae like Carmen Miranda. But this long-standing vision of Rio has changed in the course of the past several decades, transforming in step with the rise in urban violence (Freire-Medeiros 2010). The city's image as a tropical paradise has been supplanted by the more complex one in circulation today, epitomized by the popular film *City of God* (2002), featuring favela poverty, crime, and police-versus-narco violence.

The global imaging of Rio, whether in its old or new incarnation, reflects what Alexander Dent describes as one of the central features of neoliberal governance: "The perceived applicability of branding to almost everything" (2012: 30; cf. Allison 2009; Manning and Uplisashvili 2007; Murtola 2014). If capitalism always requires new markets, it is unsurprising that corporate branding has extended beyond traditional consumer goods to people, cultures, and experiences. Drawing on John Comaroff and Jean Comaroff's work on the commodification of cultural difference, *Ethnicity, Inc.* (2009), I call the newly branded version of a violent Rio that circulates in the global imaginary "Favela, Inc."[34] Favela, Inc. is made up of "media-scapes," including print media, film, television, music, and the Internet and the images and messages they carry (Appadurai 1990: 299). These highly stylized mediascapes offer a vision of what the "talk of crime" or violent "hyperreality" looks like when morphed into an entertainment genre.

The content of Favela, Inc. is not controlled by residents of the favela but is authored, with very few exceptions, by Brazilian and foreign outsiders. The lack of input and participation of the subjects of the media—residents—makes Favela, Inc. especially insidious. It adds additional layers of violence in two registers, one representational—where depictions are sensational and incomplete—and the other structural—wherein the subjects of the media see none of the profit from the circulation of their lives and hardships as a brand. Furthermore, in forming an aesthetic all their own, representations of violence work to map new forms of visual spectacle. From a consumption standpoint, Favela, Inc. offers favela violence as a recreational experience to those beyond the local setting; it allows for disembodied consumption.[35]

The circulation of the commodified, mediated favela also carries important consequences for other kinds of consumption. Favela, Inc. is not just a local commodity but a global one, with a direct relationship to favela tourism. As surprising as it may be, Rocinha is an extremely popular tourist destination, where a variety of companies proffer the embodied consumption of favela violence. The first tours began in 1998.[36] Today official estimates put visitation at around three thousand tourists per week, almost all of whom are foreigners. At the time of my residence, there were seven companies operating in Rocinha, with four major ones leading the majority of the tours. With only a few exceptions, Brazilians who live outside of the favela run the tours and very little of the profit generated goes toward improving conditions in the favela. Outsiders continue to both control the economic benefits of the practice and exercise the right to represent the favela to foreigners. There is a feedback loop between representations of the favela as envisioned in Favela, Inc. and on-the-ground tourist desires for certain types of experiences, indicative of the way in which tourism itself is not "outside of" or "exterior to" larger patterns of recreational consumption but is in fact fundamentally part of consumer participation in larger mediascapes.

Rocinha is a market commodity for tourists in two primary forms. In the first, tourists engage in "adventure tourism," where tour discourse constructs the favela as an off-the-beaten-path, edgy destination and portrays tourists as adventure seekers. In its most extreme manifestations, adventure tourism involves direct engagement with the criminal narco-world of the favela, and tourists unabashedly consume an imagined "gangsta" style through engagement with traffickers and through illicit drug use. The second, more mainstream variety of favela tourism in Rocinha is framed around education and "solidarity" with the poor and marginalized. In this form of visitation, the favela is a social problem for which the state and Brazilian elites are largely to blame. Tourism is couched as a social good, and tourists are treated as the harbingers of progress and awareness. This form of tourism, though less overtly violent, is just as fraught as those tours that openly engage with favela violence and glorify the trafficker lifestyle. Tourists are lauded for practicing a form of activism simply by bearing witness to favela violence, in armed and structural forms. Witnessing not only replaces any real action to mitigate violence, but it also works to mask what is still a highly voyeuristic encounter. In both forms of tourism, there is clear asymmetry of class and power between those who have the money and leisure to go on tour and those in the favela, who have little choice as to whether or not they become objects of the touristic gaze. In sum, tours are *about* violence, and in touring the violent favela, tourists themselves *perpetuate* violence.

After an extensive multiyear branding campaign that painted Brazil as an exotic and passionate place, Rio was selected to host both the 2014 World Cup and the 2016 Summer Olympics. Since then the city has seen a number of changes, both in terms of preparing and upgrading infrastructure and creating polices aimed at favela inclusion. Though framed as "new" and "innovative," many of the supposed transformations are slight variations on long-standing projects or derived from other previously failed ones.

A new government policy called *pacificação* has had the most impact on the favela. Pacification, or peacemaking, perfectly encapsulates the treatment of favelas like Rocinha as places that require police and military intervention to achieve some kind of peace. The policy is an attempt to transform the urban landscape of the city by allegedly improving favela security, which in its current state is incompatible with the modernization and development of Brazil that is symbolized by the awarding of the mega-events to the city. As a project of modernity, pacification goes beyond a simple remaking of security to involve changes in the physical space and local economy of the favela. Pacification subordinates the favela to the state's development goals.

State attempts to pacify the favela have a direct relationship to the continued expansion of global capitalism, since the state at work here is deeply intertwined with corporate interests. Putting the favela under (even nominal) state control allows for local markets to be formalized and services privatized (accumulation by repossession, then dispossession?). Since favela residents' exclusion has had a direct bearing on their ability to act as consumers, their transformation into a new consumer group lies at the heart of the policy of pacification. Pacification and its economic side effects are reincorporating favela residents into the formal market economy, thereby contributing to a growing and celebrated Brazilian middle class called Classe C (Neri 2012).[37]

In Rio today, implementing nominal favela "stability" allows for profitable economic expansion, both inside the favela as services are privatized and outside as increased security enables further foreign investment. In light of this pattern, uneven development here should not be understood as a by-product or a failure of neoliberalism, or of the state, but as an integral component of it (Dent 2012: 31). In this way, the pacificação of the favelas acts as a spatial fix for new iterations of capital driven by the World Cup and the Olympics in the short term and by the discovery of huge oil reserves off Rio's coast in the long term.

Given the imbrication of security and capital, it should come as no surprise that many of pacification's initiatives are being funded by powerful corporations, including Coca-Cola, the Brazilian tobacco giant Souza Cruz, and the notoriously corrupt Brazilian Football Federation (Cândida 2010). When it first began, the pacification program was also heavily subsidized by the then richest man in Brazil, Eike Batista, owner of the second largest oil company in the country. Batista contributed $US10 million to the project before his bankruptcy in 2013. In spite of pacification's link to corporate interests, public debate over the policy has been largely concerned with the alteration of the security landscape to the exclusion of its larger economic implications.[38] The spectacle of pacificação masks chains of profit and the fact that peacemaking here is still a form of militarization.

The reshaping of the geography of places like Rocinha is also bringing about important changes to the wider social landscape of the city. As favelas located near planned mega-sporting events and rich neighborhoods in the central areas are being pacified, a shifting spatial geography of crime has followed. Traffickers have fled to other still-marginal places, starting the process anew. The front lines of the state of exception are expanding beyond Rio proper. This process, however, remains a dynamic and ongoing one. As we await the outcome of Rio's current exception, this ethnography proposes a conceptualization of favela violence that not only emphasizes its performative and spectacular nature, but envisions commodification at its very heart.

ETHNOGRAPHY OF THE SPECTACULAR

To describe spectacle is always in some senses to reproduce it. But, following John MacAloon (2006: 18), to conduct an ethnography of spectacle means to defetishize and reveal the conditions that contribute to its production. The thin line here between critique and reproduction provides a valuable opportunity to question the means and the ends of ethnographic knowledge production, a topic on which I reflect as this book draws to a close. Such questions take on special urgency for research conducted in places like the favela, where violence clearly delineates social relationships. Turning the critical lens upon myself, I must ask how the ethnographic endeavor, and the process of writing about violence, implicates me (and perhaps my readers) in the overall culture of spectacle that I discuss in this book. While it might be easy to see how tourist cameras are motivated by the voyeurism of their gaze, how different really is the process of obtaining anthropological data? Are academic works like this one not complicit in the overarching structures of inequality that make some people on this planet favela residents and others mobile, relatively affluent anthropologists? Is this work just one more contribution to Favela, Inc., keeping the image of the violent favela in circulation through the authoritative voice of a "researcher" and "Western" academic? The answers to these questions, I believe, are important not only for my personal reflection but also for the larger ethnographic enterprise in an era in which violence, unfortunately, infiltrates daily life with ever more frequency.

This book does not purport to be an ethnography of all aspects of life in the favela. It is not about how residents regularly resist violence, nor is it focused on other important elements of their lives, such as family, religion, work, community.[39] My choice to write about violence is not to suggest that the spectacle is the sum of all favela life as it is experienced by each and every resident. It is only one element, among many, that influences the shape and texture of favela life. What this book is, therefore, is an ethnography that seeks to understand how spectacle and commodification are central to the production of violence in a particular place.

I moved to Rocinha in May 2008, after having conducted several preliminary visits. I spent sixteen consecutive months living in the favela and returned again in 2010 and 2011 for three separate two- to three-month visits. I then moved back to Rio for ten months during 2013–14. My long-term engagement with the community, spanning seven years now, has allowed me to capture the transformations and continuities of local dynamics over time. During my initial fieldwork, with the assistance of a local nongovernmental organization (NGO), I was able to rent an apartment from a family who over the course of my residence came to feel very much like my own. Along with contacts at various NGOs throughout Rocinha, they provided valuable insight into the history, culture, and local politics of the favela. Initially working through these networks, I was able to interview residents from all socioeconomic classes and age groups. Many people, recognizing how their own normalization of violence and poverty shapes their perception, realized that I was not accustomed to such violence, and they went out of their way to offer me interpretations and explanations so that I would feel at ease in the favela. By the end of my fieldwork, I had done eighty-five formal, structured interviews with different people and at least three times as many open-ended, more informal interviews and conversations. Subsequent research visits built on this initial data, so that this book has drawn on conversations with hundreds of people and years of shared life in Rocinha.

My experience of residency in Rocinha offered crucial insight on a number of fronts. More times than I can count during the rainy season, I waded home through *becos* (alleyways) flooded with knee-high water and sewage. I commiserated with neighbors about sleepless nights caused by the neighborhood's all night *pagode* party.[40] But I also enjoyed the strong sense of community and spent nights sitting on the stoop, chatting with neighbors and laughing. Indeed, when I lived outside of the favela during the final writing of this book in 2014, I experienced the isolation of "middle-class" condominium living and sorely missed the vibrant social life of the favela.

The house that I lived in during the first part of my fieldwork, as I mentioned in the opening vignette, was located in the heart of the favela's trafficking stronghold, a few houses away from the dono's and therefore a constant target during the sporadic police invasions that occurred over the course of my fieldwork. Though this was accidental—I had not known this was the case when I chose the apartment—residence in this part of the favela placed me in a good position from which to observe, and eventually to interact with, the scores of traffickers who frequented the area. Casual encounters eventually led to conversations, and those conversations led to interviews. I regularly conversed with an ex-trafficker neighbor who had spent over ten years in Rocinha's drug economy. This contact proved an important resource for verifying information and explaining things that others assumed I knew about the history and organization of the drug traffic. I spent a lot of time with several girlfriends of Rocinha's more important traffickers; they too became important sources. Last, I spent nearly thirty hours, stretched over a number of meetings during the latter part of my fieldwork, formally interviewing one particular trafficker, whose story is the focus of the first chapter.

I met this trafficker, Beto, through his girlfriend, who was from the Brazilian middle class and clandestinely visited Beto unbeknownst to her very protective parents. As a kind of cover story for why she was spending time in a favela, she volunteered one morning a week as an English teacher at one of the NGOs where I also taught. She knew about my study and was interested in helping me understand more of the world she was secretly a part of. She opened numerous doors for me, making the task of doing interviews feasible in terms of security since I was introduced by someone who was trusted. In many cases, she accompanied me to interviews.

There was an important gender dynamic underlying my interviews. On the one hand, my gender and my foreignness made me relatively harmless in traffickers' eyes. I was perceived as being simply too ignorant to be a tangible threat of any kind. At the same time that I was deemed relatively harmless, I was also an asset, in that I brought legitimacy and cultural capital to those I interviewed by virtue of my foreignness and educational level. It was consistently framed as an honor to be able to explain one's life and profession to someone from outside, especially to an educated academic.

This was not the case with the police. In stark contrast to the traffickers, the police had a hardness that I found almost impossible to permeate. While traffickers could capitalize on my class status, police were uninterested in conversation. They didn't view me as legitimating their work but as potentially problematic. Furthermore, my own negative and at times frightening experiences with the police—being stopped and questioned, searched and harassed while coming and going from the favela or during police invasions—left me uncomfortable with the idea of spending time with "beat cops" without some form of sponsorship or sanction from someone higher up the ranks of police power.

As a result, data on police, the topic of chapter 2, is drawn primarily from my own participant observation of police raids in Rocinha and in several other favelas in other parts of the city where I spent time. Observations also came from following ongoing newspaper and tabloid documentation and discussing this material with Rocinha residents. During the pacification process, I was able to speak informally to one BOPE officer and to several newly appointed pacification officers. In general, however, I was reticent to spend too much time talking with or attempting to interview police. Especially given my residence in the favela and my unfolding relationships with traffickers or former traffickers, it just didn't seem wise, lest I be mistaken for some kind of police spy. I was always cognizant of the fact that while I could leave the favela if things got complicated, my friends and neighbors and those who collaborated with me could not. As a consequence, the voices of the police themselves are regretfully absent from the narrative here, but this is the result of my belief and conscious decision that I could not simultaneously be a favela resident and an ethnographer of the police without compromising my safety or that of others.[41]

For the last few months of my 2008–10 fieldwork, I moved from my original residence to the other side of the favela, leaving behind the security woes of one area for the problems of another. The second neigh-borhood was widely considered the poorest and least desirable place to live in Rocinha. I chose it because it was located on the main tourist route and residence there provided me with the opportunity to observe the daily movements of tourists and to better understand residents' responses to favela tourism. It also gave me an important sense of the range of the qual-ity of life within Rocinha and alerted me to the prejudices and the hierar-chies of class and race that exist within the favela.[42]

I gathered data for the tourism portions of this study while accompany-ing tours with three of the major companies and two of the smaller ones at least once a week, sometimes more, for the duration of my fieldwork.[43] I went on hundreds of tours. I also taught English at several of the NGOs that tourists regularly visited, allowing me to experience tourism from the other side as well. As a foreign volunteer, I often found myself co-opted into the tour narrative. In all of these venues, I spoke with hundreds of tourists and favela residents regarding tourism, on and off the tour route, and interviewed twelve guides. I also worked as a receptionist at a hostel outside of the favela, where I interviewed tourists about their expectations and subsequent experiences in the favela. Toward the end of my fieldwork, a favela-based NGO asked me to help host groups of short-term volun-teers (*voluntourists*). This gave me a chance to try my hand at explicitly crafting my own version of what the favela was about for visitors and then to see how they interpreted, and at times challenged, my representations to match their own expectations and desires.

During the early stages of writing this book, Rocinha was "pacified." In the aftermath, I spent six weeks in 2012 conducting interviews about the process in Rocinha and in three other newly pacified favelas in the city. I returned again for ten months of intensive fieldwork in 2013–14, when I observed firsthand the ongoing complexities of pacification, particularly in regard to police malfeasance and intrafaction conflict. Indeed, my 2013–14 fieldwork coincided with a period of almost daily incidents of gunfire between trafficker rivals and police in the favela, a rise in petty crime, and a general climate of insecurity that stood in stark contrast to the earlier period of study.

In every aspect of this project, my residence in the favela, which was both a challenge and a privilege, was essential. While I feel a personal and professional obligation to write critically about the culture of violence in Rocinha, I also feel that it is important to insist, even while doing so, that life in the favela is so much more than the violence that infiltrates the everyday. People live out meaningful (and very quotidian) lives there, just like people anywhere else. As Nordstrom and Robben point out, as much as conducting research in areas plagued by violence induces "existential shock" for fieldworkers, so also is it an "equally powerful experience to encounter the creative and the hopeful in conditions of violence" (1995: 14). If my readers do not find abundant instances of creativity and hope in these pages, it is because of the focus I have chosen and not because they weren't a central feature of life as I experienced it in the favela. They were. And this has provided me with an ongoing source of inspiration to address the larger conditions of oppression and violence in the face of which hope stubbornly persists.

ORGANIZATION OF THE BOOK

Chapter 1 presents new ethnographic work on what I call the "trafficker state," from the perspective of traffickers themselves. I start with a brief historical and organizational background of the traffic and move to a discussion of how traffickers consolidate power in the context of the favela. I examine the quotidian mechanisms of trafficker governance, in which discourses of legitimacy are forged through interwoven spectacles of violence and wealth. In exploring the manufacture of forms of trafficker "capital"—meant here in the broadest sense—I highlight the fact that while the trafficker state often appears much like an inversion of larger carioca society, it is in fact deeply intertwined with mainstream Brazilian and global cultures.

In the second chapter, I show how police, as representatives of a larger "penal state" operating in the favela, enact and embody violent spectacle and contribute to the commodification of security. The primary actors here are two different kinds of police: the corrupt state agents who contribute directly to the vitality of the narco-trafficking economy by selling traffickers guns and taking payoffs for protection and the efficient and "modern" Batalhão de Operações Policiais Especiais (BOPE), the Elite Special Forces unit, which uses performative violence to reorder the chaos created by their colleagues in uniform. In the overall climate of insecurity in Rio, BOPE has itself become a commodity, and the squad capitalizes on this status by authoring a multiplatform integrated marketing campaign of violence and state terror, live on Facebook and Twitter.

In chapter 3 I examine the emergence of the favela as a global brand. The favela-as-commodity is consumed in two distinct but interrelated ways: in disembodied fashion, through media, and in embodied fashion, through tourism. This chapter focuses on the former, chapter 4 on the latter. Earlier tropes of the favela as a romanticized place of joy and sensuality as well as recent depictions of it as a decaying, though sexy, urban war zone entail forms of representational violence that have concrete consequences for the people who live out their real lives under the shadow of these imagined media realities. Both the new trafficker fetish and earlier representations of the poor as happy and carefree are indicative of the development of the favela as a profitable and marketable global brand. Through analysis of intersecting media forms, I show how the aesthetics and discourses of what I call Favela, Inc. obscure the larger historical, economic, and political factors that contribute to the reality they purport to represent.

The fourth chapter examines favela tourism as a form of violence. Tours in Rocinha involve a wide variety of actors configured in asymmetrical relations of power. Operated by those outside the community, favela tourism commodifies suffering and ultimately serves to further entrench stereotypes regarding favela residents. But favela tours also illuminate global inequalities between the tourist and the toured. Tourism is thus a key site for examining how violence is sold as affective recreation and how spectator-buyers, company sellers, and favela objects are aligned according to their position in a global class hierarchy. I argue that, through mimetic engagement with a glorified trafficking lifestyle or through the thinly veiled voyeurism of "witnessing," tourists are implicated in the ongoing production of favela violence and complicit in its reproduction.

Chapter 5 examines the impact of the World Cup and the Olympic Games on Rocinha, where the lead-up to these mega-events has involved a campaign of pacification. Though the program has been widely celebrated as an innovative and effective response to the challenges associated with maintaining order in Rio's favelas, my reading of Rocinha's pacification shows that the process involves far more than a simple shift in security and represents a larger project to remake the favela. I argue that "peacemaking" does not break with the tradition of violent spectacle as the modus operandi of favela governance but continues and extends extant practice through a ramped up process of economic speculation backed by militarized police power.

Finally, in the conclusion, I discuss the wider theoretical implications of my research for anthropology, particularly for the study of violence, and for Brazilian studies more generally. These considerations offer an opportunity to reflect on the ethnographic project in which I have engaged and to address issues of academic complicity.

1 The Narco-Traffic

Beto is wearing a hooded sweatshirt with the words "Thug Life" (in English) printed on it.[1] A small caliber handgun is tucked into his shorts. His bodyguards stand a few feet away sharing a large joint and admiring the panoramic view of the city before them. The lights are coming on and twinkling. "Turn on your tape recorder," he says. "I am happy to get a chance to talk, to communicate with the outside world."[2]

At twenty-eight, Beto was considered a veteran. Responsible for Rocinha's security, he oversaw the punishment of those who violated the rules for proper conduct as determined by his boss, the *dono*. This meant that he had been intimately involved with torture and murder, topics we never directly discussed. Once he told me, with a pained look, that he had done horrible things, worse than what I could imagine. Things he wasn't proud of. I didn't ask for details. In his capacity as a security agent, he was also a bodyguard for traffickers above him in the ranks, trained the soldiers under him, and worked to establish gang strategy vis-à-vis the police. Sometimes he handled police payoffs, delivering large sums of money to dirty cops. His girlfriend, Katia, eyes wide with excitement, recounted how she had once rolled naked on a bed covered with R$30,000 (about US$15,000) before it made its way to police coffers.

Tall and dark-skinned, Beto at first didn't look much different from other favela residents his age. However, his perpetual smile showed off the braces that adorned his teeth. Close examination showed other signs of wealth out of reach for most ordinary people in the community. The diamond studs he wore in both ears and his designer clothes were real, procured from boutiques in the city. Unlike most residents, Beto would never buy knock-offs from the open-air market that sprawled across the entrance to the favela.

Before entering the traffic, he had spent six years in the Special Forces wing of the military, learning from the government how to kill. One year of military service is officially obligatory for men in Brazil, but most people do not serve. Those who do are often from the lower classes and see the military as a career option. Beto took this path. He stayed on past the first year, advancing through the ranks until he left to join the traffic.

Beto's military background points to entanglements between the state and its supposed enemies, the "marginal" elements of society. In a striking example of what Jane Schneider and Peter Schneider call the *intreeccio,* or intertwining of the Mafia and the state, Beto symbolizes "that vast gray area where it is impossible to determine where one leaves off and the other begins" (Schneider and Schneider 2003: 34). Beto is at once soldier, cop, and criminal. Violent laborers, like Beto, traverse the dividing lines between legitimate and illegitimate modes of production, where they perform more or less the same sort of "work," as Beto describes it, for different bosses. Reminiscing about his military service, he explained, "I learned a lot of stuff: to shoot, to survive, to work on guns. I came out of the army like Rambo. I knew a ton. And what was I going to do with this? Who could I teach it to? I had all this knowledge inside of me and I wanted to see if all the stuff I learned about war would actually work. I already knew what my methods would be. It just took someone to say, 'Hey dude, come work with me and do these things!'"

And that's what happened. Beto was not from Rocinha but from a neighboring favela controlled by the same gang.[3] He knew someone who knew someone who said, "Hey, you want a job?" There was no deep allegiance to faction or favela here—those would come later—but rather a pragmatic desire for a different life, what he called a better *parada* (venture, adventure).

In our conversations, Beto evoked a global repertoire of images of violent, militarized masculinity. He routinely framed his own struggle against the police as similar to that of other soldiers engaged in what he described as "just" or "legal" wars worldwide. He talked constantly about the U.S.-led invasions of Afghanistan and Iraq, which he followed closely on television and in the newspaper. He fantasized about hiring himself out as a mercenary for these war efforts, where he could don desert fatigues, which he described as "beautiful," and where he could employ the most advanced technologies for killing.

Beto's awareness of the world outside the favela illustrates how traffickers are not somehow isolated from the larger society but deeply embedded in wider social spheres, consumer groups, and media cultures. In fact, global geopolitics and things like new electronics, fashion brands, or international travel were all far more interesting conversation topics to Beto than my questions about local favela and trafficker politics. He was not unique in this regard. The hunger to talk about and experience something new— to break what was described as the "monotony" of favela life—was typical of both traffickers and residents alike.

For a time, the neighborhood boca de fumo was located in the alley underneath the window of my bedroom, providing me with (often unwanted) access to the sights and sounds of trafficker business twenty-four hours a day. To my surprise, nearly every morning one particular trafficker would go to the newsstand and buy a paper. He would spend the next several hours reading articles aloud to his colleagues, pausing every so often to sell drugs to one patron or another. International news, in particular, was of interest. During the U.S. presidential election season in 2008, John McCain and the practice of waterboarding was the center of debate.[4]

For someone like Beto, who described himself as a youth "in love with war" and "in love with hand-to-hand combat and killing in cold blood," trafficking was not the only game in town. He admitted that when he left the Special Forces he could have taken the police exam, or perhaps worked in private security. These would have been appropriate venues for him to practice the skills he had acquired in the military. He laughed aloud at the irony that he could have ended up fighting for the other side, hunting a parallel version of himself. But his experiences with the government— shaped by his marginalized class and racial status—led him to believe that the drug economy actually represented a more stable and honorable employment opportunity than the police force.[5]

Beyond his unabashed proclamation that he wanted to see what it felt like to actually hurt a person and to confront a real enemy, Beto framed his decision to become a trafficker in terms of necessity: "I knew I had to make this choice because I knew what it was like to feel hunger. Other people I know, they are still hungry because they didn't have the courage to make the choice that I did. The state didn't give me any other options. " While it is somewhat difficult to believe the dire picture Beto paints here—after all, he was employed by the government and *left* to join the traffic—his use of the idiom of state neglect to explain his choice is significant. For Beto, the state itself is responsible for the ever growing number of armed youth in Rio.

This is a line of reasoning one hears frequently in the favela, as residents cite the lack of state-sponsored education and employment programs as a motivating force, if not *the* motivating force, behind the ongoing migration of young men into the traffic or into a life of crime beyond the narco-regime.[6] Trafficking, in this view, becomes a natural response to the actions of the state. The discourse of government abandonment helps to maintain trafficker power in the favela by framing trafficking as a form of politicized resistance to state oppression and placing traffickers on the front line in a battle against state tyranny.

After deserting the army, Beto advanced quickly through the ranks of Rocinha's traffic. "I never started at the bottom," he says with obvious satisfaction. "I went straight *ao lado do cara*" (to the "guy's" side, meaning he immediately began working directly for the boss). He attributes this to the value of his skill set; his knowledge of police and army strategy meant that he could train those already involved in the traffic. After all, he asked me, was there really such a big difference between the state and narco armies? Shortly thereafter, his work in Rocinha earned him a mention in an article that appeared in Rio's main daily newspaper, *O Globo*, as well as in the *New York Times*. It was just a few months after he entered the traffic. "My mom kept the clipping if you want to see it," he told me proudly. "The publication made up my mind. They had my name. Now I was on the other side [the traffic], the wrong side maybe, but there wasn't any getting out."[7]

Beto was arrested in late 2009. According to news reports, he was guilty of recruiting members of the armed forces on behalf of the traffic.

Media coverage was especially sensationalist, not because his actions were particularly shocking, but because his arrest was a painful reminder of the intimate relationship between the state and the traffic. His girlfriend, Katia, told me in a tearful phone conversation that he would get a lengthy sentence and that he was locked up in Bangu I, Rio de Janeiro's infamous high-security prison. He had a cell phone, though, and computer access, so the two were still able to instant message through their Facebook accounts.[8] Even though they had broken up a few months before, prison made Beto nostalgic for the happy times they had shared. He called often.

When I returned to the newly "pacified" favela in 2012, Beto was, inexplicably, free.[9] By coincidence we were dining in the same restaurant, I with my husband and toddler and he with a large group, many of whom I recognized as traffickers, or former traffickers. In the tenuous, high-security climate of the recent pacification, several BOPE officers were standing outside the restaurant. Beto pretended not to recognize me. He commented loudly on how cute the little blond baby was, but he would not meet my eyes. The shifting configuration of the conflict and the advent of "peace" made conversation impossible.[10]

In this chapter I examine the quotidian mechanisms of trafficker governance, in which discourses of legitimacy are forged through interwoven spectacles of violence and wealth. Rocinha's traffickers make the rules; they determine the law in the favela. When they are crossed, they respond with spectacular violence, overt displays of force enacted for the consumption of the favela audience. But trafficker power is predicated on more than the display of high-powered weapons or the direct physical violence they perpetuate. Traffickers also author and participate in a rich civic life, enhancing their legitimacy in the local milieu by attaining (and publicly flaunting) the trappings of Brazilian (and global) consumer culture. Yet, like any other governing force, traffickers experience periodic lapses in control. Trafficker "states of exception" are resolved through the same governing mechanisms—spectacle, violence, and commodification—and reveal how power is reasserted through both coercive and symbolic channels.

In exploring the manufacture of forms of trafficker "capital"—meant here in the broadest sense—I highlight the fact that while the trafficker state often appears much like an inversion of larger Rio society, it is in fact deeply intertwined with mainstream Brazilian and global cultures. Even as traffickers appear to subvert the order of things by claiming to be the kings of the morro, crowned with the glittering gold of their many necklaces, watches, and gilded pistols, their power is in fact developed in much the same ways and through the same mechanisms as those of the "legitimate" state and in dialogue with the conventions and norms of wider society. The purposeful dialogue with mainstream governance and culture signals that despite the favela's economic and social marginalization, it is integrated with the dominant logics of neoliberalism and consumption at the core of larger state and civic governance.

As Beto suggested, ongoing poverty and discrimination in Rocinha provided fertile ground for the development of the trafficker governance.[11] Persistent social segregation and lack of opportunity produce a steady stream of alienated youth like Beto willing to take up arms in search of respect and economic solvency. Though favelas have been the consistent target of police throughout their history, important changes after the fall of the military dictatorship exacerbated the situation. Gangs, forged from collaboration between political radicals and criminals, changed the landscape of organized crime in the city. Under the military dictatorship that ruled from 1964 to 1985, leftist radicals and common criminals, many of whom came from favelas, were imprisoned together in a penitentiary called Cândido Mendes, located on an island on the Costa Verde, a few hours from Rio. These two very different "threats to the nation" formed an alliance with the political prisoners organizing the criminals into politicized gangs (Penglase 2008).

This alliance, which Ben Penglase aptly dubs "the bastard child of the dictatorship" (2008), called itself the Comando Vermelho (CV), in reference to the communist ideologies of the political prisoners. It became a governing force within the prison.[12] Prisoners, upon release or escape from the island, brought their newfound organizational skills to the street, where they orchestrated organized bank robberies, stickups, car thefts, and so forth (Lima 1991). Already on the margins of the city, favelas became their strongholds. Community oriented and political, the early faction leaders of the CV built basic infrastructure in many favelas and initially presented the group as a kind of welfare state for poor residents (Penglase 2008).

In the 1980s, with an expanding market for cocaine in the North, the CV turned to drug trafficking. Rio became a transshipment and packaging location for drugs coming from neighboring Colombia and Bolivia. Cocaine provided a more lucrative and stable source of income to the factions than did random criminal acts (Leeds 1996; Gay 2005: 55–56; Gay 2009; Perlman 2010). According to local drug consumers interviewed by Alba Zaluar and Alexandre Ribeiro, the trade took off mid-decade, with 1984 jokingly referred to as the "year it snowed in Rio de Janeiro" (1995: 95). Furthermore, the movement of narcotics fostered a semantic shift: gangs were no longer composed only of *marginais* (marginal characters), *bandidos* (bandits), or *criminais* (criminals) but now also of *traficantes* (traffickers).[13]

The rise of the narcotics market, which for the first time brought significant capital to the gangs, led to the subsequent introduction of the powerful weapons of war needed to protect drug-selling sites from rebellious up-and-comers as well as rival gangs (Barcellos 2003). With more and more money to be gained from drug sales, the CV splintered into several different factions. Turf wars began to pose a real threat to everyday safety.[14] During my residence in Rocinha (2008–10), however, the reigning faction of traffickers was so entrenched that not a single resident ever expressed concern to me that another faction might take over the favela territory.[15] Indeed, the Rocinha that I describe here is in my mind emblematic of the pinnacle of established trafficker power.

Drug Bureaucracies

Favelas, under the control of a local drug boss, became ideal sites for the refinement of cocaine. After processing, drugs are weighed, measured, and packaged for sale, for both the internal and external markets (Leeds 1996; Dowdney 2003: 258).[16] The boca de fumo, where drug dealers gather to ply their trade, is the economic center of the drug trade and the public face of the traffic in favelas like Rocinha. It usually looks like a few guys (maybe one woman) sitting around on plastic chairs or on top of wooden produce boxes. Drugs are kept in faded leather fanny packs or in backpacks set on the ground beside their chairs. Boca dealers typically carry guns, but usually no weapons are visible since the focus is more on commerce than force. The boca features small quantities of drugs at prices favela residents can afford, starting at around R$5 (US$2.50). Packets of cocaine and marijuana of various quantities are laid out on a table for all to see, as are the sizable quantities of cash that the dealers handle.[17] They frequently pull out rolls of money and grandiosely count them on the table, in an obvious show of wealth.

Larger favelas host a multitude of bocas; Rocinha has around fifteen, or one in almost every major neighborhood, each with varying degrees of business. The traffic thus maintains a physical and symbolic presence in almost every part of the favela. In Rocinha, customers simply approach the dealers and exchange money for drugs. The transaction is done with complete transparency; there is no separation between payment and handoff as in big-city drug corner sales in the United States (Bourgois 1995; Venkatesh 2008). Consumption is similarly open. Wafts of marijuana smoke give the favela one of its characteristic scents, and I frequently saw cocaine users snorting in the alleys adjacent to the boca.[18]

As the public face of the traffic, the boca also reflects the security climate of the favela at any given moment. A functioning boca stocked with ample drugs and several dealers signals that all is well. An empty or nonfunctioning boca indicates that something is amiss, such as an impending police invasion, which is one of the only things that can shut a boca down. When Brazilian president Lula visited during my fieldwork, the main boca continued to operate the entire time he was in the favela, despite the presence of ample presidential security.

Though the boca serves the internal favela-based market, Beto explained that the majority of the drugs that move through Rocinha actually supply members of the middle and upper classes. These consumers usually avoid the boca because of the stigma of crime and violence (Misse and Vargas 2010: 103). As Carolina Grillo (2008) has shown in her research on the middle-class drug trade, large-scale deals are negotiated directly between middle-class trackers and their favela-based suppliers and usually take place outside the borders of the community.[19]

Though roles and the division of labor can vary according to favela, faction, and demeanor of the local dono, trafficking within Rocinha was characterized by a high degree of hierarchy and structure. On the lowest rung are the lookouts, or *olheiros,* usually teenagers, who sit at strategic points around the favela and monitor the passage of cars, motorcycles, and people. If there is something amiss, they ignite dynamite-like sticks of firecrackers to notify their comrades and the community at large of impending danger. Above the olheiros are the *vapores,* who work in the boca and sell drugs directly to consumers.[20] Both vapores and olheiros are paid monthly stipends and are supervised by a boca manager, who takes a percentage of sales from his subordinates. Precise breakdowns of boca profits are hard to determine, but Barcellos reports that in the favela he studied, 10 percent of the profit went to the *vapor,* 30 percent to the manager of the boca, and the remaining 60 percent to the dono (2003: 145).[21] Like any other kind of commission-based business, there is a spirit of competition between bocas, thereby generating greater overall profit for the "business." Team morale, if you will, is forged through the development of strong corporate identities. In the pre-pacification favela at least, the main competing bocas each had their own graffiti tag that were used to mark territory. The boss also hosted an annual soccer tournament where teams of players from different bocas competed for the championship.

Lower-rank employees are supervised by several types of managers, depending on which part of the business they work in. The manager of the white (cocaine) and the manager of the green or black (marijuana) oversee drug supplies and supervise the boca managers (Rafael 1998; Dowdney 2003). In theory, an employee starts at the bottom as an olheiro and gradually moves up through the ranks to be a manager and maybe someday even the boss. The whole apparatus, replete with a "hard work produces promotion and advancement" ethic, resembles the corporate business world, a point to which I return shortly.

Beyond those employed in the commercial wing of the trade, a security manager (like Beto) oversees a legion of *soldados,* or soldiers, whose job it is to protect the boca and the favela territory from rival gangs. The security manager is in charge of gathering intelligence on police activities and delivering police payouts, as well as keeping the dono, the head of the entire operation, informed about potential threats to his control. Soldados are also on the front lines of the gang's expansion and are periodically called upon to invade other favelas in an effort to seize their bocas, as was the case with Rocinha's soldiers several times during my fieldwork (see also Dowdney 2003: 48–54).

The dono do morro is the most important member of the trafficking hierarchy. He is protected by a special security force, comprising trusted members of his inner circle. The most important member of the inner circle is the *fiel,* or confidant (like the consigliere of the Mafia), who is the second in command and in line to inherit the dono's position should he be killed.[22] As the richest man in the favela, the wise boss relies on the loyalty of his fiel to keep him informed about potential threats to his reign. Hierarchy aside, when a boss is killed or incarcerated, power struggles among the various managers and the fiel typically ensue.

A successful dono commands the entire organization with a mixture of respect and fear and sets the tone for the offensive and defensive strategies of the favela. The demeanor of the boss affects the behavior of subordinates and influences residents. For example, people often talked about one of the most beloved bosses of the 1980s and 1990s. Even residents who were opposed to the traffic would praise him, saying that he required his employees to respect the general population and did not permit them to brandish weapons or use drugs in front of children or the elderly.[23]

Donos also cultivate varying kinds of relationships with the world outside of the favela. The kingpin, especially of a large and important favela like Rocinha, is an explicit object of media fetishization. Some donos exploit this status more than others. The dono whose reign immediately preceded my residence in Rocinha was an infamous publicity hound. He was forever giving interviews to journalists catering to the large tabloid market for glimpses of trafficker wealth. The spectacle of his illegal affluence was the product of a larger cultural fascination, but even his behavior inside the favela reflected a penchant for attention. He made special guns for his inner circle, plated (reputedly) with gold from jewelry stolen in assaults around the city. He was a prolific ladies' man and was always parading around with an entourage of admiring women.

Beto did not approve of this dono. He claimed such attention-seeking traffickers were the first to be killed. This was precisely what happened. The boss was shot at point blank during a surprise police invasion. The dono proved as flamboyant in death as he had been in life: his funeral was attended by scores of wailing, grief-stricken women, all of whom claimed to be his *primeira dama,* or first lady.[24] His demise was an important reminder that even though traffickers sometimes appear larger than life in the context of the favela, there are limits to their autonomy. Caught up in larger webs of power, they must be careful not to overstep the bounds of "acceptable" trafficker behavior or risk being taken down by someone they have offended.

While avoiding too high a profile, a successful dono must still cultivate numerous external contacts within the larger shadow network. Political allies are especially important to enabling continued leadership and control.[25] People say that a dono is killed or arrested only when a confluence of forces align against him: new political and economic alliances may demand his sacrifice, public pressure might necessitate a government response, perhaps residents no longer support him, or a jealous bodyguard might not protect him. The dono is usually taken down in spectacular style. His demise well documented, he is led away in handcuffs or photographed for the newspapers, with police standing triumphantly over his lifeless, bullet-ridden body.

Sometimes the time is right not only for a new dono, but for an entire faction change. In smaller favelas, this might be achieved through the tenacity of a group of invading soldados successfully seizing their rivals' bocas. Faction changes in larger and more complex places like Rocinha are generally protracted affairs. The one faction change in recent Rocinha history was widely described to me as the product of an elaborate, long-term strategy. Beto said that his faction (the winners) had sought out the help of the police. "Help" didn't just mean direct bribery but also involved exploiting the police presence as part of a larger military-like strategy of takeover. In light of such limitations, trafficker power must be situated within the ever-shifting dynamics of security in Rio. Individual traffickers might have the agency to influence the overall climate and tenor of the kingdom they construct, but the parameters of their rule are shaped by broader relationships, with each other, with residents, and with outside forces.[26]

DISCOURSES OF LEGITIMACY

Rocinha's traffickers make reference to two principal legitimating discourses when describing their activities. On the one hand, they employ validating paradigms of state government; they frame themselves as a parallel state. On the other hand, they talk about themselves as a successful corporation operating in a competitive marketplace. Claiming proximity to these other institutions is an exercise of self-validation. But in wanting to be like the state and the corporation, traffickers also implicitly reveal a vision of statecraft and market capitalism largely reliant on violence, spectacle, and commodification. By evoking parallels here, traffickers are not so much questioning spectacular violence as a tactic of governance as they are suggesting that the state and the corporation are able to use these tactics *legitimately* while they cannot. In claiming to be operating in the same way, traffickers seek to appropriate some of the state and corporate world's "righteous" use of spectacular violence.

Discourses of statehood and corporation were not so much distinct as complementary and overlapping. Recalling Charles Tilly's (1985) famous formulation of statecraft as the epitome of organized crime, what is notable here is perhaps not the flavor or effectiveness of these discourses but rather the manner in which they are welded together; their fusion invokes a wider reality of the enmeshment of regimes of state and corporate governance. Just as it drives the global proliferation of neoliberal approaches to government, deregulated, financialized capitalism lends an ethos of market competition—and market discipline—to the emergent trafficker "state."

Legitimating parallels are forged through everyday discourse. Beto explained, "We work as if we are another state, with another president, another secretary of defense, of health, a secretary of culture." "Listen," he said, pounding his fist on the table for emphasis. "It's as if it [the favela] was another city, with another mayor, another police station." The institutions he described are not just discursive constructs, but real entities (if a bit exaggerated) that function within the favela. For example, the "minister of health" refers to the dono's practice of subsidizing medicine for sick residents or paying for operations for disabled children, both of which are commonly cited as evidence of the benevolent nature of trafficker governance.[27] A "secretary of defense" like Beto works to keep the favela safe from outside gang members and acts as local law enforcement. Thus, these and other narco-institutions do provide some services to residents. By filling roles traditionally deemed to be the purview of the state, traffickers solidify their claim to authority in the favela.[28]

Likewise, trafficker evocations of the state are connected to their control of a discrete territory. In Rocinha, though this was different in other favelas, police did not enter trafficker territory except during large-scale raids, which occurred but three or four times per year during my research.

The rest of the time, the narco-state was left to rule over the favela as it deemed appropriate. In fact, the rhythm of daily life in the favela was so clearly established and controlled by the traffic that when the police ruptured the border between the two "states," it was spoken of in terms of an invasion, which implicitly suggested that the police were the intruders and the traffickers the rightful sovereigns.[29]

Alongside the discourse that frames the traffic as a state is a set of related assertions that frame trafficking as a business venture. Traffickers' awareness of the saliency of the corporation as a metaphor again points to the way in which they are not isolated actors but "professionals" who understand the workings of the world system. Beto explained, "This is a company. A multinational company. Why? It imports and exports and works with all of Rio. It's a business that functions almost worldwide. There is a guy that does the finances, an accountant. Don't companies have security guards like we do? It has everything! And it's all very well run."[30]

Ideas about the traffic as a corporation are so engrained that they spill over into the everyday. I frequently heard remarks that rendered criminal activity as ordinary wage labor—"I have to go to work," "I work for the firm"—and job descriptions—managers, treasurers—all of which presented trafficking as having the same basic properties as employment in the corporate world, despite the fact that "work" might involve invading the territory of a rival gang or selling cocaine.[31] Through the idiom of work, murder, torture, and other acts of violence are transformed into essential labor. The use of business metaphors imbues trafficking with a neutrality that masks the atrocities carried out by people like Beto. In drawing such "legitimating" parallels between trafficking and corporations, traffickers actually understand and even appreciate the manner in which the corporate world can yield sanctioned, socially acceptable violence and spectacle in the name of advancing capital.[32] Their attempts to borrow from this repertoire are indicative of the tenuous and arbitrary boundary between legitimate and illegitimate forms of power, coercion, and violence.

Like any other company, the traffic is often the object of worker dissatisfaction. One trafficker went so far as to complain to me that he had to work long hours with no vacation time. Beto himself regularly complained that the business never allowed for "time off." "Even when I'm not working, I can't really be relaxed," he said. "Because your head is always thinking, maybe worrying a little about how this is all going to turn out. You can go crazy. You have to find distractions." Part of the worry that Beto is referring to is the fear of being fired, which would mean losing not only his livelihood but also his life. To be sure, the corporate discourse of the traffic is laden with euphemisms, but it also suggests that people—perhaps even Beto—are not really drawn into the traffic because they have an inherent interest in violence, danger, or criminality. Rather, like everyone in a capitalist society, they have to sell their labor in order to survive, and this is one of the only options available to them.[33] This reality is reflected in the tendency to talk about trafficking as a form of wage labor or employment that should come with social benefits.

The realization that he is but one expendable worker among many felt to Beto like a denial of his humanity. "The system," as he called it, seemed to discourage meaningful human relationships among employees. In a moment of great irony, given his particular role in "firing" other unsatisfactory employees, he complained to me, "If shit gets fucked up, and they decide you're over, your 'friends' are going to execute you without even thinking twice." The feelings of social isolation that this created often left Beto melancholic and depressed. Residents feared him, and his colleagues would kill him if ordered, yet he would do, and likely did do, the very same to them.[34]

Analogies between traffickers, states, and corporations do not point simply to how traffickers legitimate their behavior or increase their individual power. Rather, trafficker imaginaries of the criminal state and of the murderous corporation pose profound questions about the entities that are the object of traffickers' self-conscious mimicry. Observed similarities between the traffic and the state, or the traffic and the multinational, are suggestive of how dominant neoliberal ideologies are legitimated by both states and corporations in pervasive discourses that thereby come to inform the character of other domains, including trafficking. In this light, the line between legal and illegal forms of governance and commerce is very thin indeed.

Spectacle and the Right to Punish

For traffickers, a key part of being a recognized governing force is having the ability to use violence and to punish legitimately. At numerous times during our conversations, Beto reminded me, "Rocinha is not a violent place." It "has no crime," he said, and children, women, and researchers are always protected and safe. The relative absurdity of this claim was punctuated by the presence of his platoon of bodyguards and his cache of weapons sitting next to him on the sofa. What Beto was so eager to point out, however, is the efficacy of something called the *lei do tráfico*, or law of the traffic: law and order both made and maintained by traffickers.[35]

In what Dowdney describes as a system of "forced reciprocity," traffickers maintain some semblance of law and order in exchange for residents' silence about their criminal activities (2003: 56–57). Reciprocity is an apt characterization. As has been noted in analogous contexts where armed, nonstate actors guarantee public order (Galeotti 2002; Gambetta 1993; Venkatesh 2008; Bourgois 1995; Taussig 2003), the law of the traffic is not founded on traffickers' altruism but rather on the fundamental premise that the maintenance of order is necessary to establish an optimal climate for their criminal activities. The law of the traffic does not, as Beto insisted, extinguish violence in Rocinha. Instead, it imbues traffickers with the right to order and control violence according to a set of norms that enhance their business interests and their personal power.

Making and upholding the law, particularly in light of the state's relative inability to do so or disinterest, is an important part of what traffickers do in the communities they control. But trafficker law, like that of the state, does not operate simply as a discourse or disembodied set of codes; its *performance* is equally important as a mechanism for the elaboration of trafficker power. Transgressions of trafficker law, far from undermining it, actually create important opportunities for performances of violence.

This is complicated by the fact that traffickers often fail to enforce the law or selectively violate it themselves as they see fit. The lack of consistency was not necessarily delegitimizing, since traffickers' ability to transcend the law if they so desired was actually an important feature of how the law was used. The right to make the rule and declare the exception—or to institute a "state of exception" in the favela as deemed necessary by the dono—is crucial to understanding how trafficker power is forged through discourses and performances of law and punishment. What should be clear here is that trafficker law is the outcome of a negotiation between several different competing interests: keeping residents happy, protecting trafficker business, and providing the trafficker state with an avenue through which to enact violence, thereby symbolizing their power and reinforcing their control.

Under the law of the traffic, murder, rape, child abuse, theft, domestic violence, and assault are forbidden in the community and in areas immediately surrounding it.[36] Residents are also prohibited from talking about traffickers' criminal activities in contexts that could lead to their arrest or capture by law enforcement. Internal discussion about trafficker violence, however, was commonplace and in some ways even encouraged, as it functioned to create a climate of deterrence. Stories and gossip about the law, and about breaches of it, were a frequent topic of conversation. While most people I spoke with felt somewhat appreciative of the degree of safety and protection traffickers provided, a sentiment that I shared since I was rarely afraid for my personal safety in the favela, they were quick to point out inconsistencies in the laws. Generally speaking, prohibitions against theft, assault, and other forms of (nonsexual) violence were aimed at keeping a sense of order in the favela that was amenable to ongoing trafficker business interests. Maintaining order was particularly important as a way of not attracting the attention of the police, whose invasions could shut down the boca. Beto explained, "The dono, he hates a thief. Sure the guy might steal a couple hundred worth of stuff, but this act, well, it might cost the dono a couple hundred *thousand*. No, he doesn't like thieves."

The laws most fraught were those that centered on regulating the private, or domestic, sphere of residents. For example, rape, child abuse, and domestic violence were explicitly forbidden under the law of the traffic. But these laws seem to be relics developed during the time when the traffic was more overtly political. Residents value them, and so traffickers pay lip service to them, but they were not consistently enforced. When rapists and child abusers were actually punished, they were usually singled out for the most spectacular castigation (see Goldstein 2003: 190–98). During my fieldwork, one alleged child abuser was tied to a telephone pole in the middle of one of the busiest thoroughfares and beaten with metal chains until he was no longer recognizable. His body was left on display for several hours. This extreme act of brutality highlights how the law of the traffic, like many state-backed legal systems, paradoxically employs inhumane forms of punishment to enforce its morality.[37]

Traffickers sometimes violated their own rules, especially in the domestic sphere. For a time, I lived next door to a trafficker who savagely beat his wife on a regular basis. Because of his social position within the favela, there was little I could do to speak up in defense of his spouse without risking my own safety, making this one of the most challenging and depressing times of my fieldwork. Beto himself had allegedly broken the law. Though I never discussed the incident directly with him, another trafficker told me that Beto had raped a prostitute at gunpoint. His colleagues disrespected him for it, but he was not punished as he might have been had he been someone else or had his victim been a more "upstanding" member of the community (cf. Arias and Rodrigues 2006). Punishing Beto was clearly not in the business interest of the dono, a calculation that Beto most likely made when weighing whether or not to commit the crime in the first place. Furthermore, the incident, though it made Beto unpopular with his peers, inadvertently bolstered his personal power. It showed that he could break the very laws that he was employed to enforce.

The idea that those who transgress the law deserve punishment, however brutal, is common among residents.[38] I once encountered traffickers marching a handcuffed and sobbing man up into the trees at gunpoint. I returned home deeply upset at what I had witnessed, but my neighbors were quick to tell me not to be scared. Yes, it's complicated, one said, but surely the man had broken a law. Another person interrupted, adding that the captive must have been a "marginal" who was probably involved with drugs and maybe gambling too (in ways that violated the gang order). Traffickers had a legitimate right to punish him. He should have known better.

Reflecting on these explanations, I realized that residents (including me) needed the law of the tráfico. Even with its inconsistencies and contradictions, it provided an explanatory framework within which to understand violence that would otherwise be too monstrous to bear. Residents themselves, by constantly locating those who transgress trafficker law at the margins of favela life, help traffickers transform these others into "bare life," which can then be extinguished.[39] By explaining the "who" and "why" of trafficker justice, residents replicated and validated the disordered order of the law in minutia. The law then became a series of mutually reinforcing understandings about who is punishable, and these understandings both reflect and reproduce wider social divisions within the favela.

Transgressions provide traffickers with valuable opportunities to perform their power through the enactment of punitive rituals, using blatant displays of force and consolidating power through fear and spectacle. When an offense is committed, traffickers act as judge, jury, and executioner (Arias and Rodrigues 2006; Goldstein 2003). Offenders are bound and gagged, often with duct tape, paraded through public thoroughfares, and then taken "up there" (*lá em cima*, a euphemism for the place[s] where killing is performed). The places of punishment fall outside the boundaries of the civilized favela, with "up there" referring to nominally secret areas of death located in the forested, more mountainous areas above the favela. Like the favela itself, which is constantly conjured by the state as a zone of lawlessness threatening larger society from within, these spaces of death and execution are similarly hinted at in everyday discourse. The fear such spaces provoke emerges in the way people talk about them. In hushed tones, they say that "up there, unpaved earth can be excavated into shallow graves," or "up there, the deep forest muffles screams."[40]

That extremely violent punishment is not hidden but rather celebrated indicates that traffickers do not fear retribution from the state. They are confident in their right to govern and to mete out punishment as they see fit. When I encountered people being marched "up there," I felt, in addition to a terror from which it took me several days to recover, that I had violated some taboo, that I had seen traffickers doing something that I wasn't supposed to see. But my presence never seemed to produce any concern. In some cases, having an audience provoked additional violent performance, as was the case when my husband ran into a prisoner being transported one morning. When the primary guard (and probable executioner) saw that he had a gringo audience, he looked my husband in the eye, grinned, and began to beat his prisoner with the butt of his gun.[41]

Given the number of gruesome stories I heard from residents about public beheadings, beatings, and torture, punishment itself was spectacular. One troubling account that I heard from several people involved the public beheading of two young thieves for assaulting and kidnapping a woman in the area just outside the favela. More recently, a woman was burned alive for cheating on her trafficker boyfriend with a policeman.

Traffickers are well aware of torture and execution techniques employed elsewhere, such as beheading, a form of execution used by insurgents in the war on terror, or "necklacing," made famous by Tontons Macoute death squads in Haiti and widely practiced in South African townships (Scheper-Hughes 1995b). Called "microwaving" in Brazil, the practice, which involves stacking tires around the offender and then lighting them on fire, has become iconic of trafficker brutality. Traffickers thus construct order through law and maintain it through spectacular violence. Their violence is not hidden, and they seem to fear no retribution. They see their use of force as legitimate, as essential to creating a climate of deterrence and terror.

Spectacle and the Ability to Consume

Traffickers do not depend on the threat of physical force alone. The establishment of power over the population entails consumptive spectacles as well. The neighborhood kids told me about Maggie while we ate popsicles on my front stoop, açaí and guava staining our lips purple. "She's a monkey," they said in excited voices, "the dono's monkey." Then, like most people do, they looked around and added, "The dono! You know, the dono? The president! The boss!" Like her owner, Maggie the monkey was a criminal. She stole a lipstick here and spare change there, weaseling her thin arms through the window bars and running off with things left on windowsills. Maggie also had bling; when I finally saw her jumping from rooftop to rooftop and skipping along the telephone wires, she was wearing a huge gold medallion around her neck that bore the initials of the gang faction. While the kids were excited about the presence of the exotic pet, the medallion was less remarkable to them. The dono's outrageous wealth, which enabled him to give a pet monkey a solid gold necklace, had long since become a normal part of life for them.

While many accounts of favelas tend to gloss over important internal class distinctions, differentiating oneself from less fortunate neighbors through conspicuous forms of consumption was a common aspect of daily behavior in Rocinha. Favela residents employed in the legal economy are avid consumers of luxury goods. Many own flat screen television sets and designer watches and wear expensive perfume. Traffickers are even more conspicuous consumers.[42] They throw lavish birthday parties for their children, their mothers live in the nicest houses, and their girlfriends and wives wear designer clothing and expensive jewelry. The desire to acquire such goods often provides the motivation for entering the traffic in the first place, as it is common knowledge that working in the drug economy is the highest-paying option for local youth.

After receiving their first paychecks, young traffickers usually begin to accumulate the signs of wealth, according to their own specific aesthetics and style. Bodies are adorned with heavy gold jewelry, medallions in the shape of dollar signs, and guns hang from heavy braided chains. High-ranking traffickers carry golden handguns, their glittering presence drawing attention both to weaponry and to wealth.

Guns, especially machine guns, are objects of prestige and tools for conversion. Beto described how young kids follow an older trafficker like him around, doing favors and looking at him with starry eyes: "They latch onto you. Even though the guy is not making any money, he just hangs around. He feels powerful being around you. And then, at some point, you get fucked up, drinking or something, and your gun is heavy and maybe you don't feel like holding it, and so you hand it to him. 'Here! Take it!' That's it. It's a done deal. Holding your gun makes him really happy."

The dono, as the wealthiest man in the favela—the CEO, as Beto called him—is expected to be the most outrageous consumer of material goods.[43] Rocinha's dono loved imported Johnny Walker whiskey (Blue Label, which retails for $175 in the United States but costs nearly triple that in Brazil) and drove a bright yellow imported motorcycle. He wore designer clothing and had a pool dug in his backyard during an especially hot summer. Living in a "mansion" hidden high up in the favela, he enjoyed playing video games on his gigantic flat screen television. His girlfriend, who reportedly had extensive plastic surgery, frequented the fanciest shopping malls in the city and had a fleet of cars and drivers. The details of the fabled couple's high-rolling lifestyle were regularly reported in the city papers. Trafficker wealth, it seems, was not only being performed for those within the favela but for those outside it as well.

While putting food on the table is a practical concern that drives some to find work in the illicit economy, many are also attracted by the promise of yet another commodity: women. "This is one of the main motivations for the guys that walk around with six or seven bodyguards, all full of guns, and who buy tons of gold chains," Beto remarked, smiling. "This attracts attention, and then they can get more ladies. There are guys who get into this business just for that reason." Beto said that most youths can't really be blamed for this behavior. After all, they learned that women care about money from television shows, produced by mainstream Brazilian culture. "How else are poor guys from the favela going to get women?," he asked me.

Pierre Bourdieu writes that "cultural needs are the product of upbringing and education" and that this "predisposes tastes to function as markers of 'class'" (1984: 1). Taste is directly related to class status in that the things we desire and consume reflect our place in a wider system of social stratification. Beto was especially eager to distinguish himself from regular residents and from "lower-class" traffickers. This was accomplished largely through the acquisition and display of material goods and through drawing distinctions between his "refined taste" and their "poor taste."

Unlike many of his peers, Beto claimed to understand how consumption is linked to social status and thought he had a more accurate reading of the items that bring prestige. He complained that gold worn in such generous quantities, the brandishing of guns, and walking around with an entourage were "tacky" and "unsophisticated" behaviors and that the women this attracted would "claw you to death" because they "just want the bling-bling" (said in English).[44] Thus, just as Beto considered lower-class traffickers' personal adornment to be beneath him, so too were shallow, cloying women.

Beto would only date *patricinhas,* wealthy girls from the city.[45] As one resident explained, "The patricinha represents that ultimate trafficker fantasy. Favela women will do everything they can to try and look like these girls, to attain the look of money. Their trafficker boyfriends pay for their designer labels, breast implants, and expensive blonde weaves and hair extensions." Just as Beto aimed for upward mobility through the strategic accumulation of high-class goods and lovers, so also did women in the favela attempt to craft status through similar self-fashioning, although the transformations required of their bodies were more drastic and painful. In the end, as Beto suggested scornfully, these women were still just girls from the favela, and they could only rise to a certain height as long as they lacked the worldly experience and culture that come from wealth.

The obvious irony here is that Beto's descriptions of these women were true of himself. He lived almost like a prisoner in the favela since to leave too often was to risk arrest.[46] He too couldn't use his money to attain experiences that would bestow real status.

Therefore, a real patricinha carries a currency beyond the beauty that money buys. She is a door to another world. Beto's patricinha, Katia, his companion for nearly two years, was from an upper middle-class family. She worked part-time for fun, making elaborate wedding cakes and pastries for parties at a ritzy beachfront hotel, and took classes in literature and poetry at the university at night. She taught Beto English words and phrases, which he laughingly, clumsily, sounded out. When she was planning a trip to Argentina with a few girlfriends, he begged her for an international phone call. "Come on, girl," he said to her while I was interviewing him. "I just want to be able to tell my buddies that I am getting a phone call from another country!" Experience beyond the borders of Brazil, symbolized here by foreign language and travel, is obviously a valuable commodity for Beto. Katia offered him education and mobility, though both are vicarious since his criminal status kept him prisoner in the favela. He dreamed about getting out of the business, about living the life she represented.

Under Katia's guidance, Beto learned to recognize a different language of wealth. He explained, "I was never able to dress nicely before. My mother didn't have money to give me nice clothes, cool clothes. And then when I got money, I was able to buy the clothes that I had always wanted— designer labels like Diesel jeans [US$400 in Brazil] and expensive cologne." He pointed his iPhone at me. "In the favela no one notices them because they haven't ever heard of them. They attract the attention of different people." To Beto, the phrase "different people" signified those who, like Katia, are sophisticated enough to recognize the subtle symbols of upper-middle-class wealth. Therefore, power and status result not from the overt display of raw gold, which he associates with poor taste, but from having the label of his jeans recognized by the right person.

Katia herself was not so different. She fetishized Beto's trafficker status. She was also a social climber. Her brushes with the danger that he represented made her the hippest and edgiest of her friends, and she took obvious pleasure in violating social taboos by coupling her whiteness with his blackness, a blackness that she said enhanced his trafficker persona for her. It was not Beto the person but rather Beto the trafficker that she found attractive, a fact that became clear when she eventually left him for a more important trafficker in another favela that was controlled by a rival gang.

The spectacle of wealth, whether gold, jeans, or beautiful women, is so central to the performance of trafficker governance that it cannot stay behind closed doors. Displays of trafficker power are played out in public venues—in the street, at the boca, and especially at the baile funk. Invented in Rio de Janeiro's favelas in the 1980s, funk is a genre of music that draws heavily on Miami bass styles and sampling. Funk has replaced Carnaval and samba music, once transgressive cultural products born in the favela but which have long since become commercialized staples of mainstream Brazilian culture, losing their radical edge along the way (Vianna 1999). Though some funk albums have gone mainstream and are now played in trendy European nightclubs (Sansone 2001), funk has its roots in favela-based performances, at funk dances.[47] These local venues play uncensored funk songs, those that are deemed too sexual for mainstream recording (*funk melody*) or that praise and extol the virtues and exploits of drug lords (*funk proibidão*) (Sansone 2001: 139).[48]

Since most traffickers were not able to leave the favela to attend social events for fear of arrest, the baile took on added importance as one of their only recreational outlets. The performance and consumption of the trafficker persona was central to the baile itself, a venue through which wealth was displayed for the larger community. Indeed, "the culture of funk music is one of the principal ways through which the legitimacy of the drug traffickers is produced and lived" (Sneed 2003: 61). At the baile, the lifestyle of the favela's traffickers was presented in spectacular fashion. Because the spectacle was of their making, they were able to craft a role for themselves as the guests of honor. With their entourage of beautiful women, body-guards, and shiny weapons, they were the center of attention. They appeared onstage with the performers or designated special VIP boxes exclusively for their entourages. Their economic and social importance was further extolled in the lyrics of the music and inscribed on the bodies of thousands of favela youths as they traced out synchronized dance steps. Huge speakers pumped bass at a deafening volume, which washed over the entire favela like waves, shaking windows and floors as it traveled.[49] Even if residents did not attend the baile, the thumping bass performed a sonic spectacle that dominated the landscape.

If funk proibidão is the national anthem of the trafficker state (Sneed 2003), the parties themselves are sites of a new "carnavalesque," as conceptualized by Bakhtin (1968). The carnavalesque is a process that subverts the dominant social order and offers up a new one through laughter and irreverence. Brazilian *carnaval*, as Roberto DaMatta (1991) has noted, is a central venue for the development of the carnavalesque. But under the sponsorship of the drug boss, who paid for the bailes, the carnavalesque process was repeated at hyperspeed, with bailes taking place once or twice a week rather than once a year like Carnaval. "The liminar [*sic*] function of the funk dance is celebrated if not exaggerated" (Sansone 2001: 140), and the possibility to break free from the oppressive social conventions was part of the baile's allure. At the baile, it seemed, anything was possible. Beto could show Katia off as his status symbol to his favela friends, and Katia could show Beto off as her status symbol when her "city" friends came up the hill to the attend the baile. Just as she was an affirmation of his status and a symbol of his wealth, so he became a commodity for her enjoyment.

Spectacle and Rites of Mourning

Both the law of the traffic and traffickers' consumptive rituals rely on performances of violence and wealth. But spectacle also features centrally in moments when this carefully constructed legitimacy threatens to erode. The public face of the traffic is one that is all-powerful and fully in control of the favela population. How, then, does the narco-regime react in the aftermath of obvious breaches in security, such as when the police kill important members of the hierarchy or when they are taken out in skirmishes with rival gangs? Responses involved both controlling the discourse in the larger community and crafting explanations that affirmed the power of the dono. In cases of high-profile deaths, elaborate funerals were staged to give fallen traffickers a hero's memorial.

Living with the everyday presence of death required the construction of an explanatory system of how, why, and who dies. This was useful for both traffickers and residents, who were continuously worried about getting caught in the middle of the trafficker-police conflict. Generally speaking, people accepted that trafficking is a high-risk profession that carries with it the probability of untimely death. Some traffickers will be killed by intimates—people they know well and work with—for some specific violation, such as rape or using crack, prohibited by the dono. Others will be in the wrong place at the wrong time during a police invasion.

In death, as in life, lower-ranking traffickers remained unnamed and largely unmemorialized by the business. However, the death of a higher-up was followed by an elaborate ritual of public mourning. Funeral and memorial practices were used to reinforce hierarchy, to reassert control, and to perform power for the population. If a trafficker was killed while invading another favela, he was presented as a hero who died in the line of duty. Such was the case with the trafficker whose funeral was held at the indoor soccer court next to my house. Hundreds of serious-faced onlookers, including scores of sobbing women, sat on the hood of the hearse and huddled around the entrance to the court. Black flags hung over the metal fencing that usually served to keep soccer balls in play, and several had been hoisted up the wires over the road.

In the days that followed, more flags appeared all over the favela, especially around the bocas. The favela was plunged into an uncanny silence, as residents strained to hear explanations that would enable them to evaluate the gravity of the situation and assess whether it posed a threat to their personal safety. The coffin contained the body of Zidane, the second in command in the trafficking hierarchy, who took his name from the French head-butting soccer player of 2006 World Cup fame. He was young, with a baby face, or so I gathered from the hundreds of T-shirts bearing his image and the word *saudades* (eternally missing you) sported all over the favela in the days and weeks after his death. An enormous mural with his face, a lion, and a starry sky was erected above the main boca. As rebellious as his namesake, Zidane had not heeded the dono's orders and had attended a baile funk in a favela called Monkey Hill. Monkey Hill had been involved in a protracted war with the neighboring community ruled by the rival gang. Enemy soldiers crept into the favela, opened fire on the baile, and killed Zidane.[50]

In explaining Zidane's demise, residents emphasized the fact that the dono had explicitly warned him not to attend the baile; his death, while unfortunate, could have been prevented if he had followed orders. The incident was thereby reframed, not as evidence of the weakness of the faction, but of its power. Beyond the political repercussions of Zidane's death, the public way in which he was mourned attests to the way in which traffickers are embedded in favela communities. They are the husbands, sons, nephews, brothers, fathers, grandchildren, and lovers of residents. Though people often lament their fall into a life of crime, for many in the favela, they are not just traffickers, but people with complex histories and multiple subjectivities.

In the summer of 2010, another spate of trafficker deaths ruptured the otherwise tranquil environment of Rocinha. Police invaded the favela from the woods one afternoon and, while storming the dono's house, interrupted a meeting attended by most of the top leadership of the favela. While numbers two, three, and four in the hierarchy were killed, the dono managed to escape. The invasion was exceptional in that it broke with an otherwise established pattern of police activity. It occurred in the afternoon, whereas most invasions took place at dawn. It involved only a small group of elite police forces, instead of the hundreds that usually participated in invasions. Clearly, the police had received valuable, accurate intelligence, since they were able to eliminate important figures in the hierarchy.

The dono did not initially appear to have had advance warning of the invasion, as he usually did with other police actions in the community. Such an exceptional event caused considerable panic among residents. Was this the beginning of a protracted war? Could a rival gang be financing the police effort? Almost immediately, however, an alternate explanation began to emerge. Since the dono himself had escaped, it had clearly been *he* who had ordered the invasion and tipped the police off as to the location of the meeting. Furthermore, he had probably done so in order to eliminate powerful subordinates who were perhaps conspiring against him. The police were simply a tool with which to reorganize his leadership cadre.

The repackaging of this event into something that added to rather than detracted from the power of the traffic dovetails with the use of public performance to communicate trafficker dominance to the wider community. Both are important strategies for (re)asserting power in the social context of the favela. Ironically, these strategies are not so different from those of the Brazilian state of exception, where discourses about the disordered and violent favela are developed in order to legitimate acts of state terror, acts that are highly performative and intended to carry the message of state omnipotence to a larger citizenry.

CONCLUSION

As I have suggested throughout this chapter, the nature of trafficker culture suggests that traffickers do not so much seek to establish a regime outside of or separate from the larger social order as to seek power and recognition in a society that has disavowed them. Traffickers use discourses of statehood, of the corporate world, and of consumer culture to form a distinct vernacular expressed through registers of violence and spectacle. Trafficker power is forged through the performative construction of order, and when that order fails, through violence. Justice as administered by traffickers is not driven by altruism but reflects the ways traffickers negotiate multiple interests in the social, political, and economic realms so as to maintain a favorable climate for the continuation of their criminal activities. Inconsistencies in trafficker law, rather than detract from their control, reflect their understanding of the utility of the "exception" in solidifying governance.

Performances of power extend beyond violence to the realm of consumption. Traffickers use consumer goods to distinguish themselves from poorer residents and to communicate that they too can acquire the signs of success. However, they misread the signs of status and the symbols of wealth. As Beto pointed out, the "tacky" gold they wear actually works to affirm, not advance, their place in the larger social order. While traffickers are prisoners in the favela, they desire encounters with people and cultures beyond it, as Beto's interactions with Katia demonstrated. Because of the constant threat of imprisonment and death at the hands of police, traffickers' options for these kinds of interactions are limited; they learn about the world vicariously—through television, the newspaper, the Internet, and talking to foreign anthropologists.

disciplinary/corrective legal used for preser.! punishment

2 The Penal State

March 2009. The night before the police invaded Rocinha my narco-trafficker neighbors were preparing for war. As the static of their walkie-talkies intermittently broke the silence in the unusually quiet favela, they donned black police uniforms and strapped on extra weapons.[1] Tipped off first by informants in the police station and then by the conspicuous movement of the hundreds of officers sent to invade the favela, the men next door took to the forest trails above the favela, taking care to leave their front door open before they left so that it would not be kicked in by the police.

At first light, several police helicopters dropped into the valley, sharp-shooters hanging off the sides, their guns poised to fire. As the ground troops advanced through one of the community's main entrances, snipers picked off a lookout, a youth in the first year of his short career as a traf-ficker, as he tried to light firecrackers to alert the population of the exact moment of the police arrival.[2] Tragically, his signal and the police effort to quell it were unnecessary; everyone in the favela knew of the *invasão* (invasion) days beforehand, word quickly spreading through the gossip channels of the grocery store, bakery, and bar.

Although the periodic police incursions I witnessed in Rocinha were always presented by local media as dangerous exchanges of gunfire

between police and traffickers, the raids themselves were oddly nonconfrontational. By the time the police arrived, the traffickers had been
warned and were hiding in the woods or relaxing watching the invasion
on television from somewhere deep within Rocinha or, as local lore had it,
from the comfort of one of the many posh beachfront apartments they
owned outside of the community.[3]

The lack of trafficker presence, however, did not diminish the scale or
spectacle of the police action. Hundreds of officers were involved in what
felt like a paramilitary scene in an action film. In front were the shock
troops, BOPE, riding in their iconic tank. The "Big Skull," as it is called, is
an enormous black armored vehicle emblazoned with the troops' signature gold and red skull and dagger insignia. Others charged up the hill on
foot, with helicopters providing air support, swooping low enough to create a windstorm that knocked the books and papers off the shelves in my
living room.

Once BOPE had secured the area, the "conventional," nonelite police
would slowly and unceremoniously climb the hill. Their leisurely posture
contrasted sharply with the combat-ready movements of their elite colleagues. Some officers stopped for a break at one of the many juice stands
that lined the main road, while others stood around watching while stolen
motorcycles were loaded onto flatbed trucks and confiscated drugs were
arranged in altarlike configurations on the hood of police cars to be photographed. Then came the journalists, wearing bulletproof vests, cameras
rolling and clicking.

While not every police invasion in every favela is a staged affair, the
majority of the police actions I observed in Rocinha were highly choreo-
graphed performances of state power. And yet the spectacle of the invasion was consistently undermined, not just by ongoing trafficker rule, but
also by the fact that corrupt police officers often provided traffickers with
advance warning of the event. Despite the absence of armed confrontation
during *invasões,* their representation as a clash between heroic forces of
the state and enemy gang members is fundamental to understanding how
the favela is policed. Both sides engaged in performative, spectacular
behavior.

Traffickers, understanding full well the spectacle of state power at play in the intermittent attempts to curtail their rule, know that the police need to claim bodies and confiscate drugs to demonstrate that they are making progress in their effort to control crime. On another memorable occasion, my trafficker neighbors simply left two tons of marijuana behind for the invading police to find, stacked in neat piles in the middle of an alleyway the police were sure to take the following morning en route to a drug boss's house. Rather than simply and cheaply loading the haul onto trucks, the drugs were flown out in a dozen helicopter trips, dangling in a huge net above the favela skyline: a picture-perfect image for the front page of the morning paper. The large haul made for a perfect media spectacle. Within a few hours of the raids, the show was over and the police were gone. Traffickers returned from the hills and paraded through the streets, guns held high and voices raised in a triumphant homecoming.

The ongoing tension between the two different faces of state security gives policing in the favela a cyclical quality.[4] The violence of one group of state actors—corrupt local police supported by traffickers—creates ongoing insecurity in poor communities. Another group of state actors, in this case, BOPE, subsequently attempts to enact "order" through the use of additional violence. Their spectacular performances of police efficacy hold a constant place on the front page, as the media endlessly reproduce the "violent favela" and the "war against the traffic," master tropes that sell papers and increase ratings. But these favela performances are short bursts of violence. While producing news-ready images of police power, they do little to challenge the ongoing dynamics of state–organized crime collusion.

In this chapter, I show how police, as representatives of the larger "penal state" operating in the favela, embody violent spectacle and contribute to the commodification of security. State violence, in its multiple forms, creates what Loïc Wacquant (2008) has described as a punitive politics of marginality. For Wacquant, the favela, like the French *banlieue* or the North American ghetto, is a site of state experimentation with forms of what he calls "advanced marginality" (2008). The penal state in Rocinha, as I see it, operates through a host of overlapping processes that together maintain favela residents' marginalization: a politics of neglect, the entrenchment of social inequality, the normalization of structural violence, police and trafficker imbrication, the consequent florescence of organized crime, the increased use of police violence to perform state order, and the expansion of the prison system.

According to Wacquant, the advancement of the penal state is a response on the part of the powerful to popular unrest resulting from the social dislocations of neoliberal policies.[5] The connection here between the violence of the penal state and the expansion of the market is a compelling and useful one, especially considering the ways in which state violence intersects with processes of commodification. In the context of overall insecurity in Rio, spectacles of violent policing have become an object of market value in several crucial ways. Behind the scenes, legions of corrupt cops and politicians thrive economically as a result of their symbiotic relationship with favela criminality. Engaging in classic profiteering schemes, they broker arms to traffickers, move drugs, and buy votes. On the other hand, BOPE capitalizes on its commodity status by self-authoring a multiplatform integrated marketing campaign of violence and state terror, broadcast live through social media.

Insecurity opens a market for "protection," both inside and outside the favela. Militias composed of off-duty police officers, prison guards, and firefighters increasingly occupy favelas, expel traffickers, and charge business owners and residents "protection fees" to supplement their government salaries.[6] Insecurity is further commodified by the enormous private security sector in Brazil, which has been growing at annual rates of between 7 and 10 percent for over a decade.[7] The number of private security agents now outnumbers police by more than a hundred thousand. Ironically, the very same police who participate in creating insecurity through collaboration with organized crime also sometimes work second shift for these companies.

While the conditions I describe in this chapter characterized Rocinha's pre-pacification period, enmeshment of state actors and organized crime continues to be the norm in the post-pacification period as well. The ramping up of the penal state as the modus operandi of favela governance is equally present in the unpacified favela and in the pacified one. What is different is that pacification itself has become the new darling of state securitization, a new form of spectacle intended to mask established punitive policies.

HISTORIES OF POLICE VIOLENCE

One spring morning the police shot the pockmark-faced trafficker while he was hiding in his bed. His body was wrapped in the sheet he slept on, which had a pattern of bluebirds faded almost to white. The cops dragged the corpse down the narrow alleyway to the road. Standing with other residents waiting for the bus, I watched as they came down the beco and stopped at the bottom, opening up the sheet momentarily for a newspaper photographer. He leaned in with his long lens and snapped quickly before they closed the sheet again and walked across the street to their cruiser, a compact Volkswagon painted with the panoptic Military Police slogan, "Com você, o tempo todo" (With you, all the time). Setting the body down with an unceremonious thud that made the onlookers visibly cringe, the two officers wiped the sweat from their brows and bickered about how to get the trafficker's body in the car. After walking to a nearby kiosk for a snack, they began to cram the body in the backseat headfirst. It didn't fit. One officer repeatedly tried to fold up the long legs while the other slammed the door. They cursed as the door kept popping open. Finally, they hit upon a solution. One officer held up the legs while the other rolled down the window. They drove off with the trafficker's bare feet hanging out, toes blowing in the breeze.

Since the early 1990s, Brazil has suffered from some of the highest murder rates in the world. Rio de Janeiro has long occupied a central place in these macabre (and notoriously unreliable, underreported) statistics. Although the city enjoyed a slight drop in reported homicides in 2013, the statewide rate remains extremely high at 23.5 per 100,000 (BPSF 2013).[8] Ongoing conflict between rival drug factions contributes to elevated incidences of death, but the police themselves are also the perpetrators of violence, predominantly directed at young black men living in favelas and on the urban peripheries of major Brazilian cities.[9] Police-perpetrated homicide is rarely investigated and is typically explained away as "self-defense." At the same time that police kill with relative impunity, they are themselves often homicide victims. To summarize the findings of a recent public security report, Brazilian police are killing *and* being killed at rates higher than in any other place in the world (BPSF 2013).[10] Police, like their trafficker counterparts, are both victims and perpetrators in the penal state.

"Law Enforcement" and Bureaucracy

The contemporary violence of the Rio police has been traced to two related but distinct moments in the force's institutional history: the formation of the first squads during the colonial era and the changes made to policing during the military dictatorship. From the time of its inception, police have been charged with upholding social inequality. According to the historian Thomas Holloway, "Unlike warfare against an external enemy on the battlefields . . . the objective [of the police] was not to exterminate or eliminate the adversary. The goal was repression and subjugation and the maintenance of an acceptable level of order and calm, enabling the city to function in the interests of the class that had made the rules and created the police to enforce them" (1993: 32; see also Lemgruber et al. 2003; Kant de Lima 1994). Policing has long been a project that reflects and maintains social divisions. The police are not meant to protect the rights of *all* citizens; police work in the favela setting in particular is centered on maintaining entrenched class divisions between the favela and the city and upholding the status quo rather than implementing some idealistic vision of the law or justice for all.[11] Thus, in the general sense, policing at the "margins" is a project wherein the favela and its residents are used to performatively reinscribe inequalities embedded in the social order. For many, the legal apparatus is experienced as a tool of persecution, not of protection.

The law of the state, though cited as positive in principle, is widely perceived by those in Rocinha as unfair and unjust in its application. State law might technically ensure *favelados'* rights, but in practice police do not enforce those rights. The differential function of law enforcement as determined by social standing was reflected in numerous statements by Rocinha residents. In many interviews, when I introduced the word *protection* as a function of the police, residents laughed out loud at my ignorance. In the words of one person, "Police come to keep things the way they are . . . to remind us that we live in a favela and they can break things and that we are not worth anything. They don't come here to change

things, no." The police treat all residents as potential or presumed criminals. As such, law enforcement is authorized to conduct humiliating
searches of residents' homes during invasions and of their purses or backpacks as they leave the favela for work. People often attribute these
searches to the fact that police do not distinguish between the different
kinds of people who live in the favela, instead lumping all residents
into an undifferentiated criminal category (Machado da Silva and Leite
2007). The law, they suggest, is blind to the important complexities of
Rocinha's social hierarchy and is perceived almost exclusively in the punitive sense.[12]

Favela residents also complain of the law's hypocrisy; they are aware of
the fact that the fluid nature of enforcement allows those with more social
capital to evade punishment. The consequences of breaking the law are
almost always negotiable—for the middle and upper classes.[13] One Rocinha
resident, Jorge, an ex-convict, explained this process to me in the following
way: "Listen, if a 'playboy' is stopped, he will call his *papai* [daddy] who
will come down to the station and pay a few fines, or make a 'donation' to
the police chief, and he will go home. No problem. Not for us people [resi-
dents]. If I am stopped there is no conversation, I don't have money to
pay."[14] The uneven distribution of justice means that while the playboy goes
free, the poor pay the price for the failings of the system, especially when it
comes to courts and prisons. A few years after Jorge made the comments
cited above, he was stopped by BOPE during the pacification of Rocinha.
He had served his sentence and had been legally released half a decade
before, but someone had not filed the correct paperwork. There was no
record that he had done his time in jail. He was taken back to the Bangu
penitentiary, where he remained for over a year, a prisoner of bureaucratic
sloppiness without the resources to hire a lawyer or the connections to contest his imprisonment.[15]

Jorge's situation illustrates yet another punitive feature of the penal
state: courts are overburdened and public defenders scarce. "Justice," one
favela-based lawyer told me, "is very, very slow." In the previous year, of the
more than two hundred cases he had open, only one had elicited any
response from the court—a notification that he had provided a copy where
an original was required. In this way, the rolling out of the penal state

doesn't just involve direct violent action but can also entail increased complacency and neglect.

Legacies of the Dictatorship

The inadequacies of the justice system and the failure to equitably enforce the law are only part of the picture. As Sarah Hautzinger has noted in her work on policing in Bahia, "Through the transition from authoritarian to democratic rule, police attitudes remain consistent in viewing social order as dependent on forceful police repression" (2007: 225). The culture of policing is marked by violence, making "disappearances" and extrajudicial executions far too common.[16]

While the administrative division between the civil and military branches of the police has existed since the colonial period, the military government in 1969, in an attempt to quell threats to its leadership, subsumed all the country's police forces under a single command (Husain 2007; Alves and Evanson 2011). During this period, "the police received special training in the application of torture and other coercive methods to control political dissidents and suspected subversives" (Hinton 2006: 95). Special death squads were formed to hunt down those that opposed the military regime, and these death squads were the precursors to the special forces of today. ROTA of São Paulo and Rio's BOPE were among the most infamous of these groups.[17]

After the transition to democracy in 1985, the police role in hunting and eliminating subversives was simply superimposed on the war against the narco-traffic, without significant alteration of the oppressive methods developed during the military state of exception. Though technically demilitarized, the police "retained the right to destroy the enemy without risking punishment" (Pinheiro 1991: 173). Furthermore, as Huggins, Haritos-Fatouros, and Zimbardo (2002) discuss in their ethnography of police torturers during the dictatorship, many of the young officers responsible for the infliction of atrocities remained with the police after the transition to democracy. Some now occupy leadership roles, fostering a climate wherein torture and violence are accepted, and even encouraged, by higher-ups.[18]

At the end of the dictatorship and with the introduction of the 1988 constitution, the police were again divided into civil and military branches, a bureaucratic structure that continues to hinder police effectiveness (Husain 2007; Hinton 2006). The civil branch is responsible for *investigating* crimes, while the military branch is responsible for maintaining public order and stopping *crimes in progress*. Competition and rivalry between the two branches undermines collaboration and fosters quarreling over territory and responsibilities.[19]

Each force is also divided internally, with differences in class and educational level separating lower-ranking street cops from officers. Disparities in pay further contribute to the maintenance of a divided and corrupt police force. While upper management earns higher salaries, the standard beat cop in the military police takes in R$2,600 a month (about US$1,100), with civil police earning slightly more, R$3,200 (BPSF 2013). With wages so low, many officers work second or even third jobs, often moonlighting in the private security sector.[20]

Substandard rates of compensation contribute to endemic corruption in all branches of the police force. Graham Denyer Willis notes, in his ethnographic work on the São Paulo police, that officers differentiate between various kinds of corruption. "Institutional corruption," "such as theft from prisoners, is quietly condoned." This is seen as police "doing what they can to make financial and professional ends meet." On the other hand, "criminal corruption," or "selling one's service weapon to criminal elements," is not condoned because it "depletes the monopoly on violence and weakens organizational capacity" (2014: 17). Regardless of these varying takes on corruption as acceptable or inacceptable, it continues to be a definitional practice, characteristic of policing in Rio, in particular. A recent government-sponsored study found the Military Police of Rio the most corrupt of any in the country, responsible for a total of 30.2 percent of all reported cases of police extortion in Brazil during 2010–11.[21]

SPECTACLES OF INEPTITUDE: "CONVENTIONAL" COPS

Police corruption in the favela comes in numerous forms. Many officers participate in extralegal markets through enmeshment with traffickers—trading information about police movements and intelligence for cash, selling arms, or agreeing to look the other way during investigations in exchange for a payout.[22] At other times, police act alone. In one oft-cited case several years before my fieldwork, the local bank in Rocinha was held up by a group of off-duty policemen. Before they could get away, traffickers apprehended them. This story was often repeated by favela residents as proof of the problematic nature of the police and by traffickers as evidence of how they were better at policing the favela than the police themselves.[23]

Not all acts of favela-based malfeasance are so spectacular. Corruption also occurs on a smaller, more quotidian scale. I heard dozens of reports of police misconduct aimed at the personal enrichment of officers at the expense of the poor. Often, police simply stole from residents, seemingly without fear of repercussion. One of my neighbors, for example, was accused of being involved with the traffic when the police searched her home during an invasion. She had recently bought a new laptop computer after saving for almost a year. However, when asked, she was unable to produce a receipt for her purchase, and the police took this as an indication that she had either stolen it or received it as compensation for doing work for the traffic. They decided to "confiscate" it. Afterward, she carefully scotch-taped the receipts she did have to her television set, iPod, and washing machine. Police also looted the houses of traffickers during the pacification of Rocinha, removing the luxury goods associated with a life of crime for their own personal use. Residents said that police were toasting each other with traffickers' expensive whiskey and were even seen taking top-of-the-line appliances and video game equipment out of the dono's house. Clearly, such behavior contributes to the overall delegitimation of police in the favela and destabilizes the divide between cops and criminals.[24]

In addition to their role as perpetrators of corruption, police were a source of constant terror to residents. Almost everyone had a story of abuse in this regard. One woman, who ran a day care center in one of the poorest parts of the favela, told me about her experience of an invasion that took place during a particularly tense period of trafficker versus trafficker conflict. Police had invaded the area in an attempt to locate hidden traffickers and make "peace." They brought tear gas. Despite the fact that the building was clearly marked as a day care center and that she was sure that the police could hear the sound of the children playing inside, officers threw canisters onto the *laje* (roof) of the building. The cloud of gas made its way into the nursery. She and her staff did the best they could to cover the eyes of the nearly fifty infants and toddlers who were in their care that day. "It was terrible," she remembered, her own eyes filling with tears. "But this is what we live with. No one cares because these are favela children. Do you think that the police could do this in a day care down there [gestures at the nice neighborhood below]?" Sometimes the threat wasn't gas but real bullets. During the same period, a police helicopter opened fire on the roof of the building. "Bullets ricocheted and scarred the walls but didn't hit anyone, *graças a deus*." Afterward, she had her son paint the words DAY CARE on the roof in large red letters so that it would be visible from the air.

Such incidents of cruel and illogical aggression attest to the violent nature of the penal state and are important for understanding residents' ongoing distrust of police. Another person described the period of police action that took place during his teenage years (late 1990s–early 2000s). At the time, the cops regularly terrorized the population in the hope of gathering intelligence, a practice still in place today, as indicated by recent incidences of police-led torture in Rocinha. He described one memorable experience.

> I was outside of the favela walking on the beach. I had heard stories of the police picking up residents down there. For example, they would find a couple making out and detain them. Sometimes they would rape the girl, because, well, you know that there are many police that do this. They would beat or kill and disappear the man. So I was scared to death when the police car stopped beside me and they told me to get inside. They began to drive around in circles. At first they said nothing. Then they started to talk to each other about me. "I bet he knows so-and-so." "I bet he knows where so-and-so lives." And I would respond, "No, no, I don't know them. I am just a student." But they continued to pressure me. Finally they stopped the car, and this was the freakiest part [*parte mais esquisito*], they started laughing, like really laughing hard. "Go ahead, get out. Go home. Go up the hill." This kind of thing happened to me many, many times. My friends would say that maybe I had the look of a bandido or something. I would get pulled off the bus or out of the van and searched and questioned. I hated them for a long time. Finally I began to understand that they are part of something larger.

As this resident astutely noted, police are not isolated or independent actors but are part of the larger punitive apparatus operating in the favela.

As subordinates, they take orders from more senior officials and, ultimately, from politicians, who establish policies that dictate the parameters of acceptable on-the-ground police behavior. If citizen confidence in the police is at an all-time low in Brazil, the only more despised group is politicians, with upwards of 95 percent of all Brazilians deeming them untrustworthy (BPSF 2013). Disdain for elected officials is especially common in the favela, where residents have decades of experience with promises made during election time and broken shortly thereafter. During my fieldwork, almost every one of the local politicians active in Rocinha was linked to corruption schemes. Residents believed several were on the trafficker payroll. Others were allegedly involved in the practice of delivering favela votes through intimidation. While one such official was eventually imprisoned and two others were murdered, the more powerful politicians that they helped to elect remain in office today. Like police, favela-based political representatives are both perpetrators and victims of larger webs of corruption and violence.

In sum, favela residents experience police primarily as sentinels who protect the boundaries between rich and poor. Largely immune from accountability for their actions in pursuit of this task, they engage in open thievery as well as quieter corruption, often undertaken in tandem with traffickers. Police also perpetrate physical and psychological violence against the favela population. They embody a penal state that inflicts harm on the poor through the enactment of direct violence and terror *and* through the passive strategies of impunity and bureaucratic incompetence.

SPECTACLES OF EFFICACY: BOPE

Daniel Goldstein, in his work on violence and spectacle in urban Bolivia, writes, "The spectacle is as much about obscuring what performers wish to conceal as it is about putting on a display" (2004: 16). Indeed, policing the favela is just as much about what is emphasized through the spectacle as it is about what is masked. As the police squad designed specifically for favela combat, BOPE is the official, overt response to the failings of the conventional forces. They are a loud, splashy expansion of hard-line social control intended to mask the underhanded practices of their colleagues.

Figure 3. BOPE officers during an invasion. Photograph by Michael Jerome Wolff.

And yet, though the elite forces are constructed as a radical break from other forms of policing at the margins, they are equal contributors to ongoing favela violence.

Violent spectacle is at the heart of BOPE's actions and takes several interrelated forms. On the one hand, the squad emphasizes its "modernity," symbolized by access to the most technologically advanced weapons of war and by exceptionally vigorous training, qualities that stand in stark contrast to the sloppy shortcomings of the conventional police forces (fig. 3).

Thus, in addition to taking on its trafficker foes, BOPE wages war against conventional cops by modeling a kind of policing constructed against the widespread illegitimacy and malfeasance of nonelite police. A parallel discourse elaborates the squad's aesthetic identity through reference to magic, terror, and triumph over death itself. These two renditions of spectacle are not contradictory but rather complementary: they intertwine modern discipline and technology with magical power (Whitehead and Finnström 2013).[25]

A direct descendant of the death squads of the dictatorship, BOPE was founded in Rio in 1978. The unit, one officer explained to me, was made to "clean" (*limpar*), an adjective that carries a neofascist connotation, conjuring up a whole host of social cleansing projects in a variety of other national and international milieus. BOPE's "cleansing" efforts primarily entail murder and torture. As the squad's official anthem states, BOPE goes to the favela to "leave bodies on the ground," executing traffickers and their associates with quick and punishing force. However, as Rocinha residents themselves were quick to note, this kind of unchecked violence, ironically, relies on an inaccurate and "unprofessional" vision of the favela that collapses all residents into potential corpses for the taking. The ideology of aggressive social cleansing isn't so much about effective policing as it is a reflection of the problematic notion that all favela bodies are disposable, acceptable casualties in the war against the traffic.

Torture is used to extract information regarding the whereabouts of traffickers. Residents widely cited torture as a central part of BOPE's calling card. Discourses about who exactly can be "legitimately" tortured are similar to those regarding trafficker violence against residents and involve the construction of narratives regarding the favela social order. For example, residents identified certain kinds of people as especially vulnerable to BOPE's violence: those associated with traffickers in some way or those who use drugs. In reality, these narratives serve to assuage residents' fears more than they reflect actual, concrete rules regarding who is susceptible to police violence.

Unlike traffickers, who are seen as motivated by "unprofessional" passion or anger, BOPE characterizes itself as guided by rules and codes. For example, their "ten commandments of behavior" demand that officers exercise "controlled aggression" and "emotional discipline," qualities that traffickers are imagined to be lacking.[26] The discourse here emphasizes the measured, and therefore positive, nature of BOPE's use of force. Its violence is supposedly used for good, not for evil.

According to a semifictional book written by the former BOPE officers André Batista and Rodrigo Pimentel (and coauthored by Luiz Eduardo Soares, former secretary of security for the state of Rio), "Every BOPE policeman leaves the barracks with a small plastic bag, which has become part of the basic kit and which is used for suffocating suspects during interrogation" (Soares, Batista, and Pimentel 2006: 30–31). The practice of torture, conceptualized by officers as "work," is allegedly undertaken with the utmost professionalism and efficiency (30).[27] In this construction, sanitized by its reference to a "hygienic" kit and standardized method of inflicting pain, even torture becomes modern.

BOPE's discourse of efficient favela cleansing is also framed as an inevitable outcome of its technological sophistication and excellent training. BOPE officers are reputed to train special forces from around the globe. They thus become a source of international pride, in contrast to the national shame associated with conventional cops. Unlike the inept and poorly equipped conventional Military or Civil Police officers, the squad has the most advanced weaponry: new guns, night vision goggles, even body armor. Officers are transported in the squad's signature armored vehicle, the *caveirão* (Big Skull), a truly impressive weapon of war that allows them to shoot freely while being protected from traffickers' bullets.[28] It provides officers with anonymity, as it is the skull itself from whence the bullets come rather than any individual officer accountable for taking lives. The spectacle of delivering death with professionalism masks the uber-present violence implicit in things like the caveirão and the plastic bag. The trappings of modernity and sterilization hide what lies behind—the brutality, the slain bodies, and the pain BOPE inflicts.[29]

BOPE's adherence to the cult of the modern is complemented by an institutional persona that emphasizes its magical qualities as well. The squad's symbol, a skull pierced by a knife and flanked by two guns, represents perpetual triumph over death as officers engage in dangerous skirmishes up and down the city's hillsides. One favela resident stated that he believed that the emblem was originally derived from the Nazi SS and was then used by the Brazilian military's death squads, rumored in Rocinha to have carved the sign of the skull into the flesh of political dissidents and other marginais during the dictatorship.[30] When asked about the skull, one officer answered, "We are the death of death." The implication, when taken together with other repertoires such as the squad anthem, is that those who bear the symbol are supernatural beings, able to overcome their mortality through their disciplined aggression and technological sophistication. The symbol of the skull is transposed onto officers themselves, who are metonymically referred to as skulls and whose physical bodies appear as skulls when in combat. Hooded and with goggles, their anonymous faces mimic the insignia.[31]

BOPE's mystical power also stems from the legendary rites of passage officers undergo to qualify for the squad. In what is widely acknowledged as one of the most difficult training processes on the planet, skulls are described as having undergone a radical transformation; they are no longer men but warriors who bring death to death itself. According to the lyrics of their anthem, under the cover of darkness they now shape-shift into "dogs of war," "beings unlike others," the "messengers of death" who "spread violence and terror." The discourse here—of a police force so strong it can defeat death itself—is especially powerful in counteracting the climate of police corruption and collaboration with criminals. BOPE's rhetoric further imbues officers with a divine right to administer justice both on the ground and in the afterlife. One verse of their anthem states that they seek not only to possess the physical bodies of their trafficker enemies but also to "steal their souls."

Concrete actions in the favela put BOPE's professional violence and its evocation of occult terror in play through performance. As Jean Comaroff and John Comaroff have noted in regard to South African policing and to problems of law and (dis)order in the postcolony more widely, "where governance is seriously compromised, law enforcement may provide a privileged site for staging efforts . . . to summon the active presence of the state into being, to render it perceptible to the public eye, to produce both rulers and subjects who recognize its legitimacy" (2006: 280). BOPE's actions on the highly visible stage of Rocinha summon an idealized but inordinately violent state into being. For the favela audience, however, it is clear that BOPE is not a solution but rather a contributor to the politics of marginalization.

BOPE's spectacular performances in Rocinha run along several principal registers. First, their occupation of the space of the favela, even for a
limited amount of time, positions the force as the natural, rightful organizers of transgressive criminality for observers outside the favela. The participation of police in ongoing favela violence is masked by their performance of order. However, the battlefield in the war against favela criminality
is not limited to the terrain of the favela itself. It also takes place in the
media imaginary. Television and social media are important fronts that
showcase state efforts for those outside the favela.[32] BOPE's victories are
exhaustively documented in the daily print and online media.

Through the reclamation of favela space, officers become the merciful
liberators of the population. One of the more common photo compositions
is of BOPE raising the squad's flag from a favela rooftop during invasions.
The act signals that the favela is now under BOPE command, and by extension that of the state. The spectacle reframes police as a victorious and transparent entity, masking their role as co-contributors to the favela's criminal
world and co-perpetrators of violence against the favela population.

As I suggested in the opening vignette, BOPE's raids, as I experienced
them in Rocinha, were remarkably nonconfrontational. Despite the
emphasis on its role as a powerful and brutal exterminating team, the
reality is that from the perspective of Rocinha, BOPE policing was as pre-
dictable as it was theatrical.[33] Nevertheless, when BOPE raises its flag
to mark the success of its invasion, it inadvertently suggests that prior to
invasion the favela was not entirely under state control, a condition to
which it will return after BOPE's departure. Such images of official victory
are hollow and ephemeral in the favela (but important ones outside it).
BOPE did not have to engage with the trafficker enemy in order to fly the
flag. Rather, the traffic chose not to fight, giving BOPE a picture-perfect
moment before returning to business as usual. Nonetheless, the imagery
perpetuates the idea of the favela as an internal enemy state, creating the
need for BOPE's return.

Despite the orchestrated elements of invasion, the success of the spectacle demands that BOPE appear as the omnipotent order that overcomes
favela chaos (see also Barnes 2014). The penal state must be performed
and the favela must appear to be a temporary war zone, with exchanges of
gunfire, from which BOPE always emerges victorious. Achieving this

appearance is no small task. In pre-pacification Rocinha, traffickers followed a strict no-engagement strategy with all police. This policy was motivated by what they perceive as the underlying purpose for invasions in the first place: a show for the newspapers. Since the image of the chaotic favela is absolutely essential to justifying and framing police action, it is up to BOPE to create the impression of disorder on the ground; the troops must appear as if they are engaging in exchanges of gunfire with a formidable enemy. BOPE's mobile, autonomous tactical units storm the urban terrain, shoot, and kick in doors, all dramatic acts that reify the idea of the chaotic favela and that are carefully documented by television crews.

Another element of BOPE performance in the favela involves utilizing visually striking images of the spoils of their invasions, like the two tons of marijuana flown out of Rocinha by helicopter. The most common genre of images are confiscation photographs in which the tools of the traffic are removed from the hands of perpetrators and separated into neat piles, a metaphoric rerendering of the tools of war. Criminal bodies, black and shirtless, are pictured, many with their heads hung in shame, eyes not meeting the camera of police photographers, in a reflection of the strategy of nonconfrontation espoused by the gang of which they are a part.

I see these photos as shrines to the productivity and effectiveness of the penal state, symbolically reordering the chaos of favela criminality and attesting to police progress. In many of them, police logos are included in the background. The photos perform an important function by offering visual proof of bodies taken and weapons confiscated. Yet the definitive victory the images convey is misleading, in that both the arrests and the spoils of war are to a certain extent permitted or sanctioned by the upper echelons of organized crime in "negotiating" the drama of the police invasion.

While the mainstream media produce invasions as a market commodity, BOPE makes its own social media, providing a privileged window onto how the squad envisions its own actions in the favela. As the performance moves into the digital realm via Twitter and Facebook, officers become complex commodities; they author another layer of spectacle. In addition to reproducing and recirculating many of the tropes discussed in the previous section, social media model certain forms of policing behavior that take on symbolic importance in the context of the climate of distrust of the regular forces.

A language of legitimacy and transparency centrally defines BOPE's social media discourse. By "language of legitimacy," I mean the manner in which BOPE presents itself not as the perpetrators of state terror but as an honest, fair, accountable police force, composed of upstanding citizens acting in the interest of the public good. Twitter, as a media platform that requires self-narration, functions to make BOPE's performances "really real" since they come directly from officers. Tweets of daily policing activities masquerade as objective reality, a reality that takes a "broadcast" form and that in some regards differs very little in content from a traditional news article or television report. The fact, however, that the posts are made in real time, purportedly by officers themselves, and often include photographic evidence of the text taken by officers' smart phones, takes the legitimacy of the broadcast to new heights.

One series of "typical" tweets is helpful for understanding the ways in which BOPE's work in the favela is constructed through narration. The broadcast begins with an announcement of officers' activities: "Officers conducted an operation this morning, Sunday the 25th, in a community known as KM32 in Nova Iguaçu." A few minutes later, there is more information about outcomes. "Officers arrest 3 and confiscate 6 guns in Nova Iguaçu." A subsequent tweet introduces causalities. "In the action, three men were injured and taken to the hospital but could not sustain their injuries." Interestingly, the semantics focus on the men being unable to "resist" their injuries; they were just not strong enough! The framing obscures the facts of how they got fatally wounded in the first place. Did BOPE shoot them in the head? Who are the deceased? The passive language of the wording paints their deaths as an unfortunate by-product of the job while depicting BOPE as humanitarian for taking them to the hospital. The final sentence mitigates BOPE's responsibility. Ultimately, it is the victim's fault that they could not resist their injuries.

The narration continues with more detail about arrests and confiscations. "BOPE captures the manager of the (narco-)traffic in community KM32." The disclosure of the rank of the person arrested presents the invasion as a highly successful one. "Another three men were arrested, among them the manager of the local traffic, known as the Fat Man [o Gordo]." And here there is a photograph of the manager replete with a nickname. The use of a nickname works to dehumanize the man in question. He isn't a concrete person, with a legal name and identity. He isn't someone's son, brother, husband. He isn't a citizen. He is reduced to o Gordo, the trafficker. In the photo, the manager, the alleged threat, doesn't really look threatening at all. Barefoot and disheveled, he looks rather pathetic. On the one hand, one might read this as an indication of BOPE's power, that their strength transformed o Gordo into the pacified figure seen in the photo. On the other hand, the photo might provoke doubts about whether the narco-trafficker was ever a formidable enemy in the first place. Finally, the series concludes, "The action was registered with the 56 precinct." And "The police confiscated 1 380, 2 9mm, 3 semi-automatic 9mm and a quantity of marijuana and crack." This concluding statement is particularly important because it shows BOPE following procedure and not taking bribes. They are arresting, not just killing. They are modeling correct behavior for the corrupt cops. Paperwork is the currency of legitimacy.

The largely unidirectional twitter broadcast is posted live, allowing for vicarious identification and participation in the conquest of the favela by BOPE's followers. And although BOPE's tweets do not allow for comments, similar reports appear as status updates on Facebook. The comment stream is also a tool for the establishment of BOPE's legitimacy. Here "friends" can thank them for their efforts and say "God bless." Sometimes BOPE "likes" these comments back, creating the veneer of a dialogue and producing a sense of mediated intimacy. This extends BOPE's imagined community and legitimates their work: "the people," or at least the people on Facebook, are unequivocally behind them. The Facebook comments affirm and recognize the new personae and brand they are creating on the web. Finally, as followers applaud their policing efforts, this confirms the legitimacy and authenticity of recent twitter/Facebook events. This makes their reports seem "really real" and not of BOPE's construction. It confirms the public's reception and acceptance of BOPE's efficient spectacle, affirming the new vision of the state in construction.

Beyond the mediated experience the broadcast of BOPE's daily activities offers, the content performs an important duty in terms of constructing ongoing transparency: the Facebook posts and tweets present an idealized image of the reordering of the favela, important against the backdrop of a larger established culture of police corruption in Rio. Thus, the use of social media refocuses BOPE's policing from torture and death to a kind of hyperaccountability and transparency complete with photographic evidence. The dialogue created then gives the impression of unqualified public support for their actions.[34]

Despite all these attempts, aesthetic and performative, live or in digital form, the fact remains that BOPE is part of, not separate from, the culture of violent policing in the favela. While cloaked in discourses of modernity and efficiency, the fact remains that violence and spectacle are at the core of BOPE's attempts to make "order" out of the disorder initiated by the intertwinement of conventional cops and the gangsta state. Security is still about violent spectacle, not about rights or protection for residents.

SPECTACLES OF PUNISHMENT: THE PRISON

When the dust settles and BOPE is gone, what happens to the bodies and objects used as visual testimonies to police efficacy? If traffickers are to be believed, the drugs and guns eventually make their way back to them, or to their rivals, as conventional cops quietly remove the spoils from evidence lockers and sell them to the Betos of the favela.[35] The bodies go either to the morgue or, more commonly, to that punitive institution that Wacquant (2003, 2008) identifies as the sibling of the "ghetto": the prison. The penal state creates a "favela-prison pipeline," where the two spaces intersect and spill over into one another (Alves 2014: 7).

As with policing in the favela context, the prison occupies a gray zone between punishment and collusion. On the one hand, it is a punitive state institution, where prisoners experience aggression and violence, as they are frequently beaten and tortured by guards (Fraga 2006: 70–72). But perhaps just as important as the infliction of direct physical harm are the punishing side effects of neglect. The result of the bureaucratic failing of the courts and the justice system is that many people, particularly poor people who lack the means to challenge their imprisonment, are detained in pretrial status (Lemgruber et al. 2013). Recent estimates indicate that almost 40 percent of the carceral population has yet to see the inside of a courtroom (BPSF 2013). Given these circumstances, it is unsurprising that Brazil has one of the largest prison populations in the world. In 2012, there were 515,482 prisoners nationwide, a population that is only expected to grow in the coming years.[36]

The rapid rise in detainees, what Wacquant (2010) dubs "carceral hyper-inflation," has produced widespread overcrowding and exceeded the penal system's capacity by 211,741 prisoners (BPSF 2013: 62). Overcrowding, in addition to producing inhumane conditions of detention, contributes to the proliferation of illness and disease. In particular, rates of tuberculosis in Rio's prisons alone are thirty-five times higher than those in the rest of the state (Diuana et al. 2008: 1888). As the "sick" social bodies of prisoners become physically sick as well, they are further isolated, as both guards and other prisoners fear contagion.

Further complicating the spectacle of punishment is the fact that the prison, the historic birthplace of the country's drug factions, is an important venue for the assertion of trafficker power. Kingpins exercise their muscle by maintaining inmate order and providing protection for affiliates, all the while continuing to command their empires from behind bars (Biondi 2010). Despite its status as an institution of state-led punishment, the prison is also a place for the elaboration of further intertwinement of organized crime and state actors. The prison echoes the duality of the favela; it is both a stronghold of organized crime and a stage for intermittent performances of state power. But just like the law outside, where social status determines application, prison conditions vary greatly across class lines. Those with more access to power and wealth (high-ranking traffickers, for example) are able to arrange luxury accommodations, off-site work release, and access to medical care if needed.[37]

These conditions and contradictions were vividly illustrated by the experience of Jose, whom I interviewed just after his release from the Bangu complex, Rio's central penitentiary, which is located in a nearby suburb. I had developed a friendship with Jose, the son of friends of mine in Rocinha. I sometimes answered the phone at their house when he called from his cell phone. (On more than one occasion he was calling to give his family advance warning of a coming police invasion!) He was imprisoned for transporting weapons for the traffic, which he claims he only did one time—the time he was caught. Jose was jailed along with other members of the same faction, a common practice intended to avoid conflict within the prison but one that also allows for the strengthening of

social ties among faction members.[38] Upon his release, Jose was unhealth-
ily skinny, with a perpetual cough and a jumpy manner. As we talked in
his living room, he got up six times in fifteen minutes to adjust the volume
on the film that was running in the background on the TV (Nicolas Cage's
The Rock, about escaping from Alcatraz). Without my asking, he started
talking at top speed, words jumbled and rushed. "We had to take turns
laying down," he said. "We had a rotation in the cell. You would stand for
a while, jammed in with the others." He jumped up and got right in my
face to demonstrate, then continued:

> Then it would be your turn for a while and you would hope you didn't get the
> last spot next to the bucket we all shat in. We all had parasites. Huge long
> worms would eat at our insides and we would eat but we would always feel
> hungry. For Christmas, the guys [the big bosses of the faction who were also
> imprisoned in the complex and who, together with a group of corrupt
> guards, controlled the entrance and sale of outside goods], they got us
> McDonalds hamburgers. You could get really anything, you know? For a
> price. And they would pay the guards not to beat you or torture you. They
> control everything. Let me tell you something.

Jose lowered his voice as if someone could hear. "Did you know that the
dono here in this favela . . . he built that fancy soccer field up there . . . well,
once a month he hosts a game and plays with the top warden at Bangu."

He stopped and got up to adjust the TV again. We watched for a few
minutes. "But that burger, it was so good it almost made me cry. The only
thing that would have been better would have been my mom's cooking." He
smiled at his mother sitting on the sofa next to him, and she began crying
softly. She was happy to have him home, but the reference to her cooking
made her cry, saddened by their troubled past. The two decided together
that she should stop visiting him because the full body cavity searches she
was subject to as she entered the prison were simply too humiliating to
endure (Drybread 2014a). "Yeah, so it was so nice when they gave us these
things, but then you also knew that later you would have to pay it back in
some way. Those burgers were like the most expensive thing in the world,
you know?" He extracted a worn piece of paper from his wallet and waved
it at me. He said it was a line-by-line itemized list of the expenses he
accrued while in Bangu. I asked him how he was going to pay the bill. He
snorted, "Probably the same way I got in there in the first place."

Jose's maudlin tale attests to the spectacle of filth, overcrowding, sickness, and corruption, but his insinuation that instead of rehabilitating the inmate, the prison binds him more tightly to the traffic is equally important. It points to the self-perpetuating, cyclical qualities of crime, policing, and punishment. The unequal application of the law, coupled with punitive and unjust incarceration, as well as the protection traffickers can provide in this context, all directly contribute to the ongoing expansion of the penal state. Prison isn't the end of criminal sociability; it's a step along the way.

CONCLUSION

As the central institution charged with maintaining social order, the police embody the mechanisms through which culturally specific modalities of law enforcement are carried out. In the Rio case, the police are undermined from the start by the fact that their charge—the maintenance of the law—is already widely perceived, especially by those within the favela, as a complicated, unjust, and uneven process. While the law itself is in question, conventional police steal, kill, and collaborate with traffickers with relative impunity. Their actions are no secret. In all segments of Rio society, conventional police are seen as a force to be feared. This is especially true among favela residents, who have decades of firsthand experience with police brutality and dishonesty.

Given these realities of local life, BOPE takes on a special symbolic role, as it performs a different kind of policing for audiences in and outside the favela. The emphasis on BOPE's magical force—which comes from declaring triumph over death itself—is complemented by its simultaneous use of the trappings of modern warfare in favela performances. The efficacy of these performances aside, BOPE's popularity and commodity status demonstrate how extreme violence on the part of the police, when deployed against the traffickers and the poor, is consumed by the public outside the favelas, even as the squad uses torture and commits widespread human rights abuses. In this climate of uncertain state control, police invasions are highly ritualized: BOPE's and traffickers' violence is patterned and overdetermined. Everyone knows their part as well as the outcome.

Traffickers understand the need for the production and circulation of images of the violent favela; in fact, they identify the generation of images of police efficacy for the media as one of the primary goals of police action in Rocinha. Therefore, they seek to meet police needs in such a way as to minimize their own revenue losses, with the understanding that they must sacrifice a few drugs, guns, and bodies. Ultimately, policing in the favela is a negotiation between the desires of police and the ways in which traffickers work to meet those desires. BOPE requires the traffic, and the chaos it represents, to carry out performances of power on the favela stage. The state can then be pictured coming into being, not as weak or inept, but as modern and efficient, performing its legitimacy for audiences beyond the favela.

The police enable the ongoing power of traffickers through corruption and through alienation of the favela population. BOPE is a source of violent spectacle that does not serve to correct the failings of the police but rather works to reenact them in a different form. Prisons close the circle. Incarceration doesn't rehabilitate. The prison is a place of punitive violence against the poor, be it through incompetence and delay or through acceptable torture of the disposable carceral population. And yet, at the same time that the prison is a stage for the enactment of performative spectacles of state punishment, it is also a place for the traffic to flex its muscle. The big bosses become altruistic protectors of a prison nation, much in the same way that they "protect" favela populations from the malfeasance and cruelty of the police apparatus. But this protection isn't born out of kindness or altruism; it is a business, and not just in prison contraband, but in continuing favors, services, and respect. Thus, behind bars, at both ends of the favela-prison complex, state actors and organized crime feed one another. All of this perpetuates both direct and structural violence against the poor, just as it generates market growth—markets for protection, markets for delivering votes, and markets for McDonald's hamburgers.

3 Favela, Inc.

Carnaval, 1959. A lively samba band parades through the dirt streets of the hillside favela, where simple wooden houses are constructed amidst a mainly rural landscape. Palm trees offer shade to playing children. Women sew brightly colored Carnaval costumes, laughing together and joking with passersby. People samba barefoot in the street, moved by the infectious beat of the band. A clean and modern city stretches out in the background. The sparkling water of Guanabara Bay below glimmers in the sun.

This snapshot of Rio comes from the classic film *Orfeu Negro* (Black Orpheus, 1959), a tropical version of the Greek tragedy *Orpheus and Eurydice* made by the French filmmaker Marcel Camus. Set in the favela of Babilônia, the picture was based on a play by the famous Brazilian author and composer Vinicius de Moraes (1954). The film historian Robert Stam describes the acclaimed film as initiating "millions of non-Brazilians into Brazilian culture, forging in the international consciousness a powerful association between three related concepts: Brazilianness, blackness and carnival" (1997: 167).

With *Orfeu's* success, the release of other films of the period such as *Flying Down to Rio* (1933), and the fame of the Brazilian screen star and "bombshell" Carmen Miranda (1940s), Brazil entered the global imaginary as a sensuous, tropical paradise. It was not, as Charles De Gaulle famously quipped, "a serious country" but rather a frivolous one awash in endless sunshine. Life was set to the soothing musical harmonies of the likes of Antônio Carlos Jobim and Astrud Gilberto (of "The Girl from Ipanema" fame). A uniquely Brazilian passion for life was at the heart of the country's emerging global brand. Indeed, this image has been deeply enduring and part of a self-conscious national marketing strategy. It is no surprise that Rio de Janeiro's recent successful Olympic bid itself was organized around the guiding theme of passion for sport.

While this vision of Brazil, and of Rio in particular, continues to be exported to the world, a new image of "the marvelous city" has developed alongside it. Rio as a place of sensuality, creativity, and simplicity, where poor but happy residents joyously celebrate Carnaval, has been juxtaposed to a vision of the city as a decaying urban war zone.[1] The sound of the samba has given way to the noise of gunfire. The favela, and in particular the Rio favela, has become iconic of this shift. As Beatriz Jaguaribe puts it, "Favelas are cast as both the locus of the 'national imagined community' and as a 'fearful stain' on the landscape of modernity" (2004: 328). And yet, this new element of the city-as-brand has not detracted from Brazil's marketability. Quite the opposite, in fact (fig. 4). Organized crime has become a source of fascination and fetish; a place where the allure of tropical Brazil merges with Rio's illicit narco-glamour.

Both the new trafficker fetish and earlier representations of the poor as happy and carefree are indicative of the development of the favela as a profitable and marketable global brand. I call the constellation of commodified images of this new brand Favela, Inc. a term inspired by John Comaroff and Jean Comaroff, referring to the process by which human identity is increasingly part of larger consumer markets in ethnic and cultural difference.[2] The favela is commodified and consumed in two different but connected ways. Media allows for disembodied consumption, whereas tourism allows for an embodied consumptive experience. This chapter examines media and the following one looks at tourism.

I observed the power of the new violent-favela-as-brand at work when the American rapper Ja Rule visited Rocinha to perform an exclusive show in 2008. In the lead-up to the performance, banners were hung all

Figure 4. The favela is being increasingly included in Brazilian pop culture and fashion. Photograph by author.

over the favela. They depicted the pop star in a white suit smoking a cigar and adorned with gold rings, diamond earrings, and a Rolex.[3]

On the night of the show, the community was abuzz with excitement. Thousands of young people packed the street outside the venue, an abandoned outdoor bus terminal. Those who were unable to afford tickets gathered in the street. Traffickers patrolled the area. They happily (and effectively) guaranteed public security the night of the show, as a crowded favela meant a sure increase in drug sales. For the kingpins, who watched the show from a special VIP box, Ja Rule's visit inadvertently affirmed their ability to maintain order during the spectacular event and worked to affirm the global visibility of their community.

The presence of an American rap star combined with the risqué trendiness of the favela as the venue attracted numerous tourists and adventurous cariocas. Limousines and luxury cars ferrying soccer stars and local music icons periodically parted the crowd that was eagerly poised to catch a glimpse of the American visitor. Ja Rule arrived three hours late and ascended the hill with his entourage in a caravan of black SUVs. He put on the show in such a state of intoxication that he forgot the words to his own songs and repeatedly groped the local backup dancers. Speaking to the crowd through a translator, he gave a rambling speech about the historical significance of being the first U.S. hip-hop artist to entertain in a favela. His announcement that he planned to build a music school for favela youth was met with cheers from the crowd.[4]

Bravado, intoxication, and charity aside, what was an internationally acclaimed rap star doing putting on a show in an abandoned bus terminal in the largest and most infamous favela in Brazil? In the days following the show, the community was asking just this question. Certainly, some residents said, it was because their favela was famous, world famous, and as he had said in his speech, he wanted the distinction of being among the first to perform there. Others said that it was because the drug boss had offered Ja Rule a fantastical sum of cash too great to refuse, plus a pound of cocaine and the services of numerous underage prostitutes. Indeed, the "corporate" sponsors for the show were composed almost entirely of businesses suspected to be drug fronts or owned by community members with close ties to the traffic.

Regardless of the financial arrangements that enabled the performance, Ja Rule was able to build both material and symbolic capital through this event. He profited financially from the show, which was widely attended. But perhaps more important, he earned the clout that came from giving a concert in a "war zone" under the supervision of real drug lords. With armed traffickers ensuring his personal security, the entire production affirmed his image as a visiting gangsta. The fact that the favela, long considered an "undesirable" and "marginal" place, was capable of imbuing Ja Rule with such street credit is a testimony to the power of the new favela chic that has coalesced around the gritty glamour of Rocinha's narco-world.

The transformation of the favela into a commodity that can be bought and sold to the likes of Ja Rule is not a neutral process. The violence of Favela, Inc. takes two forms. First, there is the matter of unequal economics: the highly asymmetric power relationships between those who author, circulate, consume, and profit from the media products and those who live in the favela. By this, I mean that the producers of the favela brand occupy very different social worlds from the marginalized subjects featured in Favela, Inc. This begs a series of questions: Is it morally acceptable to profit from depictions of others' suffering? How do the structural arrangements of production and profit amplify existing inequalities? Is it ethical for wealthy movie producers and highly paid actors to increase their fortunes by depicting poverty and structural violence? On the consumption side, is it problematic to derive pleasure from engaging with highly stylized and spectacular images of war and death among exotic peoples?

Beyond political economy is the question of the representational violence of Favela, Inc. The media have a powerful capacity to constitute reality. The postmodern theorist Jean Baudrillard called these media-made realities the "hyper-real" and argued that the media-saturated qualities of modern life are characterized by engagement with the hyper-real ([1981] 1994).[5] Though it might resemble reality in important ways, the hyper-real is a copy or representation of a "reality" that doesn't have an original. In constructing something that looks like Main Street, U.S.A., the Wild West, or the favela, the really real is distorted and "improved upon" by its designers (Eco 1986). It is made more compelling, brilliant, and vivid than the original that inspired it. On the one hand, the hyper-real seems relatively benign. After all, isn't this what entertainment media is all about, showing a fantasy version of life replete with beautiful people, high fashion, luxury cars, and interesting stories? But because of the power of the hyper-real to influence perception, to shape everyday reality, personal opinion, and even policy, it is far more than irrelevant fantasy. The hyper-real does violence to those that it purports to represent because it distorts and simplifies the lives of people rarely given the chance to represent themselves. As a result of the power and ubiquitous nature of the media, a "real" favela must then imitate the hyper-real version in order to be seen as authentic, an irony that later comes into play in tourism when favela residents perform their own authenticity through reference to the markers of the hyper-real.

Earlier representational tropes of the favela as a romanticized place of joy and sensuality and more recent representations of it as a decaying, though sexy, urban war zone entail forms of representational violence that have concrete consequences for the people who live out their real lives under the shadow of these imagined media realities. As fetishes of violence, the aesthetics and discourses of Favela, Inc. obscure the larger historical, economic, and political factors that contribute to the reality they purport to represent. Favela, Inc. does not reflect life in the favela in its complexity; the conventions of the favela aesthetic established in Favela, Inc. homogenize great differences in landscape and life quality. To put it differently, media discourses surrounding the favela are not only *about* the violence imagined to take place there, but are forms of violence *in and of themselves.*

In order to explore these representational tropes, I draw here on evidence from a variety of intersecting media forms: film, video games, toys, fashion, and celebrity circulation. For organizational purposes, I conceptualize the (cross-cutting and overlapping) aesthetics and discourses of the hyper-real favela through two primary prisms. The first pertains to the space of the favela itself: how it is marked as a place of structural violence through the use of specific visual signifiers, including the landscape and favela bodies as part of that landscape. The second involves the imagined conditions of ongoing war in the favela, in terms of residents' supposed propensity for and use of armed violence as well as the use of excessive force on the part of police.

THE FILMIC FAVELA

As a pervasive and accessible media form, film is a central agent in shaping the contours of favela hyper-reality. Through its use of visual narrative, film works to stimulate imaginary travel and is integral to structuring perceptions of faraway places and the exotic bodies of others.[6] In this chapter, I analyze seven films, all of which (with one exception) are made by middle- and upper-class Brazilians active in the national film industry and which have achieved local and international acclaim. Therefore, these depictions of favela life are constructed by outsiders, are not self-representations, and have been highly influential in shaping public perception of the favela.[7]

Orfeu Negro/Black Orpheus was remade in 1999.[8] The distance between the remake and the original is especially revealing of the transformation of the favela as brand. While the figure of the criminal is largely absent from the original film, in the remake the villain has been reimagined as a narco-trafficker.

Cidade de Deus/City of God (2002), the most popular of the Brazilian film industry's exports, was nominated for four Oscars, including Best Director, in 2004.[9] It is loosely based on a best-selling book by Paulo Lins (1997), a former resident of the City of God favela, located in the western district of Rio. The film traces the growth of the favela from the 1970s, when it was still a government relocation project on the outskirts of the city. In the process of following this growth the film charts the rise of the drug trade from an informal and mostly local phenomenon to an organized, large-scale, and increasingly violent enterprise. Almost every one of the hundreds of favela tourists I interviewed for this book had seen the film.

Tropa de elite/Elite Squad (Padilha 2008) won critical acclaim on the European film circuit and took the Grand Prize at the Berlin Film Festival.[10] It follows an Elite Special Forces (BOPE) police captain's crusade to clean up the Prazeres favela in 1997 prior to a visit from the pope. The film celebrates the violent brutality of the Special Forces while simultaneously condemning the corruption and ineptitude of the regular police squads. Since its release, it has become something of a cult classic. The sequel, *Tropa de elite 2: o inimigo agora é outro/Elite Squad 2: The Enemy Within* (Padilha 2010), was the highest grossing and most viewed film of all time in Brazil and continues with similar themes, though in relation to politicians and the emergence of militias, who now exercise control in a great number of Rio favelas.

I also include two documentary films, *Favela Rising* (Zimbalist and Mochary 2005) and *Ônibus 174/Bus 174* (Padilha and Lacerda 2002) in my analysis. *Favela Rising* is set in the community of Vigário Geral in the aftermath of the police-led massacre of civilians that took place there in 1993.[11] The event provided the impetus for the formation of the nonprofit organization Afro-Reggae, and the film tells the life story of the organization's founder, Anderson Sa. *Bus 174* chronicles the hijacking of a city bus by an ex-convict and street child, Sandro de Nascimento, in 2006, an event broadcast live on television.

I have purposely selected films that span genres, demonstrating that the spectacle of the violent favela in circulation here is not limited to fictional works but is perpetuated even by documentaries that purport to offer a more "realistic" image of life in Rio. All of the films analyzed here, except *Black Orpheus*, are based on true stories, signaling the way in which the violent favela of film is presented as an authentic commodity that "accurately" portrays real life, thereby increasing its market value. The authoritative claim of documentaries and films based on factual events gives these media forms both an entertainment and an alleged educational value—as it is through media consumption that viewers can know and understand cultural others without ever leaving the comfort of their living rooms.

All of these films, save one, are part of what Brazilian critics have called the *cinema da retomada* (cinema of return, or rebirth), a genre of film that emerged in the early 2000s and drew attention to the realities of urban marginality, particularly in Rio (Hamburger 2008: 552). The emergence of the cinema da retomada coincided with the widespread economic growth of the early Lula years. Even if living conditions and consumer power were improving, this progress was overshadowed by high levels of urban violence (551). These films, according to the Brazilian media scholar Ester Hamburger (2008), must thus be understood as statements about (in)visibility, marginality, and violence at a time when most mainstream Brazilian media were not giving attention to these problematic realities.[12] The cinema da retomada brought novel attention to the periphery even as it reinforced a number of preexisting stereotypes about the realities and the people it sought to represent.[13] Stylistically, it also embraced what the film critic Ivana Bentes called a "post-MTV language, a new, brutal Latin American realism based on high doses of adrenaline, split-second reactions created through the use of montage, total immersion of images" (2002; my translation).

Aesthetics and Discourses of Favela as Landscape

SPACE

What does the hyper-real favela look like? If we use the current media as a yardstick, it is first and foremost located in Rio de Janeiro. The focus on Rio is a continuation of the central role that the city has played in representing Brazil abroad; it has always been Rio's natural beauty and culture that has risen to the level of international icon. Though there are favelas in every major metropolitan region of Brazil and in most of the mid-size and smaller cities across the country, the exclusive setting of Rio erases other, more "marginal" geographies. And while the overwhelming majority of Rio's favelas are located on the dusty outskirts of the sprawling metropolis, the cinematically constructed favela is always on a hillside near the beach. So pervasive is the aesthetic value of the waterfront favela that the promotional materials for the documentary *Favela Rising* swap the community of Vigário Geral, where the film actually takes place, for a decidedly "cooler" one in the Zona Sul of the city—a favela with a view. The documentary itself features stories and personalities from Vigário Geral, but its imagery is largely drawn from the Zona Sul.

The breathtaking panorama of the favela on the hill not only serves to make the favela physically attractive and to locate it in Rio de Janeiro but also highlights the striking contrast between the poor and the middle and upper classes of the city. This juxtaposition is engraved on the physical landscape as towering high-rises give way to shacks and paved roads become narrow dirt alleyways. The hillside location of the cinematic slum maps a vertical transition from the orderliness represented by the city to the lawlessness and disorder represented by the favela. In both *Elite Squad* (2008) and *Black Orpheus* (1999), the sinister power of the parallel regime is most potent at the favela's apex, where traffickers mete out brutal punishment against the backdrop of Rio's famous skyline.

Favela, Inc. explicitly markets difference through the constant reiteration of the space of the favela as distinct from the normative terrain of the city. There is a notable absence of regulated services—no running water, sewage above ground in overflowing ditches, and rats' nests of electric wires (signaling illegal connections) hanging heavily from telephone poles. Other signs of "civilization" are absent as well. In both *Black*

Orpheus and *City of God,* people traverse the narrow pathways of the favela alongside livestock—usually chickens or pigs—whose beastly bodies mark the space of the favela as rural and primitive and its residents as potentially unclean. The conspicuous absence of basic sanitation and the collapse of the human-animal and urban divide carry an additional multivalent message: they underscore the conditions of structural violence under which many favela residents live and indict the state for failing to provide citizens with access to basic necessities.

Though there is a lack of urban planning in the favela, the cinematic result is often picturesque and quaint. The hyper-favela is a charming departure from the stark anonymity of middle-class condominiums and suburban apartment buildings. It is more colorful—architecturally and culturally. As the camera takes the spectator inside the community and inside residents' houses, there is a kind of cheerful poverty, where lack means simplicity rather than suffering. As one character in *Black Orpheus* (1999) puts it, "Happiness is a fridge stocked with beer and a full pot of beans." Without material possessions to fight over and in the supposed absence of internal differences of class, favelados in almost all these films are romanticized to embody a measure of unity impossible elsewhere.[14] Extended families eat meals together; children are always smiling; neighbors are friends. The idea here is that when the trappings of prosperity are removed, an imagined sense of community emerges.

BODIES

Just as the physical space of the favela adheres to constructed filmic conventions, so too are the bodies and activities of favela residents subject to cinematic imagining. Because favela residents are essentialized in these representations, they frequently appear as an unnamed and undifferentiated mass, part of the very landscape itself. Perhaps the defining element of the largely anonymous bodies on the landscape of the hyper-favela is their color. In truth, favela residents are overwhelmingly darker skinned than their nonfavela counterparts, a demographic feature reflected in the aesthetics of the actors selected for the films in question. However, the complex dynamics of race and the connection between skin color and socioeconomic status are not addressed in these films (Vargas 2004). Instead, race appears as a given, a largely taken-for-granted element of the dynamic of urban marginality. The absence of an exploration of racism and its consequences in Brazilian society means that Favela, Inc. reifies the connection between blackness, marginality, and violence for the consumer, without exploring pertinent historical issues. This stance mirrors Brazilian treatments of race (or nontreatment, as the case may be) more generally. The so-called myth of racial democracy—the idea that Brazil has minimal racial discrimination because of the high degree of racial mixing—silences discussion of the reality of racism. What emerges in film, then, is a racially inflected hyper-reality set in the favela. Favela, Inc. is therefore not only about the favela as a place but also about the imagined qualities of blackness in Brazil.[15]

Generally speaking, life in the hyper-favela appears to be a life of leisure: long afternoons are spent at the beach or playing soccer, residents frequently attend all-night funk parties. Funk music itself loses all of its political punch, as it is simplistically reduced to either a brash celebration of narco-culture or an erotic, oversexualized striptease. Indeed, there is an overt, voyeuristic focus on the sexuality of residents. Orpheus, for example, is the ultimate ladies' man who enjoys sex with numerous partners; favela women in *Elite Squad* are shown picking up handfuls of condoms at a local nonprofit; and in the beginning of *City of God* one favela woman, who gets lascivious tips on enhancing her sex life from a neighbor, is killed by her husband for subsequently trying them out with one of the local gangsters. With so much "fun" to be had, favela residents are rarely pictured engaging in any sort of meaningful work. There is a special irony here given that favela residents constitute the lower "working" classes. Most people in Rocinha were hardworking, taking three or even four jobs to support their families. But in the cinematic representation, the importance and sacrifice of the labor of the poor is dismissed and undervalued. "Work" in *Black Orpheus*, for example, is reduced to adorning Carnaval costumes with sequins or writing the latest samba tune. The only kind of labor envisioned in any extended way is the role of favela residents in the drug industry.

Even as these depictions reinforce stereotypes of the poor as lazy, they simultaneously advance the idea that marginality and blackness produce cultural creativity. Orpheus's gift for composing passionate samba numbers and the dark-skinned *carnavelescos'* fancy choreography celebrate the

vibrancy and originality of Afro-Brazilian culture. The flip side of this creativity is that virtually all of the other favela-based characters, especially those
of *City of God,* reinforce an imagined confluence of favela, blackness, and
criminality. This is particularly well illustrated by the main narco-trafficker
character from *City of God,* Lil Ze, who is based on a historical figure. While
the real-life Lil Ze was white, in the film he is replaced by a dark-skinned
actor, visually enforcing the link between blackness and criminality (Lorenz
2007; see also Zaluar 2004: 206). At one point in the film, Lil Ze's propensity for violence is linked to his lack of success in relationships. The problem,
the voice-over explains in a way that affirms hegemonic constructions of
white as beautiful, is that he is ugly (Vargas 2004: 444).

Aesthetics and Discourses of Favela Warfare

GOOD TRAFFICKERS / BAD TRAFFICKERS

Of all the features of the favela as global brand, none is as central as that
of the narco-trafficker. The drug trafficking presence is an integral part of
the aesthetic conventions of Favela, Inc. and provides the primary subject
material and plot line for nearly all of the images of the favela on the global market. In the favela landscapes pictured in the films discussed here,
gang graffiti covers the walls of the alleyways, and the high-powered guns
and the bags of cocaine and marijuana that symbolize the regime are frequent visual features. Even the documentary *Favela Rising* participates in
the sensationalization of crime, featuring several slow-motion sequences
with grainy shots of guns, gold jewelry, and drugs.

A south-of-the-border version of other likable criminals of television
and film such as Tony Soprano and Dexter, the trafficker as an object of
fascination reflects a larger cultural interest in the perpetrators of violence
as ambivalent heroes, particularly when contrasted to more purely evil
foes (Seltzer 1998, 2007; Tithecott 1997). Indeed, the figure of the trafficker in Favela, Inc. occupies an irresolute position between hero and villain, a depiction in many ways reflective of residents' view of real traffickers. In attempting to navigate the security terrain of the favela, everyone
learns who the "problem" traffickers are and who can be counted on to be
more reasonable. Nonetheless, traffickers, both good and bad, occupy far
more space in the cinematic favela than they do in real life.

The hyper-real trafficker is simultaneously altruistic and punishing, as is the case with Lucinho, the drug boss in *Black Orpheus*. The character orders the execution of an alleged rapist by microwaving.[16] With the tires still smoldering in the background, Lucinho graciously gives money to an elderly resident so he can buy medicine he could otherwise not afford. The stark contrast embodied here shows the trafficker as both merciless enforcer of favela law and benevolent agent of the narco-welfare state.

Though all the trafficking characters are interpreted ambivalently, the contrasting figures of Lil Ze and his partner Benny in *City of God* provide the clearest picture of how the good trafficker/bad trafficker motif is structured in the hyper-favela—and here we can see especially how the commodified version departs from real life to encompass essentialized and racialized depictions.[17] The character of Benny represents the quintessential "good trafficker." Growing up in much the same manner as Lil Ze, with whom he is shown killing and robbing throughout his childhood and adolescence, Benny is nonetheless able to enact extreme violence without letting it become a defining feature of his persona. After conquering the favela with Lil Ze in the first part of the film, he sets out to conquer yet another frontier—that between the favela and the city. In a manner reminiscent of that of Beto, as I discussed in chapter 1, Benny uses the wealth he accrues from trafficking to acquire the signs of middle-class affluence.

His initial transformation is signaled by shifts in costuming: he starts wearing designer clothes and sporting a hip haircut. Eventually, he falls in love with Angelica, a girl from the city.[18] In his own words, he turns into a *playboy,* a derogatory term, borrowed from English, and used by those in the favela to describe the wealthy, white members of the carioca upper class. For the good trafficker, crime is a means of class assimilation, and Benny's desire to be a playboy makes him far more likable and less threatening than Lil Ze, who does not (or cannot because of his skin color) appear to have similar aspirations. As the good trafficker, Benny maintains a stance toward violence that distinguishes him from his partner. Ever the peacemaker, he often placates Lil Ze. This makes him a hero among the favela residents, who suffer under Lil Ze's iron fist. But after Benny becomes a playboy he is no longer at home in the favela. At the end of the film, he plans to leave City of God for a romantic life in the countryside with Angelica. Ultimately, escape is not possible. He takes a bullet intended for Lil Ze and dies at his own going-away party.

Representing the "bad trafficker," Lil Ze does not appear to aspire to cross over to success in other social milieus. Even if he wanted to, he doesn't have Benny's racial phenotype and he cannot cross the boundaries to become a "playboy." The character's identity is concretely tied to his role as the drug boss, and it is only through the constant enactment of violence that he achieves empowerment. His fundamentally "evil" nature is clearly spelled out from the beginning of the film. When preparing to take over the favela's drug trade, he seeks supernatural protection by making a pact with Exu, the Candomblé orixá most often associated with the devil.[19] Throughout, he wears a necklace with the distinctive colors of Exu, symbolically reminding the viewer of his sinister allegiances.

For the bad trafficker, violence is a form of recreation. Lil Ze is not content simply controlling the favela's lucrative drug trade but consistently targets favela residents; trafficking is but a venue for the realization of his sadistic tendencies, a construction we see repeated in the case of bad cops in *Elite Squad* and *Elite Squad 2*, where law enforcement covers for an underlying enjoyment of killing and hurting others. In every scene in which he appears, Lil Ze is engaged in violence in one form or another. Angry that a character named Knockout Ned is dating a woman he is interested in, Lil Ze singles him out for a string of humiliating punishments. In one scene, he gathers his gang together and forces Ned to strip naked in front of the whole favela—an order Ned cannot refuse without risking his life. A few scenes later, Lil Ze leads his gang in the rape of Ned's girlfriend.

His penchant for violence is contagious. Among the legion of enemies that Lil Ze faces, including rival drug bosses and corrupt police, it is ultimately at the hands of a group of delinquent children called the Runts that he meets his end. At the close of the film, the Runts shoot Lil Ze dozens of times at close range, riddling his body with bullets. Despite their different relationships with violence, in the hyper-favela neither good nor bad traffickers escape from a life of crime. Afterward, the Runts jubilantly parade through the alleys of City of God, declaring victory and proclaiming ownership of the favela. Another generation of "bad traffickers" is born. The Runts' takeover works to contemporize the film, which begins in the 1970s. It is easy for the viewer to imagine the now grown-up Runts running the favela today. In the closing frame, they are shown walking triumphantly down an alley, as the words *Based on a true story* appear on the screen.

In sum, though these fictitious representations of traffickers might hold some grain of truth when measured against the reality of life in the favela, the prevalence of these characters, to the exclusion of regular, "civilian" ones, paints a very limited and noninclusive picture of favela humanity.

LOST CHILDHOOD

In the hyper-favela, the allure of a life of trafficking poses a constant danger to the favela's children, whose induction into the narco-regime threatens to undermine the larger social order.[20] Two different "types" of violent children appear in Favela, Inc.: those who are naturally violent and therefore beyond salvation and those for whom salvation is possible if the dark influences of favela violence can be mitigated.[21] Among the lost causes, again we see *City of God's* Lil Ze, or Lil Dice as he was called as a child (fig. 5). A hardened criminal from an early age, Lil Dice engages in murder with frightening cheer, as if violence is encoded in his very DNA. The character outdoes even the older gangsters in his enthusiasm. In the beginning of the film, he is left outside as a lookout while the other members of the gang rob hotel patrons. Angry that (at eight years old) he is excluded as too young to fully participate in the robbery, he returns to the hotel on his own and smilingly shoots everyone at close range.

As an adult and *City of God's* merciless drug boss, Lil Dice, now Lil Ze, works to actively convert favela youth to a life of crime. In one of the most troubling scenes in the film, Lil Ze confronts the Runts (ranging in age from four to twelve), who share his naturally violent tendencies. They have been wreaking havoc in defiance of his prohibition on robbery in the favela. He hunts them down and metes out the typical punishment for robbery—a bullet in the hand or foot of the offender. But Lil Ze also seizes the opportunity to make a child soldier out of one of the younger kids named Steak and Fries, who has been doing errands for his gang.

Steak and Fries represents the second type of child soldier in the constructed favela. He is basically a good kid for whom being in the gang means getting to hang around with hip older traffickers like Benny. Lil Ze,

Figure 5. In this screen shot used to promote *City of God*, the young Lil Ze, or Lil Dice as he is known as a child, takes apparent pleasure in wielding a gun. The tropical backdrop, complete with bunches of bananas hanging from a tree, connects pleasure of violence to the exotic landscape. Photograph from IMDb.

however, uses the confrontation with the Runts as a chance to turn Steak and Fries into a true soldier, in the process destroying his basic goodness and thus transforming the character. He tells the child to choose one of the Runts to kill. When faced with taking a life, the fear and uncertainty on the character's face is painfully obvious, but he yields to the pressure from the older traffickers and shoots the smallest of the Runts. The effect is one of history repeating itself; Lil Dice's penchant for violence is reborn in another generation.

A similar construction of endangered favela youth is commodified in *Elite Squad*. Romerito, a young boy who hangs around at the nonprofit organization run by some of the central characters of the film, struggles with his schoolwork and is shown playing in the streets long after he should be in bed. He is prime fodder for recruitment into the trafficking regime, which is presented as an easier route to prestige than schooling. Luckily for Romerito, an NGO worker and the film's police protagonist intervene on his behalf, astutely noting that the boy needs glasses and that it is his eyesight, rather than a lack of motivation, that is holding him back. After being able to "see" the favela more clearly, Romerito is able to take the right path in life.[22]

The idea that the favela is full of kids like Steak and Fries and Romerito, on whom the predatory institution of trafficking is poised to prey, is one of the most enduring and powerful features of Favela, Inc., and one that has important consequences. The image of lost childhood is central to structuring charity work, as this "at risk" population is the target for virtually all governmental and nongovernmental (both international and domestic) programs in the favela, including that of Afro-Reggae, the NGO featured in *Favela Rising*. But the focus on trafficking alone as structuring risk is misleading. Structural violence, lack of medical care, poor education, high rates of domestic violence, parents' absence from home due to work schedules, and parental drug abuse immiserate the lives of many more children than does recruitment into the traffic. The cinematic construction of risk occludes these less glamorous but very real elements of many favela childhoods. Perhaps equally problematic is the way in which these representations overlook the vast number of good parents in the favela: those who work several jobs to send their children to private schools, keep them off the streets, and give them brighter futures.

GOOD COP / BAD COP

Both protecting hero and punishing disciplinarian, police are also subject to ambivalent interpretations in Favela, Inc. In the films analyzed here, the police are responsible for perpetuating the culture of violence in several primary ways: they are corrupt and implicated in trafficking and other crimes, and they are the perpetrators of extreme violence that matches and at times exceeds that of traffickers. Like the traffickers, police in the filmic hyper-favela are divided according to a good cop (BOPE) versus bad cop (regular forces) motif.

The "conventional" police are clearly part of the problem; their failings contribute to the imagined lawlessness of the violent favela. The bad cop in Favela, Inc. is always from the regular forces; he is corrupt and inhumane and abuses the power denoted by his uniform. The main sergeant in *Black Orpheus,* who is called Stallone in reference to the tough American actor of action film fame, embodies the inhumane attitude of the police regarding favela residents. The character orders his officers to beat up residents at random and comments that he wishes he could just sterilize the whole favela to keep residents from reproducing.

While the outright murder of the popular classes by the police is portrayed as commonplace in these films (and even celebrated in *Elite Squad*), police corruption, which reverberates across all segments of carioca society, is depicted as a larger social problem. In *Elite Squad,* police levy "protection" fees on business owners, playing a key role in a citywide system of corruption. Cops kill other cops in order to take over lucrative bribe territories and engage in frequent "body dumping," where officers move bodies into other precincts so as not to have to investigate murders.[23] They even use the supposed violence of traffickers as a cover for executing their more problematic colleagues. The conventional police are also deeply implicated in the business of trafficking: they take payoffs from drug lords and sell them weapons.

These dramatic representations of police corruption and brutality pale in comparison to their real-life violence as captured in the documentary films *Bus 174* and *Favela Rising. Bus 174* uses live television news footage from bus hijacking incident to illustrate the utter disorganization and poor training of the police forces (Villarejo 2006). Police are shown simply standing around. Snipers can't get a shot off. The officers make no attempt to cordon off the area or keep the news crews away from the bus. At the end of the documentary, the viewer is told that police suffocated Sandro, the bus hijacker, in the back of their police car on the way to the station. Since the incident occurred on live television, there was little doubt as to the officers' guilt, but a jury subsequently exonerated them. Many among the general population applauded them for their actions, a reaction underscoring how readily the carioca population condones extreme violence by police against the perceived threat of violence on the part of the poor (Caldeira 2002). *Favela Rising* also addresses the problem of police brutality, and the massacre of twenty-one civilians of the Vigário Geral slum by police figures centrally in the documentary. Like *Bus 174*, the film relies on actual news footage, and the recurrent image of rows of open coffins, lined up in the central plaza of the slum, reminds the viewer of the impact of state-perpetuated violence in favela communities.

Such a disparaging view of the men in blue is juxtaposed to the positive and celebratory depiction of the men in black: BOPE. *Elite Squad* has been read as both a critique of state violence and a celebration of the squad (which some saw as fascist) (Marques and Rocha 2010; Oliveira 2008).[24] Capitão Nascimento, the BOPE captain in the *Elite Squad* films, is the ambivalent hero, based on the real-life captain who consulted on the film and coauthored the book from which it was made. Tired of fighting the war against the traffic, in the first film he suffers from panic attacks while eagerly awaiting the birth of his first child and attempting to choose a successor to lead the troops, which will enable him to retire from the Special Forces. Nascimento's anxiety, while humanizing him for the cinematic audience, contributes to and fuels his aggression. As the plot unfolds, he and his men torture and kill more and more people in the favela. The portrayal of human suffering in the film is so visceral and graphic that it threatens to undermine BOPE's heroic role. However, since BOPE's violence is legitimized by larger society as the state-sanctioned aggression necessary to defeat the trafficking enemy, the viewer is asked to excuse what is otherwise extremely revolting behavior on the part of Nascimento and his men; BOPE's use of force is necessary to quell the disorder posed by the violent hyper-favela. When interpreted in light of the equally brutal, but dishonest, regular forces, BOPE are the default heroes—the lesser of two evils.

Just as a legacy of violence is transmitted from one generation of traffickers to the next, so too does violent policing pass from senior to junior officer. Nascimento can only retire when he finds an officer who matches his capacity and zeal for eliminating traffickers. In the last scene of the film, his replacement, Mathias (a character also based on a collaborator and coauthor), shoots the drug boss in the face at close range even as he pleads for his life. His ability to deliver violent death in the face of cries for mercy qualifies him to lead BOPE. As the screen goes black, the viewer hears only the sound of the trigger being pulled. Beyond the certain death of the drug lord, the film doesn't have a clear ending, and this works to set the scene for a sequel. In the meantime, however, the viewer is left with the sense that BOPE's war against the traffic is far from over but is continuing with a new captain at its helm.

The sequel, which exceeds the original in its graphic depiction of violence, again takes up the issue of good cops versus bad cops but this time within BOPE itself. The once untouchable institution has become corrupted, and Nascimento, now promoted to a political role in the Office of the Secretary of Security, is again the ambivalent hero who must sort out the good cops from the bad. Importantly, however, the sequel addresses the rise of militias in the city, groups of off-duty police officers, firefighters, and prison guards who are increasingly taking over favela "security" while levying protection taxes on residents and profiting from various illegal schemes. The film delivers a strong critique of the participation of corrupt politicians as well. And while the picture that emerges is one that more fully captures the complexity of armed violence in Rio today, it also furthers the notion of Rio as a city plagued by conflict and corruption at all levels.

ALWAYS WAR

With the violence of both traffickers and police taking center stage in the hyper-favela, what emerges is a picture of the condition of the favela as one of perpetual war. The way in which violence is envisioned as a normal and everyday aspect of favela life marks it as a site of constant conflict. As Mark Seltzer discusses in his work on the "true crime" genre, horrific crimes are always carried out amid conditions that are otherwise normal, something he calls the "violence-normality complex" (2007: 40–45). The sun is always shining, children are happily at play. Suddenly, and without warning, atrocity tears through the fabric of the everyday.

A similar convention of unexpected violence is commodified in Favela, Inc. As the favela community in *Black Orpheus* is peacefully and happily preparing for Carnaval, their preparations are suddenly interrupted by a surprise police invasion, leaving everyone scrambling for cover. The joyous occasion of Benny's going-away party—for which the entire community turns out to bid farewell to the popular drug lord—is suddenly interrupted by gunshots. In the opening scene of *Elite Squad*, the weekly baile funk party turns into the site of a massacre, as revelers are caught in the crossfire between police and the dealers. The message is clear: the favela is a sleeping giant that at any moment can be awakened; the potential for violence is always present, and anyone can become a victim. Violent death is presented as frighteningly random. Some of the victims of the Vigário Geral massacre, the subject of *Favela Rising*, were innocently enjoying a beer together when they were gunned down by police. In *Black Orpheus*, a woman is struck by a stray bullet while sitting on her couch watching television.

The favela's violence always threatens to overflow its borders, a feature of Favela, Inc. that is key to developing discourses of real-life containment—policing or building walls around the favela. At any moment the hyper-favela can rupture the seeming calm of the city itself, just as Sandro de Nascimento did when he pulled out a gun and took hostages on bus number 174 as it was passing through the Botanical Garden District one weekday afternoon. Though Sandro had spent most of his life homeless, and so was not a direct product of the culture of the favela, the use of extended aerial shots of several large favela complexes at the beginning of the film identifies the favela as the physical place from which his violence stems. In fact, Sandro had more experience with state sponsored violence and neglect than he did with traffickers. As a child, he had witnessed his mother's murder, and he had been in and out of juvenile delinquent facilities for much of his life. On the streets, he lived on the steps of the Candelaria Church in the city's downtown, where he saw the infamous slaughter of his young friends by police in 1993.

Bus 174 also importantly illustrates the way violent spectacle functions in the Rio news media. As the documentary footage highlights, Sandro is fully aware of the way in which the live television coverage worked to protect him from the snipers' bullets; no one was going to shoot him with the whole country watching. In a life marked by social exclusion and invisibility, this was his chance to be "seen." He makes a point to tell his audience that he was at Candelaria and levels strong critiques at the police out the bus window. Sandro, and his eventual death at the hands of police, underscores yet another feature of Rio's perpetual war: violence begets violence.

Life in the hyper-favela is presented in film as consumed by armed violence, all the time. The effect of such a depiction is that it detracts from the other elements of being that take place in these communities and that structure sociability in vital ways. The spectacle and hyper-visibility of war in the favela makes not-war invisible. The characterization of the favela as a place of endless conflict is essential to constructing the favela as a place of violent disorder, thus renewing the need for the order-ing power of BOPE. While structural violence is a feature of everyday life in Rocinha, armed violence of the variety depicted in these films is spo-radic, targeted (not random), and certainly not glamorous.

CONVERGING MEDIA

The aesthetics and discourses of the hyper-favela, as I have outlined them here, are consumed in a disembodied manner. Film can be watched from anywhere around the globe, including from the favela. In addition to these cinematic forms, other iterations of the same themes are found in con-verging media. Some of these converging media allow for greater partici-pation and interaction on the part of the viewer, even if the overall experi-ence is still confined to the imagination. Also of note is that although the films that convey the aesthetics and discourses of Favela, Inc. originate in Brazil (if not in the favela), converging media are primarily authored by foreigners. In this way, converging media may also be interpreted as evi-dence for the global success of the widespread circulation of the Brazilian-made hyper-favela.

Gaming

The perpetual conflict between traffickers and police in Rio is so entrenched in the global imaginary that the favela has become a suitable backdrop for war-based video games, featured prominently in the highly successful American-made game *Modern Warfare 2*. In the game, the view of the favela comes from behind an MP5K submachine gun. The famous Christ statue appears in the distance. Through the Play Station controller, the soldier/policeman/mercenary is represented by a BOPE-esque skull and crossbones. Running through the streets, the figure passes closed businesses, burned-out cars, and abandoned concrete rowhouses. He takes cover behind the occasional palm tree to shoot at the armed drug traffickers who are hiding throughout the gamescape. Discovering the criminal stronghold, the player calls in a tactical nuclear strike. The favela explodes and bodies fall as blood splatters the screen. Victory is declared.

The aesthetics of the game reflect a number of the characteristic tropes of the hyper-favela as I have identified them here. The setting reflects the homogenized tropical, seaside favela landscape. Bodies are treated similarly. Civilians are erased all together; only traffickers appear, giving the "deserted" and "war-torn" favela an apocalyptic feeling. With the player taking the point of view of a police officer/soldier looking out from behind the barrel of a gun, the space is inscribed not as one of life, but of war and death.

Modern Warfare 2's use of the favela as an exciting place for war games is both a product of Favela, Inc.'s global circulation and a venue for its further dissemination, commodifying hyper-real favela conflict as a form of recreation.[25] And yet to play the favela sequence involves a certain entailment with the violence it depicts. Scenarios in the game constitute an especially powerful form of othering, as players experience both intimacy with and distance from the conflict depicted. They can act out various roles but can always turn off the game whenever they feel like leaving the war. This mobility, and the power of this mobility to enter and exit the hyper-favela at will, is also reflected in tourists' desire to play at, but ultimately leave behind, the "war-torn" favela they visit (see chapter 4).

Favela-based war play is not limited to the digital world. I purchased a Lego miniature on eBay, where it was advertised as a "favela drug trafficker" (guns sold separately). With a bandanna partially covering his face, the figure does not possess features that specifically identify him as either Brazilian or as a favela-based trafficker. Rather, he reflects an imagined transnational gangster aesthetic, which could just as well be seen in Mexico or Los Angeles as in Brazil. Although there are notable regional, historical, and cultural differences between narco-regimes, the Lego bandido is suggestive of how these differences are being collapsed to form a stereotype of the Latin American trafficker.

In other cases, toys are more specifically rooted in the Brazilian setting, as is the case with the toy version of the caveirão used by BOPE. The caveirão is a popular Brazilian toy, widely available in the chain stores Casas Bahia and Casa e Video (equivalent to Target or Walmart). When I asked salespeople who bought the toy, they said it was purchased by children both inside and outside favelas. While in some senses playing at cops and bandidos is not dissimilar from playing with G.I. Joes or other activities that take war and conflict as the topic of play, one must also ask about the subjectivity and relationship between who is playing and what their relationship is with the particular war in question. Does the experience of play differ for those who only know the hyper-favela and those who live in the favela and can draw from their own repertoire of real experiences with the caveirão or traffickers? Interestingly, my observation of these games (both digital and otherwise) as they are played inside the favela reveals a certain ambiguity, at the crux of the really real and the hyper-real. When favela kids play, nobody wants to be the cop.[26]

Beauty and Fashion

Even as it is continuously marketed as a place of poverty and violence, the hyper-favela takes on a gritty yet appealing quality; it is edgy and transgressive precisely by virtue of its elaboration as a place of lack and risk. Importantly, however, this formulation does not find the favela compelling in and of itself; rather, it is useful as a point of contrast against which other more conventional commodities are cast. This is especially apparent in how the favela is used in the marketing of fashion and merchandising.

For example, a certain kind of surf shorts was widely sold by street vendors and in boutiques across Rio during the time of my fieldwork. A photo of a "typical" hillside favela makes up the background. Superimposed on the characteristic brick buildings are the iconic images of the war on drugs. On one side is the "Big Skull" and on the other side is a masked, heavily armed man, gun stretched across his chest defensively. He could be a trafficker or a policeman, an anonymous figure reminiscent of the unidentified "Latin" Lego gangster. The inclusion of the word *Paz* (Peace) on the shorts references the commodified victimhood of favela residents, since during times of intense crisis in the favela residents frequently raise banners calling for peace.

Favela violence is both normalized and made into an acceptable motif for fashion. The shorts also homogenize the landscape, cast all residents in the overly simplistic role of either the perpetrators or the victims of

Figure 6. Favela Duvet Cover by Geronimo Studios for Deny Designs.

violence, and visually reinforce the imagined centrality of war and conflict in favela life while erasing all other forms of subjectivity. Fashion products like this both reflect the violent favela as brand and put the visual markers of this brand into further circulation as they are worn around the city and purchased by tourists as souvenirs (fig. 6).

In some cases, the aesthetics of favela deprivation are used by fashion designers and marketers to emphasize the beauty of their models.[27] This quality characterizes a photo shoot staged by the U.S. television reality show *America's Next Top Model*. In a 2009 episode, judge Tyra Banks and the contestants travel to Brazil. While technically filmed in São Paulo, there are confusing, geographically impossible shots of the Rio beach thrown in as well, again homogenizing the Brazilian landscape through reference to the coastline. The contestants do a photo shoot in a favela, where the architecture and the bodies of residents, mostly dark-skinned children kicking a soccer ball, appear out of focus, as background to the models in the foreground. In yet another expression of how Brazil is imagined as a tropical place, the contestants are dressed as none other than . . . Carmen Miranda!

Finally, the idea of the aesthetic of the favela landscape as a useful point of contrast in order to highlight beauty or high fashion extends to uses of the bodies of favela residents as well. In an extremely high-profile event in June 2013, a bricklayer's assistant was taken from his home in the poorest part of Rocinha by police and questioned. He never came home. Though police claimed to have released him, it later came out that nearly twenty officers, including the chief of the local precinct, tortured him to death, "disappeared" his body, and orchestrated a complex cover-up. In the aftermath and accompanying publicity storm, during which the bricklayer assistant's family repeatedly appeared in the media, his son was "discovered" by a prominent Rio-based modeling agency. "He is a diamond in the rough," explained the photographer who launched his career.[28]

Though the son's modeling work will certainly help a family that lost its primary breadwinner to police violence, his marketability is undoubtedly tied to his role as a victim. His photo portfolio, which was publicized in the daily paper, consists of posed images of a serious, apparently grief-stricken, and angry face. In this case, then, we see not only the commodification of the body of the favela resident for what it signifies in terms of skin color and class but also the commodification of the identity of the particular model whose body is marked with the characteristic tropes of the hyper-favela: crime, lost childhood, and state violence.

Celebrities

A number of pop stars have used the favela as a backdrop for music videos, thus introducing it to an MTV audience and widely circulating the favela as a brand. Most famously, Michael Jackson visited the community of Dona Marta and filmed the video for the song "They Don't Care about Us" in 1996. Jackson's visit, taken together with the message of the song (which made explicit references to racism and police brutality), drew attention to the plight and disenfranchisement of favela residents. In the clip, the social justice message of the lyrics is enhanced by references to poor policing and through Jackson's dance moves, in which he makes guns out of his fingers and shoots repeatedly. The nobler, even if somewhat fraught, nature of Jackson's performance of social solidarity contrasts sharply with that of Ja Rule's use of the favela to accumulate the social currency of traffickers. And yet both singers appropriated the global brand of the violent favela.

While the mere fact that Jackson felt the favela and Rio de Janeiro was an appropriate venue for the video is a testament to the success of the violent favela as a global brand, the video also works to reaffirm the image of the favela as a marginal, dangerous location and its residents as hapless victims. Jackson's video perpetuated the image of poor favela residents as innately creative artists and musicians. The well-known Afro-Brazilian band Olodum, composed of hundreds of percussionists with painted African drums, paraded through the streets as Jackson's backup band. The brightly colored buildings of the historic district of the Pelourinho, located in the northeastern city of Salvador, far from Rio, was used to convey the favela's cheerful poverty. Again, we see confused geography lending itself to the communication of a romanticized, if problematic, Brazil.

Celebrity uses of the favela are also gendered in important ways. In the aftermath of the King of Pop's death, Alicia Keyes and Beyoncé revisited Dona Marta and filmed a video for "Put It in a Love Song" in the same parts of the favela where Jackson had originally performed. (Incidentally, they used what has come to be a tourist destination known as the rooftop of Michael Jackson, which is now complete with a bronze bust of the pop star.) However, the lyrics of the song and the photo stills of the video (yet to be released) suggest that the gritty backdrop of the favela was being used much in the same sense as it is in fashion—to accent the beauty and elegance of the female stars rather than to convey a political or social message. Dona Marta appears quaint as Keyes dances down alleys swept clean, pausing to sit on plastic, brightly colored beer crates. Beyoncé leans out of a broken-down vintage bus. The favela's landscape of urban decay can be strategically employed, not as a place of value in its own right, but rather as a setting against which beauty can be highlighted and displayed.

When put in the same framework with other, more conventionally beautiful things, the favela becomes chic.

CONCLUSION

Brazil has long been famous for its stunning beaches, erotic samba, beautiful people, and endless tropical sunshine. While this vision of Brazil, and of Rio de Janeiro, continues to be exported to the world, a new image of the city is emerging alongside it—one that celebrates the spectacular violence characteristic of the ongoing war between police and traffickers in the city's favelas. The favela is fast becoming an iconic feature of Rio. There is now a growing market for the favela as a global brand and a substantial audience interested in consuming representations of the violent favela through media and a variety of other leisure-based practices and products.

These media are consumed not only by outsiders but by insiders as well. The audience is not limited to those in the "formal" city or abroad but includes members of favela communities themselves. Though further research is needed on internal consumption, it does not appear that residents reject the hyper-favela's images; instead, they seem to enjoy them. Nor are they passive consumers but highly participatory ones, constantly discussing and critiquing the video and verbal texts. When I watched *Elite Squad* with a group of favela friends (it had been pirated prior to release), I was surprised to find that almost everyone laughed throughout the film. They laughed, they said, because the oppressive behavior of BOPE toward those in the favela was just "so true" that there was nothing to do but laugh. As other literature on the representation of marginality in film has shown (see Cobb et al. 2003), disenfranchised people are at times eager for images of themselves, unconsciously embracing stereotypes and even creating an overlay of hyper-reality in their own lives. It is also possible that in consuming the cinematic favela, viewers don't see themselves in the depictions but instead (as I was told in different conversations) see "other" people, in "other favelas" worse than the one they live in.

As I have shown in this chapter, Favela, Inc. creates a hyper-favela with a distinct set of aesthetics and discourses crafted by outsiders and circulated globally. The aesthetics and discourses of the favela-as-brand do not reflect the complexities of local existence but rather homogenize and sensationalize favela landscapes, bodies, and violence (both physical and structural). The power of these mediated representations lies in their ability to define what favela life looks like for the audience, feeding stereotypes that come to inform policy. The favela-as-brand generates considerable wealth, little of which is redirected toward improving the dismal realities. In this way, Favela, Inc. entails representational violence and deepens structural inequality. Clearly, these processes are not unique to Brazil but are implicit in the production and consumption of images of structural and physical violence in a variety of settings.

Favela, Inc. is central to developing an understanding of favela tourism not as an exceptional form of travel, separate from everyday life, but rather as imbricated with wider cultural behavior related to the consumption of images of the bodies and lives of exotic others. Favela, Inc. enables imaginary travel on a scale far exceeding the actual movement of visiting tourists. I do not, however, see Favela, Inc. as the sole source of causation here. It would be an overstatement to say that travelers come to Rio *only* because of the allure of the violent favela as constructed by media. Nevertheless, as I show in the next chapter, media imaginaries do shape desire and experience in important ways. Disembodied media consumption and embodied tourist consumption inform one another. Both use spectacle to transform favela violence into a commodity form, albeit in different, yet intertwined, ways. Both media producers and tour companies are wont to point out that the products they proffer work to raise global awareness of violence and suffering. But even if they manage to achieve this in some small measure, they also thin out and distort human experience by romanticizing, aestheticizing, and commodifying violence.

4 The Tourists

March 2008. The film *City of God* begins with a chicken destined to be dinner at a favela barbeque. The camera takes in the chicken's strut as it moves among the raucous crowd and then zooms in on the hand of the drug boss sharpening a knife against a grindstone. Sensing its impending death, the chicken takes off down one of the favela's narrow alleyways as the boss and his guests give chase. As the tempo of the music builds, the camera shifts to Rocket, the protagonist of the film, who is himself running through the alleys of the favela, believing the gang is after him. At the foot of the favela, all three parties collide and are joined by a fourth—an advancing group of less than honest policemen. Now intertwined, Rocket's fate and that of the rebellious chicken unfold backward from this initial moment. The image of the runaway chicken has become iconic of *City of God* and is commonly used in promotional materials for the film. I had forgotten about the chicken when Leonardo, who worked as a tour guide in the favela, took a long drag off one of his menthols and asked me if I remembered the opening sequence of the movie. It was a Sunday afternoon, and the favela was humming with the sound of music and people basking in the summer sun. With families cooking together on their rooftops, the scene was reminiscent of the one to which he was referring. "That chicken," he remarked, "nearly got me killed recently."

Leonardo was one of the only tour guides who actually resided in the community, and he would often bring small groups of tourists to the favela after typical tour hours for funk parties and drinks on weekend nights. On more than one occasion, after overindulging in the seductively sweet low-grade *cachaça caipirinhas*—the drink of choice in the favela—a tourist did something brash. The previous weekend, Leonardo had been with just such a tourist. Suddenly the man jumped from his chair and took off running down an alley adjacent to the bar. In Rocinha running is something that tends to attract attention, and a gringo running through the same dark alley that housed the neighborhood's drug-selling site quickly led to a group of traffickers pointing their machine guns at him and ordering him to stop. Leonardo followed the sound of the commotion and found his tourist on his knees, his hands behind his head, with several angry traffickers standing over him, firing questions.

The terrified tourist was only able to gesture weakly toward a lone chicken, just barely visible under the flickering street light. "Luckily," Leonardo said with a wry smile, "this was not my first encounter with tourists and chickens, and I was able to explain to the 'guys' [traffickers] that the man had been trying to get a snapshot with the chicken. You know, from *City of God*, I said." "Oh, right . . . from *City of God*," they replied, laughing, as one guy lowered his gun, grabbed the chicken, handed it to the tourist, and said, "Go ahead, man, get your picture." The moment that the tourist had been trying to capture—a simple photo with a chicken, intended to connect his own experience as a favela tourist to the gritty violence of the film—was now enhanced by a more spectacular encounter with real traffickers and the potential for real violence. The incident Leonardo described was but one among scores that I witnessed and heard about in which visitors' expectations of what the favela would be like, and the kinds of images and ideas they had developed prior to travel, came to influence the experiences sought out while visiting. As the confluence of guide, tourist, and chicken suggest, the locality of the favela does not simply await discovery by the intrepid traveler. Rather, the favela-as-tourist-destination, like any commodity in the global market, is produced for consumption. Tourism represents the embodied consumption of the violent favela as a global brand.

Favela tourism is far more than a benign leisure practice. It *produces violence* in a number of ways, both economic and representational. Both the process of commodification of favela violence by tour companies and guides and its embodied consumption by tourists are violent. On the commodification side, the organization of the tour companies and the flow of profit they generate enrich outsiders at the expense of favela residents. The political economy of the industry thus reflects, and extends, local class inequalities, hierarchies, and forms of consumption. Equally important are issues of representation. Nonfavela residents—guides, company owners, and tourists—figure powerfully as authors and interpreters of the touristic favela, thereby problematically concentrating the power to speak for the favela beyond the reach of those who actually live there.

In addition to the local inequalities that favela tourism perpetuates, the presence of tourists attests to the centrality of larger, global structural inequalities, where only certain populations have the means to travel and where the misery of some has become a commodity for others.[1] And finally, the process of touristic consumption of favela violence in both its physical and structural forms produces a disconnect between violence as a touristic spectacle and the very real and crucial experience of structural violence—poverty, lack of opportunity, discrimination—as a lived reality in the favela.

Favela tourism, like other forms of cultural tourism generally, is driven by the desire to know and consume "authentic" and "exotic" others. This view of tourism, derived from Dean MacCannell's (1976) classic formulation, sees "First World" tourists as suffering from a form of disillusionment and alienation symptomatic of advanced capitalism. Tourist ennui drives an ongoing search for more rewarding ways of being and living, imagined to be present in the realities of less evolved or developed others. Consequently, the consumption of the authentic favela (remembering here that authenticity is very much linked to the favela's violence) offers tourists a means through which to assuage the disillusionment of their lives.

By examining favela tours within the larger framework of violence in Rio, my work departs from previous scholarship that has framed favela tourism as consuming poverty rather than violence. In this formulation, Bianca Freire-Medeiros (2009, 2013), in one of the only published studies on the topic, places favela tourism within an emerging niche travel market called "poorism," "poverty tourism," or "slum tourism" (Butler 2010; Booyens 2010; Manfred 2010; Odede 2010; Weiner 2008; Frenzel, Koens, and Steinbrink 2012). In her fascinating monograph, *Gringo na laje* (Gringo on the Rooftop), she argues that favela tourism is driven by tourists' desires to see and to consume impoverished carioca slums: "Brazilian poverty, while never a secret, has now become an incontestable tourist attraction" (2009: 19). By framing the practice as such, she envisions tourism in the favela as analytically similar to visiting impoverished destinations in other corners of the world, such as Soweto, Johannesburg, or the slums of Mumbai and Buenos Aires (Freire Medeiros 2009, 2013; Freire-Medeiros and Menezes 2009).

While this comparative perspective is useful for an analysis of poorism, neither popular interest in poverty as a spectacle nor tourists' utopian fantasies about their solidarity with the poor is sufficient to explain the growing rise in favela visitors. Poverty-as-attraction does not account for or explain the violence-focused media's influence in structuring tourist desires and encounters. Likewise, poorism alone does not account for the market in tours more explicitly engaged with the favela's narco-world. Favela tours are unique in this regard as other poorism destinations are typically not under the explicit governance of narco-traffickers. Tourism in Rocinha, therefore, is better understood through its relationship with favela violence, of which poverty, as a form of structural violence, is but one facet.[2] Thus, rather than envision poverty as the central attraction and favela tourism as poorism, I interpret poverty as one kind of violence, albeit one that features centrally in the construction of favela authenticity.

TOURISTIC BUREAUCRACIES

Organized tourism in Rocinha began in 1992.[3] As tourist interest in the violent favela increased, the industry grew and diversified to accommodate it. Freire-Medeiros estimated that in 2009 there were around 3,500 tourists per month riding in jeeps along Rocinha's main road and walking through its narrow alleyways (2009: 10).[4] According to several of the tour guides I interviewed, after the Cristo statue, Sugar Loaf Mountain, and

Copacabana Beach, Rocinha is the most popular tourist destination in the city. All of the major international guidebooks—*Lonely Planet, Frommer's, Rough Guides*—have standard entries on favela tours. Tourists typically purchase tours through their hotels and hostels, with management taking a percentage of the price from favela tour companies for referring their guests.[5] For some visitors, such as those taking day trips from cruise ships, the favela tour is included as part of a city package, signaling its rise in importance as a destination that is now part of what it means to "see" Rio.[6]

As a result of the sustained and regular tourist presence in Rocinha, tourists themselves have become an expected and almost unremarkable feature of the favela landscape. Tour itineraries run along established routes, at established times, so that everyone in the community knows when and where to expect tourists. During my fieldwork there were five well-established companies operating in Rocinha, though this number has changed slightly over time. The five main agencies accounted for the majority of the tourist traffic in the favela, with regular tours taking place twice a day, morning and afternoon.[7] All except one of these companies began with tours to other destinations around the city, only adding favela tours as a result of the growing market.

Members of the Brazilian middle and upper classes own every one of the large agencies that operate in the favela. Upper management has varying degrees of interaction with daily operations. One of the five owners I talked with had never even been to a favela, let alone the one his company was operating in, a fact that is suggestive of the disconnect between management and the on-the-ground functioning of the tours. It also signals that tours do not always, as their proponents claim (including this particular man's guides), challenge extant social divides. In contrast, another owner, who resided in the neighborhood adjacent to the favela, often led the tours himself and was highly engaged and committed to social projects. That said, this owner was very much the exception, and other operators characterized him as self-righteous and annoying.

With the majority of company owners taking a more distant role and providing little oversight of tour discourses and practice, the flavor of favela tourism is determined largely by the forty-some guides employed by the major agencies. Of these forty, only three were Rocinha residents.[8] The rest came from the Brazilian middle classes. Historically, business, industry, and even the domestic spheres of Rio's more affluent society members have always depended on the labor of the favela. In this way, the dynamics of favela tourism represent historical continuity. But the new twist here is that it is not the labor of residents in the traditional sense that fuels profit but the brand of the favela itself. With negligible numbers of locals leading tours, and with owners concentrated beyond the borders of the favela, the economics and representational politics of favela tourism are highly problematic in that they reflect and extend existing social and class divides in Brazilian society.[9]

SPECTACLE AND STAGED AUTHENTICITY

Favela tourism is a lucrative enterprise. Tour prices range from R$35 to R$75 (US$20–45). Given that the average monthly salary of favela residents is around R$403 per month (US$199) (Pacheco 2011), tour companies generate equivalent revenue in just a few hours.[10] Except for one owner, who donates sizable sums to an after-school program for children in a nearby favela, financial contributions to the community on the part of the agencies are negligible. When I brought this up in interviews, one company owner, Carlos, explained to me that he didn't believe in giving regular donations, which he felt "could lead to dangerous forms of dependence and paternalism." He believed it was better to perform what he called (in English) "random acts of kindness." For example, he had once built a house for a needy favela family in the poor area of Rocinha. His random act of charity just so happened to be situated along his company's tour route and became part of a larger performance and narrative of touristic charity. The grateful recipients were often called upon to perform their gratitude for his tourists.

Carlos asserted that unlike other company owners, he did an important service for the community in that his tours were designed to "stimulate the favela economy." In truth, he structured tours so as to facilitate *tourist* contributions to the betterment of the community, in lieu of his own. He used the local form of transportation (motorcycle taxis), the tours stopped at a bakery where tourists could buy a snack, and he subsidized local artists by taking tourists to an art studio, though he took a commission of

sales. At the art studio, he got free use of a rooftop for tourists to take photos. Other companies had to pay residents for the use of rooftops. In short,
Carlos outsourced the financial obligation to improve the favela to tourists
and made an additional profit on their expenditures.[11]

Though Carlos's arrogant posture was more overt than that of the other
owners, his tour reflects the larger injustices of the tour business. Financially
speaking, tourism produces little material change in the favela, despite
the fact that owners and guides often claim otherwise. When asked, not
one of the hundreds of favela residents I interviewed could cite a single
example of concrete improvement in Rocinha as a result of the presence of
tourists.

In addition to the exploitative economics that underlie tour organization, all forms of favela tourism enable outsiders to continue to shape the
discourse surrounding local life; tours are themselves a form of Favela, Inc.
and a means through which nonfavelados continue to craft the dominant
image of the favela in the cultural imaginary. Though the search for the
"real" is one of the main motivations of tourists, the practice of tourism
necessarily involves "staged authenticity" (MacCannell 1976). Life is assem-
bled and narrated in certain ways for the tourist to experience. Staged
authenticity is the bread and butter of favela tours; the favela performs
itself as a place of poverty and violence.

The way in which favela authenticity is staged for visitors is dependent
not only on the spoken narrative of guides but also on the physical journey
through the space of the city. In their design, and in their movement between
the city and the favela, tours capture what Jaguaribe and Hetherington
describe as "two sides of a tropical modernity" (2004: 325). The tour begins
in the heart of the tourist district, at the expensive waterfront hotels set
against the famous Copacabana and Ipanema beaches. Even if the tourist is
not staying in one of these pricey accommodations, most companies only
pick up at some prearranged point on the beach. Whether intentionally or
not, the favela tour starts at the most expensive square footage in all of
Brazil. Moving through the city to Rocinha, even if the guides sometimes fail
to point it out, tourists cannot miss the gated and guarded condominiums,
the architecture of fear in a "city of walls," as Teresa Caldeira (2001) has
described it for São Paulo. From the outset, the tours reify a divided model
of the city rather than trace the continuous and vital movements of capital,

labor, and culture between the condominiums of the Zona Sul and the handful of favelas nestled among the high-rises.

When taken as a whole, the content of favela tours hinges on contrast— be it an explicit, stated contrast between Brazil's haves and have-nots or an implicit and silent contrast between the favela and the tourists' own at-home reality. If an explicit contrast is drawn between city and favela on tour, so also is a certain kind of story told by the passage through the favela, and by its emphases and omissions. Rocinha is far from homogeneous, and one's positioning on the physical landscape of the morro itself signals placement in the internal class hierarchy of the community. In general, the nicer areas along the road and closer to commerce are the most expensive and "middle class"; those higher up or located in the interior away from the road are the poorest. At the same time, however, appearances can be deceiving. A dilapidated exterior might hide interior luxury, with flat screen TVs and state-of-the-art appliances. The favela that tourists see on any tour is necessarily partial, due to the manner in which enormous variations in quality of life are both concealed and mapped unevenly onto the landscape.

The mode of transportation that the tourist uses to visit the favela is controversial. Riding tours, in which visitors simply ride down the main road in a vehicle and descend every so often to see something right next to the road, are criticized by residents for making the favela look too nice and downplaying the poverty just beyond tourists' view. "No one goes around like that!," one resident criticized. Indeed, I often thought that if it was authenticity they desired, tourists should be given the experience of walking *up* the steep hillside.

Several companies make the descent along the road in jeeps. Almost all local observers cited the jeep as the defining symbol of the exploitative nature of favela tours. With its open top, camouflage paint job, and associations with the safari, residents felt that the jeep turned the favela into a zoo and residents into wild animals running loose around an urban jungle. In fact, the jeep has become such a potent symbol of the voyeuristic potential of the tours that several companies explicitly advertise the fact that they *do not* use them.

Just as the riding tours are scorned for providing an overly prosperous image of Rocinha, walking tours are cited by some residents as focusing excessively on poverty. Most walking tours took visitors to one of the poorest parts of the favela, a place called "Dirty Clothes," where people were supposedly too poor to have laundry soap and the steep hillside made for scarce access to water.[12] Detractors contended that these routes gave tourists the false impression that the reality in these areas was representative of the favela at large. Such complaints came from more affluent favela residents who felt that taking tourists to Dirty Clothes emphasized the poverty of the community while ignoring the struggles of residents like themselves who had managed to enter the (favela) middle class.

While residents do not have the power to influence the physical trajectory of the tours, they are excluded from participation in the spoken discourse, which is typically conducted in English. Because of the language barrier, they can neither join the conversation nor determine what is said about them to foreigners. This uneasiness was amplified by the fact that many were deeply distrustful of the guides, who came from the "asphalt" (a euphemism for the gentrified city).[13] How could guides know what life in the favela was like if they didn't even live there? These two factors combined led to uneasy speculation about what the guides were saying.

In my own experiences on tour, much of what was said was relatively accurate, but I also heard numerous errors and inventions. For example, one guide, gesturing toward the famous *gatos*, or rats' nests of electrical and telephone wires, always made a point to say that *all* favela residents stole their electricity since they were too poor to pay for it. For many residents, this was an insult, as the fact that they received and paid a monthly electric bill was not only a source of pride but also a factor that shaped their conception of themselves as citizens.[14]

Another guide repeatedly pointed out the kids flying kites on their rooftops, a common leisure activity in the favela, stating that they were employed by traffickers and were sending coded messages with their kites. While traffickers may have used kites in the past, fireworks, cell phones, and walkie-talkies have long since replaced such a primitive mode of communication. But with hundreds of kites flying in the air above the favela on a sunny day, the guide's statements gave tourists the impression that the community was teeming with child soldiers, an idea that had already been prefigured by the prevalence of violent, murderous children in pre-tour media (see chapter 3).

The need for such sensationalism on the part of the guide brings me to an important fact about tours: they are actually extremely safe.[15] Tourists are not in danger, even though guides may manufacture an experience that suggests otherwise according to the desires of their tourists. At least in the pre-pacification favela, traffickers posed very little threat to tourists, though every so often I observed a problematic encounter involving a tourist (usually accidentally) taking a picture of the boca or an armed soldier. Media commentators and members of wider carioca society, however, frequently misunderstand tour companies' relationships with traffickers, thinking that favela tours are the product of some kind of negotiation (perhaps a monetary one) between guides and the favela's drug boss.[16] Though this is not the case, the discourse is nonetheless revealing of the fact that for outsider observers, the favela is imagined to be so completely subordinate to the desires of traffickers that every movement within its borders must be negotiated with the dono.

Many of the traffickers I talked with about the tourist presence took it as a compliment. The tourism industry's growth and success was cited as proof of how ordered and civilized the favela was under their governance. While tourist robberies and assaults at other attractions throughout the city are relatively common, traffickers were proud that tourists were safe in the favela.[17] Beto even expressed regret that he couldn't talk to the tourists: "All of us [traffickers] are interested in getting to know them. Maybe learn what countries they come from. Take a photo together, you know? But the guides, they are real afraid of us; they don't let the tourists come near."[18] Fear is not the only motivating factor in keeping tourists and traffickers apart. Guides who get too close to traffickers risk legal ramifications as well.[19]

In the absence of the dramatic armed conflict that is so centrally featured in Favela, Inc., subtler, and often invented, symbols of favela violence, like the kites, have to stand in for open gunfire. Sometimes guides go further. I often observed one particular guide actively working to sensationalize the danger posed by traffickers, even where it was not present. He liked to repeat "No pictures, no pictures" in hushed tones throughout the tour, while looking around anxiously, after having told tourists upon arrival in the favela that photography was forbidden in certain places and that they were being watched by the traffickers to ensure compliance. This fabrication, in my experience, effectively instilled a sense of danger among tour groups.[20] Tourists are placed in a situation where their imagination can conjure a violence that is otherwise largely absent. The manufacture of risk allowed tourists to have an exciting brush with danger without getting too close. Yet while some guides work to promote feelings of fear and excitement on tours, the act of tourism itself, as a negotiation between guides and the desires of tourists, also crafts new forms of spectacle that contribute to favela violence.

VARIETIES OF COMMODIFICATION

Although sharing the patterns of discourse that I have outlined above, tour content and emphasis come in two distinct varieties: those that frame the visit to Rocinha as a wild, urban adventure and those more explicitly focused on social justice in alleged solidarity with the poor. With so many guides and so many varying narratives, there is sometimes slippage between these broad categories. In general, though, the difference between adventure- and solidarity-oriented tours is reflected in the marketing rhetoric on company websites, in what the owners and guides told me in interviews, and in tourist desires and behaviors.[21] While both varieties market and sell the violent favela, they do so in different ways.

"Adventure tours" (which include "gangland" and "drug tours"), marketed to the young, backpacker set, present authentic favela life as dangerous, risky, and illicit. They openly and unabashedly commodify and romanticize the transgressive criminality of the narco-traffic and sensationalize the threat of violence. By focusing on the spectacle of trafficker/state violence, these tours occlude less spectacular but no less important realities of everyday structural violence—poverty, lack of opportunity, racial discrimination, and so on. Alternatively, the larger, and more mainstream, variety of favela tourism in Rocinha, what I call "solidarity tourism," is centered on "education" and "awareness"; the favela is presented as a social problem for which the state and Brazilian elites are largely to blame. And yet, as I will show, trafficking remains at the center of these narratives of exclusion. Solidarity tours are presented as educational excursions, where tourists are positioned as "witnesses" to violence. Tourism is framed almost as a form of activism, marketed to the more mature tourist. Both varieties of tourism, however, frame the favela as a fundamentally violent place and provide tourists with a recreational venue through which to engage with it as spectacle. In both cases tourists do more than passively observe life in the favela. As tourists pay to reenact trafficker violence, or to reinforce structural inequality by playing the role of charitable visitor, they perpetuate the conditions in which violence is produced.

Adventure Tourism

"Blow is much cheaper here than in Copacabana," says our tour guide as we sip lukewarm sodas, the November sun warming our backs. "If anyone wants to get their vacation off to a good start, I can hook you up. You know, make the tour a little more fun? A little more *real*?" He raises his eyebrows and grins. A show of hands reveals that nearly all of the European twenty-something hostelers are eager to accompany him on the cocaine buy. Afterward, sitting at the lookout point at the very top of the favela, he passes around their purchase. When a few of the tourists look nervous about such open drug consumption, he quickly puts them at ease: "It's OK, it's legal here" ("here" meaning the trafficker-controlled favela). The ease and levity with which the drugs are first acquired, then consumed, normalizes drug use and disconnects the tourists' recreational use from the guns and bullet holes in the buildings that surround them.

Next we begin the long, winding descent through the favela's labyrinthine alleys. Halfway down, another attraction: we can take a photo with a loaded AK-47 for a fifteen-euro "suggested donation" to the owner of the gun, a sleepy-eyed drug trafficker. We had to knock at his door for a full five minutes before he answered, since, the guide explains, a shootout with police earlier in the morning had driven most of the gang into hiding. In fact, there had been no shootouts that day. This was an outright lie intended to make the tour appear more dangerous. After rousing the owner of the AK-47, the guide picked up the gun and struck a couple of poses with it to demonstrate. "Just like *Charlie's Angels*," he says to the girls in the group.[22] "Make sure you get the favela in the background of the picture!" he instructed. He grabbed a grenade from his trafficker buddy and laughingly pretended to lob it off the steep hillside.

"You might think this is wrong," he says to me in a low voice, "but, hey, I'm only catering to the market." The upper-middle-class son of an American father and a Brazilian mother, this guide lives in Ipanema. He does the tours more for fun than for money. "I don't need to hold a gun," he laughs, "but you gringos are crazy about it." Given the popularity of his underground (and highly illegal tour), I didn't doubt his claim.[23] On this particular tour, guests did indeed seem to enjoy playing at the dangerous life of a trafficker. Hence my surprise at their reaction to the gun. Even though they had been talking all morning about taking a souvenir photo with guns, just like their friends who had recommended the tour, when presented with the loaded AK-47 there was just a lot of nervous laughter. Favela violence had suddenly become a little too authentic.

While tourists openly and unabashedly purchase intimate encounters with the guns and cocaine that symbolize the narco-regime, they also play at and reenact the spectacle of the drug war that is portrayed in the movie, television, and video game depictions of the favela that are circulated all over the globe. A related attraction channels this desire in a more direct way, offering tourists a chance to play "cops and traffickers" in live-action paintball games. The location of these games is particularly significant because the favela in which they take place has been "pacified" and is the site of the Batalhão de Operações Policiais Especiais headquarters and training grounds. Tourists playing cops and traffickers become a simulation of BOPE training exercises.

The performative and embodied engagement with imagined police and trafficker warfare produces yet another layer of spectacle.[24] "Gangland" and "favela war" tours like these capitalize on the image of violence that makes favelas famous: selling drugs, encounters with traffickers, and the simulation of war to tourists eager to experience favela life as depicted in movies like *City of God*. In doing so, the tours glamorize the criminal life; and the spectacle that results covers up the painful struggles inherent in favela "warfare." Tourists cannot see the poverty and lack of opportunity that makes trafficking a viable option for youth, the long history of police abuse and state terror that often motivates people to take up arms, the desire for wealth and respect, or the experience of losing friends and loved ones to armed violence that marks the life of all traffickers.[25] The men who traffic are reduced to a singular role, criminal, a highly simplistic representation that does not account for the fact that these people are also fathers, husbands, and sons.

Beyond the specific subjectivity of traffickers themselves, adventure tours such as these render invisible the daily struggles of the vast majority of the residents who chose not to engage with crime. Tourists cannot see the acute (and vastly more common) challenges of favela life: trying to get by on minimum wages; negotiating ongoing discrimination because of place of residence, skin color, or regional origin; or the negative health effects of poverty and the abysmal public health care system that is the only option for the poor.

The ability to consume the drugs that finance organized crime in the favela and to play with the guns that protect cocaine shipments from rival gangs and law enforcement reifies the violent favela and makes it available for affective tourist experience. And yet, as much as the favela experienced by the coked-out tourist represents the epitome of staged authenticity, so also does the touristic consumption of this version of the slum reaffirm the authenticity of yet another form of alterity. In the eyes of favela residents, affluent white tourists, as representations of an imagined European and American habitus, act out their part as the users of the favela's drugs. Favela residents, like tourists, are consumers of global media, much of which emanates from the United States. Hyper-real depictions of North American life made for TV are, ironically, confirmed as "real" for residents by tourists' behavior. Resident's see evidence of their idea that everyone is rich in the expensive cameras tourists carry and the designer clothing they wear. A natural penchant for drug use and "partying," which they have already observed on television, are confirmed in light of tourist actions.

But what do tourists do with these experiences? Are they able to analyze their actions with any critical distance? The answer to this question is no, not really. Most openly welcome the chance to be "be locals, not gringos," as one company's slogan framed it. They do not question the veracity of the "local" with which they are presented. In interviews, tourist reactions to the favela as an adventure experience fall along the lines of affirming their experience as edgy or risqué: "That was so crazy, man!" "Rio totally lives up to its reputation as a party city!" Furthermore, tourists do not seem to think that their behavior is either suspect or embarrassing. In fact there didn't seem to be any attempt to hide their activities in the favela, illegal though they were. Instead, some tourists said that the experiences would be complete only when they could be documented on social media after returning to the hostel wifi connection: "I can't wait to write about this on my blog. No one is going to believe this." "This is going to be a wicked Facebook profile pic." On all the adventure tours that I accompanied, there was only one tourist who openly expressed her discomfort. Even then, her discomfort was circumscribed. She felt bad that the people in the favela saw her both consuming drugs and consuming their poverty. "I just feel kinda weird," she said. "I mean, what do *they* think of *me*?" She gestured toward an older woman and a young mother nursing her baby on the stoop outside their house as the tour passed by. It is possible that the group setting made it hard for tourists to express discomfort and that on some tours their intoxicated state made it harder still. But for the most part, the sentiment was that this was reality, and they weren't responsible for the content of that reality.

Adventure tours such as these, which voyeuristically engage with favela violence and the spectacle of trafficker guns, focus on the consumption of violence as a commodity. As the opening vignette about the runaway chicken illustrates, tours are often seen as a natural extension and continuation of pretour media. However, by snorting cocaine and photographing one another with AK-47s, tourists are forging a new kind of violent spectacle. Their ability to play at the trafficker life but then leave it behind underscores the power of mobility. Adventure tourists become both consumers of violence and perpetrators of it.

Solidarity Tourism

"Philippe! Philippe! Run and get some other kids, quick! The tourists are coming!," said João to his ten-year-old nephew, Philippe. João ran a small nonprofit organization, Art over Trafficking.[26] Within ten minutes, by the time the group of elderly Danish "solidarity" tourists had stepped out of the rain into the brightly painted but ramshackle art studio that housed the organization, a small group of kids sat serenely painting at a large table, a classic samba tune playing softly in the background. Because he was always short on art supplies and didn't have the money to buy new materials, João quickly constructed a hyper-real scene: he sprinkled water on already completed watercolors, instructing the children to run their paintbrushes over the lines to give the appearance of spontaneous originality.

The tourists made the expected complimentary remarks about the children's pictures and exclaimed over the small models of the favela that lined the walls, which were made entirely from trash the children had scavenged from the trash pit around the corner. After looking around a bit, the Danes began to engage in something that by that time in my fieldwork I instantly recognized as a "ritual of charity." One woman cheerfully implored her husband to take a picture of her making a donation, her hand poised above the donation box as she smilingly put a R$2 bill in the slot (about one U.S. dollar). Several others rummaged in their pockets and came up with some change, one by one photographing themselves in the act of "helping out" the budding artists.[27] Afterward, João and I dumped out the box, shaking the coins out one by one. "I don't understand," he said. "They come from a rich country. Why do they give so little?"

Residents have come to use the industry to profit in small ways from donations, as João's calculated performance for the tourists suggests. Cunning aside, he is still entrenched in a cycle of poverty so precarious that he must co-opt the neighborhood children to make fake paintings in order keep his social project afloat and his family fed. At the time of the Danes' visit João had just had a part of his leg amputated. A Type 2 diabetic, a disease linked to poverty and poor diet, he had cut his leg and the cut refused to heal. For weeks, he made daily visits to the public hospital to be examined, but given the triage model of medical care, his problem was never considered serious enough to warrant treatment. Finally, when about a third of his leg developed gangrene, he was admitted.

In tourism, these sorts of complexities and experiences of structural violence are transformed by *both sides* into a simplistic and reductionist narrative about trafficking and crime. Performative encounters, from both residents and tourists alike, rely on a vision of the violent favela, and especially on a sympathetic vision of favela children, to produce a spectacle that tourists recognize and respond to in ritualized ways.

"Solidarity"-oriented favela tours, like the one that visited João's studio, commodify nonprofits in the favela, where residents and children perform charitable versions of themselves so as to inspire tourist donations. In fact, none of the children painting that day were actually traffickers or former traffickers. While they are indeed "at risk," they are more at risk of becoming teenage parents than they are of taking up arms. One of the boys who was painting on this day was homeless and lived out of a cardboard box under the overpass in front of the favela. These realities get left out—both because they don't fit with tourist expectation and because residents and NGO leaders don't see them as as effective as narratives about armed violence.

Instead, social projects like João's refer back to the idea of the inherently violent childhood that is so prevalent in the global media. As I discussed in chapter 3, media representations of the violent favela characterize young residents either as cold-blooded "natural" killers or as innocent potential converts to a life of crime. Nonprofits reluctantly depend on such problematic constructions of endangered youth for funding, hence the performance of the creative and artistic yet "at risk" childhood that is consistently rolled out for tourists.

Companies that tour the favela in the name of solidarity see their work as educational. One agency even refers to its tours as "sociological." While these agencies may in some cases perform the minimal educational work of raising the awareness of tourists, especially when contrasted with the garish sensationalism of adventure tourism, the marginalizing discourses and global inequalities that they reproduce are no less suspect. Voyeuristic qualities are masked by the fact that the tone of solidarity tours is decidedly upbeat, with guides celebrating favelado perseverance in the face of oppressive life conditions. But with actual favela residents making only brief cameo experiences on the solidarity itinerary, guides' laudatory remarks often feel especially hypocritical.

The exclusion of residents is a natural outcome of the fact that solidarity tourism is really not about favela realities at all; rather, it is all about the experience of the tourist. Favela residents are but a means to the end of tourist education. As one guide liked to say, "Our goal today is to recognize our common humanity." The concern here with *tourists'* recognition of favelados is revealing of the challenges associated with solidarity tourism more generally. Tourists are positioned as empathetic observers whose role in the favela is to bear witness to the violence and suffering found there and, in doing so, achieve greater awareness of Brazil's problems. Tour rhetoric extols them for crossing a social divide few Brazilians are willing to traverse: their presence itself becomes a mode of charity.

Furthermore, since tour guides often tell tourists that the social projects they visit are supported with the money they pay for the tour, they do not feel the need to make additional cash donations. Such an orientation to the tourist helps to explain the meager donations João received. The "witnessing" objective of the solidarity tour frees tourists from feeling a financial obligation to assist in the betterment of the favela; charity requires only the giving of spare change since the tourists' mere presence stands for something more than money. Performances of charity, however, are photographed so as to provide visual evidence of what tourists believe they are doing: bearing witness, raising their own awareness, and applauding residents' struggles for dignity and respect, all acts that confer status on the gracious visitors.

Though solidarity tourism brings essential, if minimal, revenue to Rocinha's nonprofit organizations, tourists' ideas about the proper uses of donated funds further reveal how tourism's economic benefits are oriented to the desires, judgments, and opinions of tourists. On one memorable occasion, a group was asked to give money to an after-school program for the purchase of chocolate Easter eggs for the children, a Brazilian holiday tradition. Several flat-out refused, arguing that chocolate was not an appropriate way for the organization to spend money in such a precarious environment. One tourist explained, "If they had asked for food, I would have gladly given it [the money], but I don't think the eggs seem like a necessity." This incident signals the tension between conflicting ideas of "development" in the favela. Solidarity tourists, in particular, often felt that they knew what was best for the favela and its residents and limited their donations (of both time and money) accordingly. Their paternalism was both insulting and frustrating for residents. In conversations with people like João, I found that many residents recognize the power dynamics inherent in "solidarity" as it is practiced here, but the tour agencies' small donations and the tourists' spare change were still an important source of funding in a climate where resources always fell short of need.

At other times, however, the tours posed more serious challenges for local nonprofit organizations, by devolving into unkind and humiliating spectacles. One day care center struggled with allowing tourism because of the behavior of one of the company owners. When visiting with a group of tourists, he would pull down the pants of the boy toddlers, "pantsing" them. The kids would then teeter and fall over as their legs caught in their pants, something that he found especially humorous and at which he encouraged tourists to laugh along with him. His actions put the day care center in a tough spot. On the one hand, they thought his behavior was deplorable; on the other, they depended on the small monthly deliveries of food he provided. Instead of confronting him about the problem, which they feared would have negative consequences, they developed a blanket rule that the children could not be touched at all. Tourists could only observe the kids playing from the windows, something that gave the whole exchange a truly zoological effect. Again, although the management of the nonprofit was aware of this side effect, they felt they had limited options. The organization needed the money that the tourist visits generated. Here one sees, in stark relief, how the greater structures of inequality and poverty that underlie the tours play out and yet also how residents are able to challenge those relationships in important, if insufficient (by their own estimation), ways.

On a more theoretical level, the use of favelados as a tool for the education of the global leisure class suggests a troubling connection between the experience of violence and the production of suffering as a commodity. Joan Kleinman and Arthur Kleinman write that the "globalization of suffering is one of the more troubling signs of the cultural transformations of the current era: troubling because experience is being used as a commodity, and through this cultural representation of suffering, experience is being remade, thinned out, and distorted" (1996: 1–2). Also problematic in the case of the favela tour is the way in which the thinning out or distorting of suffering is marshaled primarily for the affluent tourist's personal growth or self-realization. Solidarity appears hollow in this light.

Tourist self-realization is taken by tourists and the industry as a good in and of itself; it replaces real action. One tourist told me at the end of a tour, "I am so happy that I came and saw how life is here. I am glad that I saw it, even if I cannot do anything about it." Voyeuristic contemplation of the favela's problems and challenges, paradoxically, produces feelings of happiness for the tourist. This blithe statement made in the tour van on the way back to the ritzy beachfront hotel zone perfectly encapsulates the violence inherent in the practice of solidarity tourism. As solidarity is reduced to looking, tourism perpetuates favela violence in that it encourages voyeurism under the guise of "social justice." The poor and violent favelados recede into the invisible background once again, having served their purpose as refractory mirages used to make the tourist feel good about herself. The tourist's contented complacency replaces any feelings of obligation to actually *do* something in response to the violence witnessed. Just knowing, just consuming, is enough. As a result, although it might seem on the surface like a good thing, solidarity tourism is just as insidious as those tours that openly engage with favela violence and glorify the trafficker lifestyle.

LOCAL RESPONSES

Despite the extremely problematic nature of tourism, many favela residents support the presence of foreigners in their community. Time and time again people told me that they felt honored that tourists would come from across the world to see their community, one the residents almost unanimously see as a nice place with many amenities lacking in other favelas. Outside interest confirms their feelings of satisfaction with many aspects of Rocinha life. Most people I spoke with were extremely proud of their houses, which, while they appeared ramshackle and improvised to tourists, were the fruit of much sacrifice and labor on the part of residents. The residents are pleased that their community is world-famous, though famous for what they often are not exactly sure. Other people found the interest of tourists downright baffling but not really unpleasant.

Understanding these local interpretations of tourism requires an appreciation of the larger context of social marginalization residents face. Favelados suffer constantly from ongoing discrimination as a result of their status.[28] Their place of residence becomes a marker that supersedes many facets of what are complex identities, just like any other. People become reduced to signs of violence and poverty. Given this experience of marginalization, residents interpret visits from affluent foreigners in a positive light because they appear, on the surface at least, to break with the unfortunate conventions of Rio's urban segregation.

However, many of the residents who espoused enthusiasm for the tours had little or no actual contact with tourists. They were also unaware that tourists paid substantial sums for the tours. When I brought up this point, many residents could not even imagine that people would *pay* to see the favela. The more contact with tours and guides that residents had and the more information they had about economics, the less favorable their opinion tended to be. Those who lived along the crowded tour routes were often more critical, and some would even swear at the tourists as they passed or comment on their voyeuristic behavior, saying things like, "Why don't you go visit a favela in your own country?" "Oh, so you have come to see my little shack, now have you?" "Why don't you pay me to take a picture?" Of course, guides don't translate such commentary, as it would work against the solidarity tour message. Proximity to tourists and knowledge of the economic arrangements of tourism generally anger residents, who, though embittered, have little recourse to stop the tours. Nonetheless, even their untranslated comments represent a challenge to tourist objectification.

Sometimes residents used humor and farce to critique tourist behavior (cf. Goldstein 2003). Teenagers in a photography class I participated in decided to do what they called a "gringo photo series." They went around, laughing as they went, taking pictures of the things that they had seen gringos photograph—stray dogs, piles of garbage, half-naked children without shoes, open sewage ditches, bullet holes in concrete walls, gang graffiti—all things that were outside of their usual repertoire of photographic subjects. Afterward, they engaged in a mock exhibition of the photos: "Oooo Fabino, I just love the colors you have captured in the *lixeiro* [dump]." Or my favorite: "Gabriela, the sun shining off the dog poop is just so inspiring." The ability to both mimic tourist behavior and to make light of it represents a form of resistance to touristic objectification.

Contrary to the image of unity and community that figures prominently in the discourse of favela tours, the organizational dynamics of Rocinha's tourism industry create deep fissures. The few local businesses and organizations (a bakery where tourists buy a snack, an art gallery where they buy souvenirs) that do profit from tourist visits fiercely protect their territory and do not want to share their small slice of profits with other residents or other business owners. The fact that tours generated revenue for certain residents and not others was frequently cited by a vocal group of favela leaders when discussing the financial exploitation they believed to be endemic to the tours.[29] In 2008 and again at the end of 2010, the

Resident's Association, the formal local governing body of the favela, tried to regulate tourism in the community in order to rectify what they viewed as unfair practices detrimental to the community's dignity.[30] Several public meetings were called to discuss the development of favela-run tours and numerous community leaders denounced the existing tourism industry for conducting a "tourism of exploitation" and for "getting rich off of Rocinha's problems."

The president of the Resident's Association announced a plan to impose an R$5 "entrance fee" (to be deducted from each agency's profits) for each tourist who entered the favela. The revenue would go to the association to use to improve the community as they saw fit. Although it quickly became apparent that the association was just one more party that sought to concentrate potential wealth from tours in the hands of a chosen few inside the favela, some people nonetheless agreed that the residents or their "leaders" should decide how the income would be spent. The accusation that companies were making a profit from the violence and misery of the favela further raised the ire of solidarity tour owners, who envisioned their tours as using charitable work and education in an indirect campaign against the reign of the traffic. Ultimately, the proposed entrance fee proved impossible to implement. There was no way to levy the tax without calling on the traffickers to force companies to pay, an act that would have carried complications for an association already struggling with issues of credibility because of its historical link to organized crime.

Toward the end of my fieldwork, another favela-based group, mainly composed of business owners and a few people with loose ties to the traffic and money laundering (or so the gossip went), again proposed a tourism-related project. The project coincided with a larger federally funded development program that was taking place in the favela.[31] Funds had been earmarked for a bed-and-breakfast program that would train residents to host visitors under a more sustainable tourism model. The company owners were called to a meeting (which none attended), and a group of Rocinha representatives was quickly appointed to oversee the implementation of the project. Two years later nothing had come of the proposal. People told me that the board had created the structure of a community-run agency merely in order to obtain the federal funds and that they had never really planned to open the project at all.[32] Even if unsuccessful, these efforts to develop alternative tours signal that it is not just outsiders making a business of commodifying the favela; internal actors will also do so if it means generating a profit.

As a result of these sorts of challenges, community-run tourism remains relatively undeveloped in Rocinha, though several entrepreneurial resident guides have started their own small companies that are just beginning to attract tourists. Local critics of the favela tourism industry say that placing Rocinha's tours under resident control would eliminate their exploitative nature. I wholeheartedly agree that locally run tourism is preferable from an organizational and financial standpoint. At least revenues would go to some local people, not outsiders. A shift to resident-run tours would do little, however, to alter the problematic preconceptions of tourists, the conflation of witnessing and voyeurism, or the perpetuation of favela suffering through its commodification as spectacle.[33]

When Rocinha residents do participate in the tourist industry it is often in circumscribed or stereotypical roles. Resident guides in some ways challenge the status quo; for example, they offer tourists a chance to have a meaningful interaction with someone with life experience in the favela. However, as employees of the larger agencies they often find themselves co-opted into reproducing the discourses of owners and guides who are outsiders. Resident guides struggle to negotiate both the value-added quality of their status as residents and the way in which residency and its accompanying associations are limiting.

Resident-run tours seemingly offer the ultimate authentic experience: tourists can see the favela through the eyes of someone who actually lives there. Unfortunately, though, the markers of authenticity have been written by outside authors, and unsurprisingly, they center on trafficking and violence. I got to know one guide who had been employed by one of the larger favela tour companies that purported to train local youths as guides as part of its social mission in the favela. He told me about a time the company's owner invited him to appear with her on a popular television program, where she was to be lauded for her role in saving favela children through tourism. While they were waiting to go onstage, she instructed him to say that he had been a trafficker and that, through involvement with her organization and through the skills he acquired with her help, he had been saved from what would have otherwise been sure imprisonment or an early death. "She had the power, and I didn't know what would happen to my job if I said no," he explained wistfully. "But afterward my mother was furious at me since I had never been involved with trafficking and getting on TV and saying that, well, it made my family look bad."

Ironically, this guide was quite a "success story" all on his own, despite this belittling experience. He had taught himself several languages, had earned a tourism credential that enabled him to work in any sector of the city, and was a responsible and charismatic independent guide. Nonetheless, this particular narrative of favelado success was clearly not the one the company owner wanted; the young man was more useful to her as a stereotype consonant with the images of violence tourists bring with them, projected to enhance her image and elevate her NGO rather than as evidence of self-motivation, self-reliance, and hard work. The guide's inability to refuse, even if it meant detracting from all of his hard-won achievements, is indicative of the way in which those few favela residents who do manage to find work in the tourism industry still find themselves subordinate to larger power dynamics.

At the same time that resident status, albeit of a certain prefabricated variety, can be valued, it is also limiting. A guide named Edilson worked intermittently for one of the larger companies. He complained that although he had the proper certification and skills to do tours anywhere in the city, he was only called upon by the company to conduct favela tours. He felt that this was because the company owners did not think he could do a good job leading tours in other, nicer parts of the city, since they presumed he had never really spent time anywhere outside of the favela.

Edilson was an incredibly insightful and astute guide. He had taught himself five languages and was more than capable of leading groups anywhere in the city. In trying to understand his situation, I asked the opinion of one of the nonresident guides. He said bluntly, "He might be nice and all, but really he has a *cara de favelado*." In one sense, *cara* means "face" and refers to someone's physical appearance; *cara* signaled that he was black. But "cara de favelado" also refers to a range of other performative markers of someone's "character," including class, way of speaking, mannerisms, and clothing. In the eyes of his Brazilian superiors, these elements of Edilson's "cara" were glaringly obvious. While his role as a resident (and one with a cara de favelado to boot!) gave him an authority other guides lacked when touring Rocinha, outside it, the same features disqualified him.

When conducting tours in the favela, resident guides cannot show whatever version of the favela they deem representative of life there, though to do so would clearly constitute one take on authenticity. Instead, they must negotiate between their own narratives and the expectations of tourists. Time and time again, I observed ways in which tourists' preconceived ideas about the favela as defined by armed violence determined their experiences, even as resident guides actively tried to complicate this predetermined image. In one memorable instance, despite the fact that the question of trafficking and armed conflict had been almost entirely absent from the tour narrative, and the group had not seen any traffickers at all, when it came time to buy souvenirs it was clear from the visitors' choices that this image still dominated. One traveler proudly showed me a painting he had purchased at one of the open-air stands that sell art, a frequent tour stop. A large red canvas was covered with headlines and pictures of invading police, dead bodies, and burning vehicles, all of which were drawn mostly from other favelas and not from the one he had toured. Overlaying the gruesome images was additional red paint splattered like blood.[34]

Furthermore, as I often noted on resident-run tours, tourists did not actually want a resident's perspective and felt uncomfortable with the resident guides. They preferred to have the experience of favela life explained by someone more like them. As an anthropologist-researcher and a favela resident, albeit a temporary one, guides and tourists constantly elicited my perspective on Rocinha while on tour.[35] It was assumed that I would be better able to "translate" the favela, and it was easier for tourists to ask me the kinds of frank questions about life that they could not politely pose to residents. (For example, I often got questions like, "How do you stand to live here?") The way in which both guides and tourists continuously cast me in the role of translator is a testament, I believe, to the potential of ethnography as an act of cultural translation seen by the "Western" public as generating the most authentic information about favela others. Another reason I was able to occupy this role when guides could not was because I had also been a tourist myself. My mobility gave me a perspective that resident guides, who could not afford to travel, could not achieve.

Just as tourists consume residents as representatives of the "authentic" favela, so too do resident guides consume tourists as representatives of different countries and cultures. The key difference of course is one that is at the heart of the injustice of mass tourism more generally. Who has the means to travel and who does not largely reflects entrenched (local and global) class lines. Yet those in the favela do not accept this limitation at face value. And whether it was traffickers watching the Travel Channel on television, asking me to bring them U.S. luxury goods, or guides engaging in imaginary travel, mobility was a sign of prosperity and an experience of class status.

Edilson, in particular, was a frequent imaginary traveler who caught fleeting glimpses of the larger world through the descriptions of tourists. He poignantly explained to me, "I am a poor black man who lives in a favela. I am never going to be able to go anywhere. I am never going to be able to travel to Europe. Even if I had the money, they would never give me a visa. But by taking Germans on a tour, by talking with Germans, maybe I can know a little bit of what it's like to visit Germany. I can feel the cold, the snow . . . " Another resident guide, Ivan, explained that his interaction with tourists offered a respite from the everyday violence of the favela.

> Listen, gringos come here thinking it is so cool. There are traffickers, drugs are easy to get, and it seems like a huge party. But listen, Rocinha is a heavy place, a very heavy place. I feel this all the time. When I spent some time outside of the community and then I come back, I notice this heaviness again as soon as I get off the bus and cross the road. People here talk too much about trafficking, about violence [he gestures at the boca visible outside the window next to the restaurant where we are talking]. The gossip goes on all the time. When I hang out with foreigners, there is something new to learn, new to talk about. It's a "lighter" life.

Edilson's and Ivan's reflections belie the emancipatory ambitions of their imaginary travel by underscoring the sad fact that favelados themselves often lack the means to leave the favela. It is therefore in such statements that the truly violent nature of favela tourism is revealed. The global structural inequalities between the tourist and the toured—and those who forge the narrative that connects them—are centered on uneven access to mobility. To see other places, to explore far-flung corners of the world, to move beyond the favela are the defining features of power. Residents can only travel vicariously, or experience "lightness" as Ivan puts it, in the secondhand descriptions and cheerful banter of the tourists who come to see and to consume the violent favela through their "authentic" interpretive lens.

The intertwining of travel and desire here cuts across all groups: everyone is commodifying and consuming everyone else. Ivan's "lightness" recalls Beto's interactions with his middle-class girlfriend, Katia: how she provided him with an ability to escape the violence of the everyday in Rocinha, to experience levity and the possibility of movement and freedom.[36] Travel is the ultimate expression of these things. It means not only to move oneself through space but also to be able to play with identity and to be transformed. The desire for this runs both ways. Just as Katia wants to travel into Beto's world, he wants to travel into hers. So too is it with tourists, who find value in playing trafficker, a freedom to take on a new role without consequences in a favela on the other side of the world.

CONCLUSION

Favela violence is not limited to the exchange of gunfire between enemies or the spectacular punishment ordered by the dono when someone transgresses trafficker law. It is also inherent in the process of transforming these Rocinha realities into spectacles for consumption. Enterprising tour company owners, with an awareness of the global market for the favela, sell their understanding of favela violence to eager tourists. The product they offer is mitigated and shaped by larger mediascapes, as the runaway chicken at the beginning of the chapter suggests. The spectacle of the experience on tour masks the conditions that produce the favela, occludes the factors that produce the tours themselves, and mystifies the global structures that make some people tourists while others lack the mobility to leave. Tourism is at once a product of favela hyper-reality and a vector for its further circulation, as tourists blog about and photograph favela "reality" as they experienced it.

The economic relations that inform the spectacle of the violent favela as it is sold to tourists are deeply problematic. Residents are excluded from the process at all levels, save in situations where they are needed to communicate authenticity to tourists. The favela is marshaled in the name of touristic desire; tours are not so much about the favela itself as about what Rocinha can reveal to tourists, about tourists. Herein lies the greatest violence of tourism. Rocinha, replete with all its challenges, is *used* for tourist "education," "awareness," and even "fun."

The tourism scholars J. John Lennon and Malcolm Foley, writing about the practice of "dark tourism," or tourism in places associated with violence and death, claim that the practice is organized around the contemplation of the failures of modernity (2000: 11). Favela tours engage with modernity's discontents on several levels. Almost every tour makes a critique of the paradigms of modern governance, either explicitly through tour discourse or implicitly by underscoring the obvious exclusion and marginalization that marks favela life. Police brutality, corruption, and the failures associated with bad policy further call the modern state project into question. The presence of armed traffickers running the favela adds another layer of complexity to the picture, offering a dystopian alternative to Brazilian "order and progress."[37] Yet at the same time that the tours feature a marked anxiety about the overall project of modernity, a competing version of favela life is advanced. Favela violence is "cool." Traffickers are rebels who refuse to play by the rules of the system that exploits them.

Tourists' romantic misreadings map the favela as a place of freedom, both because of organized crime's perceived and imagined distance from the state and because of the imagined unity of the community in the alleged absence of wealth disparities and class stratification. The tourist tropes developed here, of longing, of desire for the other (which cuts both ways), are not unique to favela tourism but are embodiments of how the figure of the other can be romanticized and exoticized (Pratt 1992; Said 1979). Romantic depictions of the favela as a community, where families live together and neighbors take care of one another, also work to assuage tourist fears as they arise during the contemplation of the failed Brazilian urbanscape. The favela, as a space of violent alterity so central to the tour narrative, is recaptured. As anxiety regarding the failures of modernity slips into the background in the face of the poor but cheerful, or defiant and cool, favelados, tourists reflect on their own experiences of disconnection and ennui at home in contrast to the perceived or projected vibrancy of favela life. Yet the spectacular favela far exceeds outsiders' understandings of it. Like every place, it is a social and historical product—in some senses made by favelados but through a process of negotiation with the state, the media, guides, and tourist desires.

5 "Peace"

November 2011. In the days prior to the pacification of Rocinha, the traffickers who had long controlled the community held a number of lavish farewell parties for themselves. With DJs playing the latest funk beats and free beer for all, these parties represented the last hurrah of one of the most stable and powerful drug regimes in Rio's recent history. The high-profile traffickers packed their things, bid their constituents an intoxicated, emotional farewell, and left Rocinha in anticipation of the permanent presence of the so-called pacifying police forces. Minor players who could fly under police radar stayed behind to covertly continue the trafficking enterprise in the post-takeover favela.

While the traffickers were partying, other kinds of commercial outlets were caught up in preparations for the coming police invasion, as the presence of the UPP, the community policing units, promised to reconfigure the largely informal favela economy. On every street corner, vendors selling pirated DVDs held massive inventory liquidation sales. Residents scrambled to disconnect their pirated cable and Internet utilities, fearing that they would be arrested for having purchased the trafficker-subsidized service, even though it was the only one available.

At dawn, legions of armored police tanks began advancing and met no resistance. In one of the most media-saturated and spectacular performances of state power the city had ever seen, police "liberated" the favela's more than one hundred thousand residents from a quarter century of narco-trafficker rule without firing a single shot. Shortly, behind the lines of tanks and the advancing Special Forces (BOPE), came another army: Internet and TV service providers. Eager to tap the lucrative favela market, corporate representatives outnumbered the invading police threefold. Before victory had even been declared, salespeople were busy passing out flyers for bundled service packages.

In this chapter I draw on ethnographic material from several distinct moments: the pre-pacified favela between 2008 and 2010, the immediate period after pacification in 2011, and again fifteen months later, in 2013. I argue that there are three central ways in which Rocinha is being reordered under the aegis of pacification: (1) through the implementation of new forms of state-led security, (2) through changes to community infrastructure, and (3) through the opening of the favela economy to corporate interests. Although represented by its principal architects as triumphantly bringing both order and progress to a new favela middle class, pacification is in fact the love child of militarized state power and elite corporate interest.[1] Wacquant has described this process of global neoliberalism as "the 'iron fist' of the penal state mating with the 'invisible hand' of the market" (2012: 67). Enhanced entanglement of state and corporate agendas in the Rio case is apparent not just in the details of pacification as I describe them here but also in the who's who list of its major funders. Eike Batista— once the richest Brazilian, a powerhouse venture capitalist, oil tycoon, real estate magnate, and mining mogul—initially funded pacification to the tune of US$12 million per year.[2] Coca-Cola, the number one sponsor of both the World Cup and the Olympics, is also contributing, as are Big Tobacco and the notoriously corrupt Brazilian Football Federation.

Pacification depends on a new rationale—what I call the Olympic exception—for the same old variety of oppressive state action in the favela.[3] The Olympic exception is not the exclusive invention of Rio de Janeiro but is present whenever mega-events come to a town, as evidenced by recent host cities such as London, Beijing, Johannesburg, and Sochi

(Broudehoux 2007, 2010; Davis 2006; Zirin 2014).[4] It capitalizes on the burgeoning nationalist pride inherent in hosting prestigious global sporting events and targets threats to a successful Games and World Cup—urban disorder, crime, and a lack of adequate infrastructure. With success hanging in the balance, the pressure to be ready to host the world enables the transformation of the cityscape with a speed and tenor otherwise financially and politically impossible. Favelas, long the symbol of urban "backwardness" and "primitiveness" in the eyes of city planners and carioca elites, are an obvious target. Those located in the tourist zones and near major event venues have been designated for special attention.

It is worth reflecting here on the historical use of the term *pacification* by the Brazilian state, which attempted (militarily, culturally, and religiously) to bring indigenous Brazilians into the fold of "modernity" using the exact same term. The reemergence of pacification in this new context indicates how similar tropes of "progress" and "civilization" are being transmuted to encompass the favela as an imagined space, a threat to still-elusive Brazilian modernity. Others have suggested that the policy "pacifies" not only the favela but also the historically truculent military police (Henrique and Ramos 2011: 2) and, in addition, that it functions to "pacify" the anxieties of the middle classes (Cavalcanti 2013: 205).

SPECTACULAR (IN)SECURITY

When I first began fieldwork in Rocinha in 2008, traffickers were the primary "security" presence, with police entering the favela in sporadic "invasions" at three- or four-month intervals.[5] Despite some shortcomings in trafficker-based security, residents by and large reported feeling an overwhelming sense of personal safety under trafficker rule, especially since it repressed crimes like rape and robbery.

Pacification purports to challenge trafficker hegemony and transfer security from traffickers to the state. It begins when politicians announce that police action is forthcoming in a certain favela, thereby allowing traffickers a chance to flee and minimizing the chance of armed resistance. Then, on the appointed day, BOPE invades, in some cases with military backing, to perform the initial conquest of enemy territory.[6] After BOPE has "cleared" the favela, a process that usually takes several weeks, the focus shifts to the implantation of the UPP. UPP officers are distinct in that they are supposed to be novice recruits, outsiders to the combat ethos long characteristic of the conventional police battalions of both the Civil and Military Police squads.[7] The allegedly kinder and gentler UPP units are charged with transforming local attitudes of hostility and distrust into relationships of collaboration and cooperation. It is no small irony, however, that even while officers are charged with keeping order and protecting favela residents, the term *pacification* itself marks the favela as a place that requires violence to achieve peace (fig. 7).

BOPE has made it a practice to appropriate the precise geographic locations of trafficker power for the establishment of their headquarters, and later these same spaces are used to house the more permanent UPP. This practice was shown clearly in Rocinha, where police took over the residence of the head trafficker.[8] In this symbolic act they recast themselves as the new donos de morro. The use of these trafficker-constructed spaces is problematic, however, in that it is emblematic of the way in which pacification entails the ousting of one armed force simply to replace it with another, a frequent critique by residents, who say that the only thing that has changed is that the guns have moved from guys in swimming trunks and Havaianas to guys in uniforms.

In Rocinha, from the very beginning, it was clear that pacification did *not* constitute a radical break from previous policies but was made possible precisely through the same old police and trafficker collusion. While the news networks broadcast images of the decisive police victory and government officials touted pacification successes as a sign of total resident support for the state, the situation on the ground was far more complex. Only a small handful of the approximately three hundred traffickers who were believed to have been operating in the community were captured. Many were reportedly smuggled past barricades and roadblocks with the assistance of police officers themselves, who hid the fugitive traffickers in the trunks of their cars in exchange for bribes. And while some successfully fled, many more remained, rendering the government and media discourse regarding the "the liberation of the favela" laughable.

Figure 7. Pacification forces at work. Photograph by Rosângela Lago.

When I visited Rocinha a few weeks after pacification, I saw traffickers everywhere. Some had even traded in their machine guns for clipboards and BlackBerry smartphones and were working for the cable companies doing door-to-door sales—of legal *and* illegal goods (and thus becoming truly indistinguishable from the formal corporate employees). Then, just a few short weeks after pacification, a bloody intergang struggle for control of the "pacified" favela began. Under the nose of the supposedly all-powerful BOPE, warring traffickers engaged in open gunfights and dumped the decapitated bodies of their rivals in public venues around Rocinha. The brazen presence of the traffickers and the persistence of the drug trade (even if less public) undermined the state effort, as residents were forced to keep a cool distance from police for fear that they would be punished when traffickers retook the favela. Indeed, the permanence of the state was (and still is) a central concern for residents who described pacification as a response to the security pressures of the upcoming mega-sporting events, rather than a policy born out of an earnest concern with their welfare.

If an ongoing trafficker presence was one factor impeding the success of pacification, a number of police shortcomings also made residents skeptical of the peace effort. A wave of assaults and homicides (resulting allegedly from bar fights and old feuds) swept Rocinha, crimes that had been practically unheard of in the favela during trafficker rule, adding to residents' growing insecurity.[9] At the time of my initial fieldwork (2008–10), much of Rocinha's community life took place on people's stoops and in the alleyways in front of their houses, often at night after residents returned from work. This vibrant street life has all but disappeared. Many people were (and still are) afraid to let their children play outside and now lock their doors for the first time in their lives. After 10 p.m., the favela is eerily silent. In the absence of police protection from crime within the favela, residents slowly began to approach the remaining traffickers to arbitrate disputes or discipline other residents. By turning to traffickers to exercise their historical function, residents reactivated ties of paternalism, control, and respect that had been under threat by pacification.

In many cases, it was not only the failure of police to protect residents from criminals that increased insecurity, but police behavior as well. Indeed, pacification in Rocinha marked the advent of state security. Anonymous and impersonal, state security creates the sort of stability recognizable to international media and foreign investors but is in stark contrast to previous forms of trafficker order based on internal favela social structure. The state security apparatus, for example, consistently reduced residents to a single category. Residents complained of police harassment when officers couldn't distinguish between the legitimately

employed and the traffickers with the same acuity as the traffickers themselves, who were based in the community and could easily differentiate
between different kinds of residents. Young men in particular were regularly "profiled" by police, stopped and subjected to humiliating searches.[10]
To make matters worse, there were widespread reports that BOPE had
taken over the traffickers' former execution grounds in the woods at the
top of the community and were torturing "suspected bandidos" on a regular basis. This suspicion on the part of residents was confirmed by the
high-profile death of Amarildo de Souza, a bricklayer's assistant, in June
2013. Amarildo's death, which coincided with widespread political upris-
ings across Brazil in the lead-up to the Confederation Cup (a World Cup
preevent), drew national and international attention to the reality of
police violence in Rocinha.

During a police operation in Rocinha, Amarildo was removed from his
home by a group of UPP officers and taken to one of the local police headquarters inside the favela. There, at the behest of the UPP commander,
former BOPE officer Edilson Santos, he was tortured by UPP officers, who
sought information about the location of some of the traffickers purportedly
hiding in the same area of the favela where Amarildo resided.[11] The torture
session lasted several hours. It was witnessed by more than two dozen UPP
officers, none of whom intervened, and resulted in Amarildo's death. The
police then promptly disappeared his body, which was most likely removed
from the favela in the Big Skull that was called in during the wee hours of
the morning by Edilson. Over the days and weeks that followed, Edilson
and others (unsuccessfully) instituted a cover-up that allegedly included the
embezzlement of "private donations" from megabusinesses operating in
the favela to pay bribes. Nonetheless, the story came out and has resulted in
the indictment of more than twenty-five officers. Although Rio Security
Secretary Beltrame ordered an overhaul of the program in the wake of the
scandal, he continued to insist that the incident has not damaged the cred-
ibility of the UPP project.[12] Residents' trust in the police and the government, already tenuous at best, is now at an all-time low.

Even before the Amarildo scandal broke, those residents who were
basically happy to have the traffickers "officially" gone began to express a
quiet narco-nostalgia. One resident, an elderly woman who had once
complained to me about the volume of the traffickers' funk music in the

neighborhood in which she lived expressed a sentiment that I heard time and time again: "I am not saying that the way it was before [under trafficker control] was right. I know that it wasn't. But now Rocinha is a no-man's-land [*terra de ninguém*]. It was better before. You knew what to expect."

A focus group of twenty teenagers one year after the UPP was officially inaugurated revealed a similar sentiment. Only one person felt that the favela had improved in any identifiable way. This reflection is particularly telling in that in much of the state rhetoric regarding pacification, it is precisely this generation of favela residents that is identified as the primary benefactors of the new relationship between favela and state.[13]

Many residents said that their worst fears about pacification had been confirmed: the process had actually *enhanced* the power sharing between police and traffickers in an almost farcical fashion. By 2013–14, the division of power was mapped rather obviously on the landscape. Police continue to control parts of the lower half of the community, showing off a visible and permanent state presence through regular patrols. From this strategic vantage point, they can, in the words of one resident, "parade around" at the bottom of the favela for the cameras and visiting dignitaries. But the traffic continues to exert control in the "no-man's-land," the narrow alleyways where the police will not go.[14] One longtime resident told me that even in broad daylight she was afraid to walk in the favela's becos because she might get caught in a shoot-out between rival traffickers or between traffickers and corrupt cops. It is widely believed by residents that the two warring groups of traffickers are using the police against each other and that whoever comes out ahead will do so because of the involvement and intervention of the police.[15]

Collusion extends beyond the division of territory. Police continue to collaborate with the traffic, skimming off the profits from the continuing drug trade. Certain officers use their sirens constantly, giving dealers an audible warning of their approach so as to avoid direct confrontation. Later, these same cops pick up a weekly payoff from traffickers, one of whom referred to the UPP as his "new manager." What is not clear is whether such arrangements are institutionalized or are the work of a few bad apples; the latter is surely the discourse that will be embraced if the story ever hits the press.[16] Given all of these complexities, pacification's security element has not brought about the integration of the community into the larger society, nor does it mean that Rocinha residents are truly protected by police.

COMMODIFICATION OF THE LANDSCAPE

A second mechanism of pacification has an impact on Rocinha's infrastructure by encouraging residents to map their community in new ways and by constructing new facilities and socialities. Pacification thus reenvisions the state role in the landscape of Rocinha as one of active intervention rather than neglect. Through discourses of improvement, progress, and state benevolence, the state asserts its right to "modernize" an area that it historically neglected.

The transformation of the physical favela began well in advance of the concerted military/police action. Along with a handful of other communities in Rio, Rocinha was designated a recipient of the federally funded Programa de Aceleração do Crescimento, or PAC, an initiative implemented under Lula (starting in 2010) that designated "underdeveloped" areas for improvement.[17] PAC thus takes the responsibility for urban planning away from favela residents and authorities such as the local Resident's Associations and exercises both symbolic and literal control over the development and organization of space.

PAC is a project of winning favela hearts and minds but is also, crucially, a political performance for outside audiences, tied to party politics and election cycles. Pacification as a political project is embodied by the construction of an enormous billboard installed at the base of the favela, adjacent to and visible from the major highway that runs out front. The sign announced the arrival of PAC, with the most prominent part being the amount of money the government was investing in the favela. Much of the initial PAC work took place during my residence, so I saw firsthand how the program turned the favela into a revolving construction site. There was obvious collusion with traffickers. Some of the PAC workers were themselves traffickers, who donned hard hats and reportedly kept an eye on things since rumor had it that the dono was concerned that PAC was a project designed to spy on him and gather intelligence for later police action. I was told on numerous occasions by high-ranking traffickers that almost a million dollars in PAC funds were paid to the traffic as bribes to allow the construction to take place.

One of the most significant PAC projects in Rocinha involved the construction of what would come to be called the *rua nova*, or new road. Prior to its construction, the community only had one thoroughfare wide enough for cars. The rest of the favela was a network of narrow alleyways.[18] Many residents cynically linked the rua nova to the advent of state security initiatives; the new road was not only wide enough for cars but for tanks and militarized vehicles as well. A successful police takeover depended on better vehicular access, especially through the heart of the favela where the road was constructed. But the road required the relocation of hundreds of families. Removal had important historical echoes, as many residents had been struggling for rights and legal deeds to their homes and to protection from eviction for decades (Fischer 2008). As imperfect as it may be in the eyes of urban planners, residents see the built environment of the favela through the prism of resistance and resilience. PAC overlooked this quality of favela space and failed to take resident input into consideration when implementing changes.

The transformation of the physical landscape could only be achieved by dividing the population and by removing some people to the periphery of the city. The process of deciding on these partitions was fraught with controversy. Residents with connections to narco-traffickers and other community leaders were resettled in several apartment buildings constructed along the new road.[19] Now a central architectural feature of the favela landscape, the apartments were painted bright colors in an attempt to visually remake the favela's classic brick and mortar, cloaking poverty in a more cheerful aesthetic. By default, the new residences rendered the self-constructed houses of the "old" favela style inadequate and ugly. Despite the happy facade, residents wryly noted contradictions in the new favela landscape, paying particular attention to how the workers painted only the sides of the buildings that were visible from the rich neighborhoods and alleyways below. (Eventually the unfinished sides of the buildings were painted as well.)

The road project was accompanied by efforts to encourage people to envision favela space in a new fashion. A post-pacification contest sponsored by the government asked residents to give names to the favela's rua nova and to some of its major alleyways, thus giving residents a sense of agency and involvement in the creation of state spaces. After most people just wanted to call it the "new road," government officials chose other names themselves. I saw alleyways called Peace, Tranquillity, Love, and Happiness. Residents were not buying it. Both the bright colors and the blithe names are illustrative of a local expression that is used to describe pacification's outcomes. Locals say that the favela now wears "makeup," makeup that masks the ongoing reality of violence and poverty.

The neighborhood around the new road quickly became one of the most desirable places in the favela to live. Residents who didn't have the connections to get a government-issue house on Tranquillity or Peace Street were compelled to accept a cash payout for their houses, which were quickly razed to make room for the rua nova. Those who were bought out quickly discovered, however, that government compensation did not match Rocinha's rising prices. Across the city, pacification was producing widespread real estate inflation, both inside and adjacent to favelas (Frischtak and Mandel 2012; Neri 2012). In the community of Complexo de Alemão, for example, it was reported that there were increases in rent of over 100 percent, leaving hundreds of families homeless.[20]

Several entrepreneurial residents I knew on the rua nova moved back into old, dilapidated quarters with family members in order to rent their government-issue apartments to gringos vacationing in the city. The presence of gringos renting and buying in the favela is emblematic of the way in which pacification works in tandem with gentrification. In a compelling instance of what David Harvey (1987) has characterized as war on a spatial level, gentrification and its accompanying real estate speculation expelled people from desirable areas of the city faster than years of armed violence (see also Smith 1996). The process of "upgrading" in Rocinha in the name of favela progress meant that the government was able to legitimately remove people who had been fighting for land rights for decades (Fischer 2008; Cavalcanti 2007). Hundreds of Rocinha residents relocated to other favelas. Two families I knew who had been removed went to Praça Seca and Campo Grande, respectively, far from work, which meant an added, costly commute. Now geographically marginalized, they also faced heightened insecurity as limited economic options led them to purchase new homes in favelas under the control of heavy-handed, extralegal militia groups.

Spatial pacification is not just about removing and relocating poor people and attracting new kinds of residents; it is also about winning over those who remain by convincing them that state intervention is in their interest. Here pacification takes its cue from global counterinsurgency theory, where building new facilities is envisioned as a way to garner the support of local residents—the "build" in the "clear, hold, build" strategy for upping local support for military interventions (U.S. Counterinsurgency Field Manual 2006). In this vein, PAC built an urgent care center, a sports complex, and a footbridge over the freeway adjacent to the favela, designed by the famous Brazilian architect Oscar Niemeyer. These services, however, have not convinced residents that the government is firmly committed to improving their lives, or that the state presence is real or lasting. The projects instead proved to be attention-grabbing publicity centerpieces developed without local consultation. The enormous (and very expensive) footbridge linking the favela with an adjacent wealthy neighborhood is an especially apt illustration of how PAC projects perform improvement and favela integration with the rest of the city in spectacular fashion but yield minimal benefits to favela residents (Cavalcanti 2013: 203).

Though at first many residents cited PAC as evidence of a true government commitment to improve living conditions in the community, with time cracks appeared in this facade. Among the list of residents' complaints is that the sports complex has not created jobs for residents, as it is staffed principally by employees from outside the favela. One community leader complained that the complex's focus on youth programming is a poor substitute for a decent educational system; none of the existing schools were upgraded or expanded under PAC. The urgent care center, Unidade de Pronto Atendimento, or UPA, did in fact reflect a real need in a community where heath care concerns are paramount; however, it is seriously underresourced, lacking supplies and doctors. One resident told me that on the one day she visited they had run out of painkillers. "I couldn't even get an aspirin," she lamented, jokingly playing on the acronym and referring to it as the Unidade de Péssimo Atendimento (Unit for Terrible Treatment).

These critiques aside, the most telling aspect of the PAC projects is that despite the millions of dollars spent on infrastructure in Rocinha—and millions more spent in every other pacified favela—basic sanitation issues have not been addressed. Trash collection is insufficient, rats run rampant, and sewage runs aboveground and overflows when it rains. Addressing these problems would make the most difference in improving the lives of residents but would not contribute as efficiently to the elaboration and marketing of the pacified favela as a global brand, since it isn't visible from the outside.[21]

PACIFYING THE FAVELA ECONOMY

A third mechanism of pacification is centered on the economy. Pacification frames favela markets in two crucial ways. First, it disrupts local economies and extracts taxes from a previously unregulated system, increasing state revenue. Second, it captures new consumer markets, thereby generating corporate wealth. Contrary to the stereotypical image of a favela as a place of abject poverty, favela residents have a substantial amount of purchasing power. A recent study revealed that Rio's favelas alone represent a combined GDP of US$13 billion annually (excluding the drug traffic), more than several Brazilian states (Flor and Marinho 2013). Under the guise of social inclusion, pacification creates new territories of consumption via the material redirection of the favela and its residents.

Rocinha is unique among favelas in that it is a thriving commercial center with an estimated one thousand small businesses. When I lived there, I could get sushi, Chinese food, or pizza delivered to my apartment in a matter of minutes. On every corner, there were beauty salons, mom-and-pop groceries, produce markets, Internet cafés, video game arcades, and so on. As part of an informal economy, many of these businesses have historically operated outside of official channels and have not been entirely subject to permitting or taxation. The relative lack of costs associated with formalization has kept overhead low, allowing for business owners to offer affordable goods and services for their favela customer base. In this way, informal commerce has played an absolutely crucial role in sustaining both merchants and consumers within the favela (Perlman 2010: 159).

Though the process is still unfolding, pacification through economic formalization is expected to alter long-standing features of local commerce. One of the first instances of aggressive formalization came as part of what was called "the Shock of Order," implemented under Rio mayor Eduardo Paes.[22] With its origins in Giuliani-era New York City, the policy is based on the "broken windows" theory, which envisions acts of vandalism or other small-scale deviance as gateways to larger criminal behavior.[23] The illicit market in legal goods so important to favela livelihood is reframed through this lens; informality is increasingly envisioned as the driving force behind a supposed urban degradation antithetical to hosting the World Cup and Olympics.

The Shock of Order targeted Rocinha's economy on several levels. At first, effects were largely diffuse, affecting only favela residents who worked in the informal sector in Rio. Beach vendors, in particular, were apprehended by authorities if they didn't have the proper license to sell their wares. One Rocinha resident I interviewed sold bikinis along the strip of beach between Leblon and Ipanema. He had been fined and lost days of work as a result of the Shock of Order.[24] "What kind of government persecutes honest, hardworking people?," he asked indignantly. Given that (at the time of our interview) Rocinha had not yet been militarily pacified, he was especially outraged at the hypocrisy of being punished for doing honest (albeit informal) work while a high degree of *bandidagem* (criminality) was simultaneously being tolerated by the state.

The Shock of Order also periodically intervened in one of Rocinha's major local markets, the Camelódromo da Passarela, which runs along the favela's entrance adjacent to the highway. The Camelódromo's location on the border zone between the favela and the formal city put it at the front lines of the city's new battle against the "perils" of informal urbanism. But "periodic raids by police together with 'Urban Order' stewards" brought more disorder than order (Doherty and Lino e Silva 2011: 30). Vendors fled the police, stalls were sacked, and merchandise was broken. Beyond the more tangible disorder surrounding the Shock, a kind of conceptual chaos accompanied attempts to police informal commerce. Doherty and Silva describe one merchant who "got a formal loan from a formal bank to sell food in an informal settlement without paying formal taxes on her business but bought products from a formal supermarket in the formal city" (2011: 34–35). The tension and contradiction here between competing forms of acceptable/unacceptable, licit/illicit commerce is at the heart of the economic pacification of the favela and suggests the arbitrary nature of the Shock of Order.

Just as with state-led security initiatives, the Shock of Order has remained concentrated at the bottom of the favela and along the main road. Community business owners, however, continue to express concern that the coming cost of formalization will render a serious blow to internal commerce at some point in the near future. It remains unclear whether the "domestic" market of Rocinha can survive under regulation by the government and what impact this will have on favela consumers, particularly those in the lowest income brackets.

Although local establishments are under threat, residents are able to exercise their growing spending power in new venues. The presence of the UPP further opened the favela to a number of domestic and multinational franchises (Subway, for example), including pharmacies, supermarkets, and, recently, the mega home store Casas Bahia.[25] Casas Bahia has historically enjoyed a strong favela customer base but was unable to realize its full market potential in the unpacified favela because previous security concerns labeled most of the favela an "area of risk" outside the jurisdiction of the store's home delivery services. Since the grand opening, the smaller, locally owned furniture stores—the only ones that would deliver—have been unable to compete, and almost all of them have gone out of business. In some of my initial interviews with merchants after pacification, they complained about two things that they saw as crucial to the decline in their revenue. The first was that there was less narco-money in circulation, so they were selling less luxury goods. Second, they felt that pacification rhetoric had wrongly promised them new customers from nearby nonfavela neighborhoods who would frequent their stores since the favela was "safe."

Pacification also brought dramatic alterations in the provision of electricity, cable, and Internet. Overnight, the utility companies had thousands of new customers and a veritable monopoly on service provision when trafficker-backed options were disconnected. The interplay between the militarized state and corporate interest is perhaps most transparent with regard to these providers, as the government removed local competition for corporate actors at no cost by targeting the informal markets that had previously provided services to residents. The privatized electric company Light has been providing power to Rocinha and many of the city's other favelas for over a decade, and many residents had been paying electricity bills through standard channels for years. However, some residents did (and still do) use *gatos*, illegal connections made by siphoning power from the legal line of a paying customer. According to a U.S. Embassy cable leaked by Wikileaks in 2011, favela gatos cost Light an estimated US$200 million in lost revenue per year (Hearne 2009). It had been difficult for Light to police these illegal connections, in part because in Rocinha they were condoned by traffickers, who said the practice was a form of righteous appropriation from the "robber barons" of Light.[26] With the UPP presence and the diminishing dominion of the traffic, Light can better control the proliferation of gatos, not only because the permanent police presence means that it is easier for the company itself to investigate, but also because residents themselves are more concerned about being caught for tapping into their neighbors' connections. The bottom line here is that pacification has brought Light significant profits, with post-pacification Rocinha alone expected to generate about US$12 million annually, up from US$1.1 million before the process began. CEDAE, which supplies water and sewer to the community, has also formalized service in some places and is expected to grow from US$150,000 to US$1.5 million with pacification (Leite 2011).[27]

Similarly, pacification has produced a dramatic shift in the provision of (typically bundled) cable television and Internet service, which until 2011 was only available through informal channels. When I lived in Rocinha, I purchased service from a relative of the drug boss; his cousin was responsible for supplying my neighborhood. He came over and literally shook some wires around in front of my apartment, gave me an Internet password, and I had fifty-some TV channels (including four HBO channels) and relatively reliable Internet for about R$30 (US$15), which I had to pay in cash when he came to collect once a month. Representatives of the corporate giants Skye and Embratel began to compete for the lucrative business of the previously untapped market of favela consumers within hours of the initial police takeover. Despite the high cost of the new service offered by these companies, residents rushed to get reconnected since pacification happened to coincide with the finale of a highly popular novela and an especially juicy scandal on the program *Big Brother Brasil*.[28]

Two parallel discourses have galvanized around the formalization of utilities. On the one hand, class status and citizens' rights are linked to formal market consumption (O'Dougherty 2002), as residents seek what Alexander Dent has described as a "fully consummated commodity experience" (2012: 32). For those who have long been excluded, an electric or cable bill becomes a sign of citizenship based on legitimate consumption. On the other hand, the dramatic cost increase associated with the consumption of licit utilities is producing narco-nostalgia, a longing for a return to the times of the traffic and to the economic side effects of their rule. One elderly evangelical Christian I interviewed stated that she was firmly opposed to pacification and wished the traffickers would come back since she now had to pay double the monthly rate for her cable service, which didn't even include her favorite channel—the *Big Brother* twenty-four-hour camera. According to my informants, prices jumped from R$30 to R$120 (US$15–$60).

The capture of consumers through pacification has brought an expansion in the availability of consumer credit for residents. In the pre-pacification favela, I only knew one person who was able to get a credit card, which required a legitimate nonfavela address, that is, an address outside the "area of risk," and formal (*carteira assinada*) employment.[29] She regularly shared her account with others who lived on her alleyway, allowing neighbors to charge items as needed and make monthly payments. With pacification, four people in the alley were able to secure their own credit cards. While this can be attributed in part to some small gains in upward mobility on the part of these new cardholders, it is also, they told me, much easier to secure a credit card than it was just a year earlier since the favela is increasingly regarded as part of the "formal" city. Even residents with bad credit are able to access a new kind of credit card, based on having a qualifying cosigner.

With the boom in available credit among many young favela residents, it has been possible to observe emerging patterns of consumption. One person told me that with a newly cosigned credit card, several young women he knew had paid for breast augmentation. "I think it's kind of sad," he explained. "They might have these beautiful breasts, but at home there might be so many people living in a small space that they can barely find somewhere to sleep on the crowded floor." While this pattern of prioritizing status-imbuing consumer goods, including changes to one's body as a commodity, was always commonplace in the favela, pacification and the emergent formal and credit-heavy economy have enhanced this process.

While favela commodification has long been the norm, especially in communities near the wealthy parts of the city, the Olympic exception coupled with a rise in foreign investment in the city has heightened stakes. Ongoing social inequality needs to be not only "acceptable" but also aesthetically palpable in a city increasingly made for TV. The pacified favela is emerging as a valuable city brand, especially when pacification is understood as a somewhat paradoxical mix of government benevolence and bootstrapping, self-reliant entrepreneurship by motivated residents. Indeed, economic pacification has been accompanied by a discourse of entrepreneurship, in which residents are expected to market and sell themselves as part of the ever-increasing commodification of the favela landscape.[30] A variety of new micro-finance organizations have opened in Rocinha and are making loans available to residents to realize their entrepreneurial potential.

Both the domestic and international media have been central in circulating the pacified favela as a global brand, particularly through the highly selective representation of pacification's complexities—largely reifying the spectacle of the pacified favela, in lieu of critiquing the ongoing challenges of (in)security. Most of the time, press coverage is laudatory and focuses on the positive transformations afoot. Where the Rio media has always featured exhaustive, sensational coverage of favela violence, the ongoing failures of pacification, including the complex and problematic power sharing it has engendered, have generated relatively little mainstream press coverage. In 2014, the only place that consistently reports gunfire is Rocinha's own small-scale social media news sites or residents' Twitter or Facebook pages. Such media engineering does not help residents seek greater accountability from pacification's architects, but it does ensure that the elite and corporate sponsors will get a good return on their "marvelous" investment. Pacification, however incomplete and unsuccessful, is estimated to grow the regional economy by US$21 billion (Hearne 2009).[31]

CONCLUSION

Pacification has created insecurity through the promotion of security. It has changed space for outside viewers and police strategists but has left residents wading through sewage every time it rains. It has implanted an economic system that puts local enterprises out of business while letting corporate economies and investment capital flourish. In *The War Machines* (2011), Danny Hoffman offers a Marxist reading of Deleuze and Guattari, in which exclusion and integration are critical to capitalist expansion. He writes, "Capital, at least in its current manifestations, generates a unique form of surplus by continuously unproducing what it produces. It must deterritorialize what it previously territorialized only to territorialize it again" (10; see also Harvey 2003 on "accumulation by dispossession"). This dynamic is at the heart of pacification. Uneven development in Rio should not be understood as a by-product or failure of neoliberalism, or of the state, but a purposeful and integral component of it, just as the violence that has accompanied it isn't "an outcome" or a "response to" but an actual engine of capital. In this way, the pacification of Rio's favelas is especially revealing of what Neil Whitehead (2011) has described as the cannibalistic features of the modern state, a state that has been "structurally adjusted" by what he calls the "off shore pirate class," a mobile, global elite who use the scaffolding of the state to expand their fortunes. The pacification of the favela acts as a spatial fix for new iterations of neoliberal capital driven by the Olympics and the promise of Brazilian modernity.

And yet, remembering that capital always needs a crisis, pacification also entails a process of division, of successive cycles of exclusion and integration. This is apparent in both the changing socioeconomic hierarchies within pacified favelas and the spatial reverberations that selective pacification has brought to the wider city landscape. There are heightened divisions inside the pacified favela as the growing cost of formalization is fortifying already existing fissures along class lines. Although this feature of favela sociality has often been overlooked by observers, communities have always been internally heterogeneous places with their own unique class structures. With pacification and its accompanying shifts, poorer people are being removed, relocated, or pushed out by gentrification and rising rents. The remaining middle- and "upper"-class Rocinha residents, who are experiencing material enfranchisement and heightened access to conspicuous goods, are increasingly reproducing an ideology of consumption as the key to claiming class status. It remains to be seen whether the new consumptive habits of this group will bestow enough "distinction" on these upwardly mobile residents or whether their skin color and place of residence will trump their acquisition of the markers of middle- or upper-class status (Bourdieu 1984).

Real estate value also hinges on the stability of the peacemaking efforts.[32] While home values have risen in favelas as a result of pacification, this should not be mistaken as a sign that their worth is getting closer to that of residences in the rest of the city. On the contrary, the neighborhoods directly adjacent to Rocinha have seen astronomical growth in market value, with São Conrado apartments in particular enjoying a nearly 200 percent increase since pacification.[33] The real estate bubble is ossifying, rather than challenging, urban inequality.

As communities located near planned mega sporting events and rich neighborhoods in the central areas are pacified, a shifting spatial geography of crime and marginalization has followed. Traffickers from many of the pacified favelas fled to other still unpacified places controlled by the same gang, adding to the peripheral population yet to be captured by both the police and the corporate market. While centrally located favelas have the "privilege" of the UPP, the more than one thousand unpacified favelas in Rio continue to function as staging grounds for BOPE's violent and oppressive tactics. Thus, while one kind of favela is lauded as a success, albeit a beleaguered one, a new front line of the state of exception is being forged outside of Rio proper, in places largely out of sight of the media and the International Olympic Committee.

Epilogue

May 2009. It is dark by the time the car turns up the bumpy road to the dump. We ride in silence, noting the empty trucks lumbering past us, coming out of Jardim Gramacho, the largest garbage dump in Latin America.[1] We slow at the entrance, where Curtis tries to explain our visit, finally turning to me to explain for him, pulling some forms with stamps and signatures out of his camera bag. "They are American journalists," I say. "I am the translator. We have come to do interviews in the dump. They were just here this morning but wanted to come back at night, to see how it is to pick garbage in the dark." With a bored look, the guard takes Curtis's forms. Through the window I can see him dialing an old rotary phone and nodding. He comes back. "Yes, it's OK, but you have to take one of us with you. You will need someone to make sure you are safe." I move over and let the guard into the backseat. He is young and smells like too much cologne. Making small talk, I learn that guards don't last long. He has only been on the job a few weeks. "How did you get here?," he asks me. "Are you a journalist too? Like them?" He nods toward the front seat. "No, an anthropologist. I met Curtis on a favela tour. I live in Rocinha." He nods his head. Of course he knows of it. "Curtis needed a translator. I need money. Not for me but for someone else. Someone who is sick . . ." I let my sentence trail off.[2] The driver navigates the potholes as we head to one of the many picking areas. The dump spreads out endlessly before us. The night hides the garbage that forms peaks and valleys in all directions. The small lights of the pickers' flashlights form a milky way of stars. We park next to several security vehicles and a few more guards surround us. They order us in no uncertain terms not to wander off. It is hard to predict the behavior of the pickers, they warn, as if referring to wild animals.

The smell is overwhelming. The sound of Curtis gagging punctuates the silence between the roaring of the diesel engines of the trucks and the whoosh of tons of garbage falling upon tons more. Curtis pulls expensive camera equipment from the trunk, on loan from the major American TV network that is financing the production of the story. His wife sets up a floodlight. He has spent the past few years as a correspondent in Iraq, she in Gaza. They are supposed to be in Rio on vacation. But he can't take vacation anymore, she tells me when he is not listening. Together, we walk deeper into the dump. We wait for a truck. The camera rolls and Curtis wades deeper in, capturing the surge of the pickers as they race to be the first to find a gem among the garbage. Metal? Paper? Glass? They sort urgently through the new merchandise, according to a system of value that eludes me, placing things into the large sacks they carry.

The pickers are not especially happy to see the floodlight or the camera. Curtis is going to have a tough time getting interviews, I think. Several people hurl obscenities at him. "I didn't give you permission to film me. Get that #@!%$@ camera out of my face!" As I start to render their anger into English, a guard touches my arm. "Don't," he says. "Don't listen to them. The owner of the dump is who decides these things, not them. He says you can. They don't get to say no." I finish my sentence anyway, but Curtis ignores me, his eye on the story. He finds a man who agrees to be interviewed. He squints into the Curtis's floodlight. "Why do you pick at night?," Curtis asks loudly. I translate: "It's cooler." The man adds, "The vultures don't bother us as much." In the silence of the car ride back to the favela, I think about this answer. Exactly which vultures did he mean? The scavengers that circle endlessly above the dump, clawing through the garbage for rotting food? Or us, with our cameras and our questions?

THE ANTHROPOLOGY OF VIOLENCE AND
THE VIOLENCE OF ANTHROPOLOGY

The challenging experience that night at the dump introduces some of the concluding points I would like to make. Our presence at Gramacho raises questions about the goal of trying to comprehend people's experiences in the context of violence and poverty. Curtis would say that the camera authorizes him, that his story celebrates the ingenuity and work ethic of pickers as they find a way to eke out a living and that it educates the larger world about their plight. (Whether the larger world really cares is another story.) This discourse mirrors that of many favela tourists, who claim to be visiting Rocinha in the name of education and witnessing. But the spectacle of Gramacho, along with the process that lies behind the production of Curtis's images, also provides a valuable opportunity to question the means and the ends of ethnographic knowledge production. While it is easy to see how Curtis's camera is akin to the hungry eye of the vulture, how different really is the process of obtaining anthropological data? In places like the dump or the favela more generally, where structural violence surrounds and informs social relationships, questions about the ethics of spectatorship must be taken very seriously. Because ethnographic research involves social relationships, it too becomes enmeshed in the structures of spectacle, violence, and commodification.

Gramacho forced me to reflect anew on the moral dimensions of inequality that underlie so much of what I discuss in this book. After such an extended period of time in Rocinha, I had normalized the violence of everyday life there and lost the critical distance necessary to more self-consciously interrogate my own presence as an anthropologist.[3] That I had agreed to participate in the Gramacho spectacle, for whatever reason, reawakened me to the need for a critical examination of my complicity in the very structures of violence that I had sought to critique. The fact that it took being confronted with something so extreme that it made Rocinha seem luxurious is revealing of the ethical complexities of doing research on violence and suffering.[4]

As anthropologists have long known, the regimes of knowledge that undergird the ethnographic enterprise are problematic, especially in places where violence defines daily life.[5] Books like this one and researchers like me play an important role in representing the favela to the world; we too "invent" the favela, as Licia Valladares (2008) has so astutely argued. Critical and engaged observation and writing are thus especially important in this context, as is being conscious of and sensitive to how power relations inform research. There is no doubt that there were (and continue to be) significant inequalities between my favela-based collaborators and me as an ethnographer.[6] The practice of ethnography implicitly capitalizes on these power divides. It is far easier to insert oneself into the lives of the marginalized; imbalances of power make it easier for me to study favelas than to "study up," and it would be virtually impossible for a favela resident to come to the United States to study me (Nader 1969). This is well illustrated by the fact that even traffickers, due to their class position, were more accessible to me than were BOPE personnel.

Power dynamics fundamentally influence the quality of relationships with research subjects as well. Despite the fact that I formed lasting friendships with many people in Rocinha, many of whom I consider "family," the profundity of these relationships never completely effaces the differences between us. These differences are not just about language or culture but also about our differential access to capital, in all its forms. Although during my long-term residence in Rocinha I was a "poor" graduate student, I was still a member of the U.S. middle class who could afford the luxury of spending years studying for a PhD. Unlike my interlocutors in the favela, I could continue my education during this period of my life instead of working full time.

My class position signified that I enjoyed a mobility that other favela residents did not. I could *choose* to live in a favela. While residence as an ethnographic method was based on my understanding of the tenets of anthropological fieldwork, it was still illustrative of the power differential between me and other residents. The fact that I had the ability to make a choice to experience violence by living in Rocinha meant that I could also leave and go somewhere else when things got rough. I could always, in the end, get on a plane and go home. And much as the struggles of daily life in Rocinha became mine during my fieldwork, my access to greater mobility always formed a subtle subtext. This privilege revealed itself in especially stark relief when, during the writing of this book, I lived in a nice neighborhood in Rio, outside of the favela.[7] Every time I saw an old friend or acquaintance in Rocinha and they asked where I was living, I experienced a sinking sense of guilt that I was somehow not acting in solidarity with them by not living in the favela. To respond meant to openly acknowledge the differences between us, even if these differences had always been there.

Furthermore, like favela tour guides, I had and have the power to represent the favela to outsiders. Anthropology is not a neutral chronicling of reality but an act of translation: it involves translating experience as a field-worker, as well as the words and thoughts of others, into something that is understandable for readers elsewhere. The ethical quandaries and power dynamics that I alluded to above make being attentive to the content of translation especially important. The end product of scholarship in the favela setting (books like this one) is unavoidably part of Favela, Inc., because it puts the favela (and, in this case, its violence) into global circulation. For this reason, though I recognize that the interpretations of readers are ultimately beyond a writer's control, I have tried to avoid sensationalism by being especially attentive to my subject position and to the development of my narrative.

For me, challenging favela violence through ethnography has meant continuously redrawing the connections that are hidden in the production of favela violence as spectacle, including those of the power dynamics between ethnographer and ethnographic subject. I have tried to write against favela violence (to denaturalize it by translating it into the language of ethnography) by making visible that which is supposed to go unseen, unacknowledged, and unsaid. I have outlined these connections in two registers. One strategy has been to insist on reporting the imbrication of criminal and state violence, to argue against the idea of one as more legitimate than the other, framing both as forces of terror and suffering. I have purposely sought to call attention to traffickers as people whose multifaceted subjectivities are so often erased by simplistic depictions of them as "enemies of the state." My goal has been to suggest how someone like Beto enters into and thinks about his profession, to reveal something of how he thinks about violence, and to note how his violence is intertwined with, even part of, larger modes of state governance and intertwined as well with the consumer regimes that touch lives around the globe. This is not to romanticize or glorify traffickers but rather to ask the reader to consider a critical empathy—without which we cannot imagine, let alone realize, an end to the states of exception that enable violence in so many parts of the world today.

A second strategy has been to insist on the connections between favela violence and the violence inherent in structural inequality (global and local), including that of anthropology and the ethnographic enterprise. This means insisting on the connection between "our" violence and "their" violence, showing how those who enjoy the privileges of global capitalism contribute to the conditions that produce the favela (as well as to those that make garbage picking an invisible reality worldwide). It is my hope that by insisting on these comparisons, I have not reproduced the spectacle but rather helped to demystify it—to turn attention away from the favela's exotic, dazzling properties and toward the stories of fellow humans.

Finally, in thinking about engaged anthropology in the setting of the favela, it is worth reflecting on what motivates the writing of books like this one. Most certainly, its production has been informed by a human desire to challenge inequality, and by outrage, compassion, and a desire for transformation and change. But it is also the case that this task is linked to my own career trajectory—to grants, degrees, tenure. This does not mean that activism is impossible, but it does mean that as academics we are beholden to institutional expectations. Engaged scholarship means not letting one trump the other, holding each in balance. It means publishing books not just for academic peers but also for students, and writing for the general public as well. It means not considering one's own knowledge to be an end in and of itself. Anything less, I believe, puts the ethnographer back in the tourist slot—where it's just about looking and doing nothing—or mistaking one's own understanding (and that of one's highly valued and well-educated peers) for some kind of meaningful change.

VIOLENCE, SPECTACLE, AND COMMODIFICATION

My goal in this book has been to show how favela conflict is embedded in larger sociopolitical relationships. Violence in Rocinha, I have argued, is rooted in local realities of inequality, prejudice, and penality. The construction of the favela as a place of danger and disease, so key to late nineteenth- and early twentieth-century carioca thought, has found new life in popular representations today. Trafficking, as a form of "social illness," undermines the legitimacy of the state and threatens Brazil's ascent to the status of a global economic and political powerhouse. Just as the colonial regime utilized the image of the savage to justify atrocity and the military regime relied on the figure of the subversive to enact a state of exception, so also has a "postauthoritarian" regime anchored its authority on the elimination of the trafficker. The state of exception as it exists today is authorized to torture individual "criminal" bodies while depriving and neglecting the collective body of the poor and marginal. With the advent of Mega-Event Rio, the state of exception is shifting to promote radical urban transformation in the name of being ready to host the world, being ready to embody the modernity signaled by the arrival of these spectacles.

In the favela, the punishing face of the state is embodied by BOPE, with its magical technomodern professionalism. Techniques of warfare are channeled into ritual performances of violence that deliver shock and awe not only for the local favela audience but also for the rest of the country and the world via the television camera and social media. While notions of traffickers as savages or primitives inform BOPE's actions on the favela stage, traffickers like Beto describe a criminal culture that is equally adamant in *its* claims to professionalism and modernity. Employing metaphors of government and of the market, traffickers envision themselves as righteous warriors, kings of the morro. They forge a unique cultural imaginary within the borders of Rocinha, drawing on the larger symbols of societal wealth to stake their claims to legitimacy and visibility.

Traffickers are frequently magnanimous to the favela population, embodying that traditionally paternalistic and clientelistic role so central historically to the functioning of Brazilian politics. But when their power fails, they are quick to take up punitive measures, torturing and killing those who break their rules. Ever ambivalent figures, they "combine elements of both predation and welfare" (Davis 2008: xi). The resistance and rebellion traffickers represent—after all, there are not that many places left on the planet that appear to be outside the control of governments and corporations—is simultaneously interpreted as a threat to national security and romanticized in films like *City of God*. Such romanticization feeds tourist desires, as the "freedom" and "sense of community" believed to be natural to the favela is especially appealing to those members of the middle and upper classes of Western countries who recognize in their lives and in the lives of others the great disappointments of modernity. Again, however, this image of the favela is specious; uncritical terms like *freedom* and *community* mask the harsh realities of life under the cocaine economy.

Today, the favela is one of many "concrete deserts of neoliberalism" (Davis 2008: xvi). Traffickers do not seek to establish alternative lives outside of "the system" but rather long to be included in it, even if it is based on ideologies that exclude them. And, in fact, included they are, albeit in an especially perverse and asymmetric form. Their image is appropriated and commodified, infusing Brazil's exotic glamour with a dose of gritty, urban reality. While traffickers are still prisoners in the favela, tour operators cash in on gringo desires. The pervasive hyper-favela circulates on the Internet, in the cinema, and even in the toy store.

This book, as an ethnography of commodified spectacular violence, has argued for a new interpretation of the factors that contribute to violence in Rocinha. By linking the production of favela violence to its commodification, I have demonstrated how the media are implicated in the ongoing production and commodification of war. Favela tourism signals how violence is transformed into spectacle and how discourses of witnessing but thinly veil the practice of voyeurism on favela tours. My ethnographic data show that violence and commodification must be located within one analytical framework, with spectacle as the vernacular by which these forces communicate and articulate. This matters for how we study violence anthropologically because it means that mediation and consumption of violence must be considered not as offshoots or outgrowths of conflict but as integral parts of structural aggression and violence itself. War cannot be separated from its representation and consumption, on TV or in ethnography.

Likewise, to look only at incidents of localized armed violence is to miss the critical influence of larger global movements of capital and consumption. Mediation and commodification of violence are fundamental to making the favela what it is, something that is especially well illustrated by the case study of Rocinha. One cannot understand trafficking without understanding how traffickers experience desire for commodities and how they are themselves commodified. Policing cannot be understood without looking at its imbrication with crime or without attention to the way that it has itself become spectacular performance on an ever-expanding security market. The consumption of these dynamics, be they in embodied (touristic) or disembodied (media) form, is a fundamental part of the story; localized violence cannot be extricated from its global circulation. As I have insisted throughout this book, the perpetual war in Rio offers a particularly spectacular context for thinking through these issues. At the same time, the construction of savage others, the violent imposition of state order, the incessant production of the media, and the consumption of suffering through recreational activities are not at all unique to Rio but are a global phenomenon. My work in Rocinha thus offers a model for thinking about and conducting research on violence more generally.

"DEVELOPMENTS" IN RIO

Developments in Rio in the lead-up to the 2014 World Cup allow one to see the ongoing evolution of spectacle and commodification: the continuing failure of favela pacification, the resurgence of widespread beach holdups called *arrastões* (sing. *arrastão*), and a new movement, the *rolezinho*, in which favela residents conduct organized "strolls" through the elite spaces of the city's luxury shopping malls.

As the trafficker state of exception gives way to the Olympic one, the pressures of achieving modernity mean that the project of instituting "order" in spaces of criminality and informality is ever more pressing.[8] Pacification, represented as a shift to more humane policing practices with the goal of integrating favelas into the larger social fabric, has been central to this project. But pacification in Rocinha, as elsewhere, has been a rather spectacular failure. Recently released statistics suggest that once declining homicide rates are again on the rise (ISP 2013). The numbers of disappearances in favelas are higher than ever, a fact that suggests the long-standing role of the police in delivering death to suspected bandidos has not been eliminated but simply reinvented in a covert form more palatable to the public (Andrade 2013).[9] The police themselves are far from "pacified," and the same is true of most of the favelas under UPP jurisdiction. With each passing day, UPPs across the city are facing even greater challenges than they did at the time of their initial implantation. Crippled by allegations of police abuse and corruption and with low resident trust (all of this by the UPP's own admission), they are now under constant armed attack from traffickers. In some favelas, as residents have feared since the advent of the UPP, traffickers have been returning to the morro, sensing, perhaps, the shifting political tide. Pacification is no longer such a valuable political commodity.

The weakening of pacification as a policy has enabled constant skirmishes between traffickers and police. Bursts of gunfire echo in the hills above the Zona Sul, in the picturesque favelas of Cantagalo (Ipanema) and Pavao-Pavaozinho (Copacabana), even on the eve of Carnaval 2014 as the city started to fill with revelers. In Complexo de Alemão and Rocinha, traffickers who never left when the police arrived are now becoming more brazen in their attacks on UPP officers. In response, police are returning to their iron fist tactics of leaving bodies on the ground, killing, for example, eight people ("suspected traffickers") in one favela during one incursion in February 2014. The newly appointed police chief has announced plans to continue on the warpath against the faction that controls the area. The official return to war, invasion, and spectacular (not community) policing models is suggestive of the end of the era of the UPP as a solution, at least in propaganda if not practice. In Rocinha, meanwhile, already enfeebled police claims to control have been undermined by recent events. On Christmas Day 2013, angry residents threw bottles and garbage at a group of officers on regular patrol and broke all the windows of their cruiser. In late January 2014, the traffic responded to the UPP killing of two suspected traffickers by ordering all of the businesses in the favela to close for two days in tribute and in protest—something they did, even the banks and the newly opened multinational sandwich shop.

Yet, paradoxically, even with these important cornerstone favelas of the UPP project in crisis, the government announced that it would honor a plan to extend the UPP to Rio's satellite cities of Niterói and São Gonçalo. Though this makes little sense strategically, the expansion of the UPP is suspected to be part of a 2014 election-related promise made to these cities' strongmen and vote deliverers.[10] The suburban expansion affirms the centrality of the UPP in backdoor political deals, confirming what many in the favela have long suspected—that the program and, by extension, their very security are but pawns for the maneuvering of the powerful. Pacification and favela violence appear as commodities once again.

But the interconnection of spectacle, violence, and commodification is not limited to the favela. Across Rio, the summer of 2014 was marked by growing insecurity. Among the more attention-grabbing incidents was the resurgence of gang robberies, called *arrastões*. These were prevalent during the 1990s and central to support of the state of exception and violence against the favela at the time. On scores of occasions, poor, preteen kids from far-flung favelas came by bus to the affluent Zona Sul, where they surrounded wealthy Brazilians and tourists, taking smartphones, jewelry, and cash off people standing helpless in bikinis and speedos. Several of the largest of these events were captured on film by passersby and have been circulated endlessly on news and true crime television programs. Pundits have explored whether these children are acting on their own initiative, are in cahoots with opposition politicians wanting to undermine the government in the lead-up to elections, or are in the employ of trafficking factions wanting to undermine public security and embarrass the country as the World Cup approached. Regardless of their motivation, the rise in public insecurity, it seems, has infected almost everyone with an extra dose of narco-nostalgia: everyone from favela residents to rich old ladies in the nail salon outside Rocinha now openly express how much they miss the dono.

Government reactions to the arrastões have been spectacular, if unsurprising. Buses coming from the Zona Norte and Oeste (the "real" margins of the city) are being targeted: police are racially profiling passengers, and minors without an accompanying adult are presumed criminals and sent off to juvenile detention facilities.[11] Policing along the beachfront has increased radically, with spectacular, if slightly comedic, patrols of heavily clad, bulletproof-vested and combat boot–wearing police walking between the beach umbrellas as if expecting an invasion from the sea.

Arrastões on the beach, however, haven't been the only instances of ongoing violent spectacle. In December 2013 and January 2014 another phenomenon swept the city, the "rolezinho," or lower-class stroll through the luxury shopping malls of major Brazilian cities, in greatest force in São Paulo (Pinheiro-Machado 2014). The presence, en masse, of the "favela"

Rolezinho de gringo na favela é "chique"

Rolezinho de favelado no Shopping burguês...
Ah pô, mas aí já é vandalismo...

Figure 8. A popular Facebook meme that surfaced around the time of the Shopping Leblon rolezinho. The text reads: "Gringos strolling in the favela is 'chic.' Favela residents strolling in the bourgeois Shopping . . . Damn, that's just 'vandalism.'" Adapted from Facebook meme by author.

or "periphery" in these enclaves of elite consumption produced panic on several fronts. Patrons fled, certain that the presence of so many nonwhite youths was part of an arrastão. Police and private mall security took violent action against the rolezinhos through aggressive crowd control measures, and legal proceedings (replete with the threat of hefty fines) were instituted against those who dared to enter a shopping center in a group intending to stroll. And in some cases owners even closed down and boarded up their establishments altogether rather than allow the event to take place. Citing legal proceedings against the rolezinhos, Facebook has continuously shut down their event pages.

Fundamentally, these reactions have been concerned with continuing a long-established practice of denying mobility to the poor, the irony of which is beautifully illustrated by the image and commentary in figure 8, which decries the contradiction of foreign tourists being free to stroll in the favela while favela-led strolls are criminalized.

News pundits, cultural commentators, and academics have all been quick to assess the political and social significance of the rolezinho. In the Rio context, even though the movement never quite got off the ground, leftist groups have been appropriating (and therefore commodifying) the practice as confirmation of what they have long been fighting against. They frame the rolezinho as both a concerted protest against racial discrimination (a sad reality in Brazil) and a critique of rampant capitalism in Brazilian society. The true motivation of the rolezinho organizers and participants who hail from the favela, however, is far from clear.

The one major Rio rolezinho was held at the upscale Shopping Leblon, home to some of the most expensive commercial venues in the city. Shopping Leblon closed its doors on the day of the event after some nine thousand people RSVP'd on Facebook. In the end, there were only about fifty people standing outside boarded-up windows, very few of whom came from the favela but were instead there in solidarity with the idea of the rolezinho. When I asked people in Rocinha about the Leblon event, some residents suggested that since the rolezinho was about being able to enter and enjoy the luxury of the mall and the consumer experience it offered, they simply weren't interested in standing outside protesting in the hot street. This line of interpretation questions ideas about the rolezinho as a concerted political action aimed at calling attention to racism and suggests that the movement wasn't so much politically radical as it was about the right to comsume. One resident laughingly sang his critique: "Don't you know that old samba song, 'Quem gosta de miséria é intelectual, pobre gosta de luxo' [Only intellectuals like poverty, the poor like luxury]?" In this view, the rolezinho was not a critique of capitalism. Quite the opposite. It was about favela youth wanting to get access to consumer goods, especially the brand and designer names that they saw as representative of access and inclusion. Youths wanted to buy these items, not in the favela, but in the same air-conditioned, sparkling clean, perfumed places as the middle and upper classes. But what the rolezinho and its subsequent repression revealed is that despite the entrance of these youths into the new middle class by virtue of their increased spending power, the conditions of their consumption were still going to be policed, as much through spectacular state violence as by the tactics of the retail outlets themselves.

Failing UPPs, arrastões, rolezinhos—all suggest that violence, spectacle, and commodification will continue to be central to unfolding social dynamics in Rio de Janeiro. In 2012, I asked Beto what he thought would come from pacification, the World Cup, and the Olympics. He offered a prognostication. People will continue to play their parts, he surmised. Traffickers will challenge pacification. Cops will break things, abuse residents, and steal—that is their job. Politicians will lie. The government will never really "pacify" Rocinha. Its riches hold too much promise. It is too useful. But it doesn't matter. Tourists will still come. So will *futebol* fans and Olympic athletes.

Sadly, he has been all too correct. But even in the wake of this cynicism, the people I have come to know in Rocinha are not engulfed by sorrow or rage but continue to face ongoing violence with resilience. Their resilience is rooted in the hope that drives many lives lived in the margins: the hope that one day their lives will be different.

Notes

1. Over the course of my fieldwork, I volunteered for three different nonprofit organizations as an English teacher. In addition to allowing me to give back to the community that hosted me as a researcher, my connection with these organizations was essential in helping me to gain access to the favela, to make the contacts necessary to do research, and to stay safe in the community. In general, the role of anthropologist was one that didn't make much sense to people; an English teacher who was also doing research was more acceptable.

Names of all research participants have been changed and in many cases, given the sensitive subject matter, are presented simply as "residents," with no other potentially identifying information. Though it is common to mask the location of the community of research as well (Guenther 2009), many of Rocinha's distinguishing features (including the presence of tourists) made it impossible to do so in this case. Taking to heart Scheper-Hughes's (2000) reflections on the politics of naming, using the real name of the community forced me as an author to write more carefully knowing that I was also more accountable without the use of a pseudonym.

2. In this text I maintain the use of the Portuguese word *favela*, which translates roughly into English as "slum." While other scholars (Scheper-Hughes 1995; Goldstein 2003) use the somewhat prettier translation "shantytown," I believe that *slum* better captures the slightly derogatory undertone that the word *favela*

carries in Portuguese. Furthermore, as favelas have developed over time into more permanent settlements, residences no longer resemble improvised shanties but are made of brick and mortar. Though "favela" refers to a physical location defined largely by a lack of services and informality, it can also be used to denote a space of marginalization vis-à-vis more affluent surrounding areas (Roth Gordon 2009: 58).

3. *Bailes funk* are dances that are held weekly in the favela. I discuss them at length in chapter 1 as one of the central social venues for the performance of trafficker power.

4. This figure includes those that were widely known in the favela or reported in the newspapers. It is likely that there were more deaths that occurred internally but were not public knowledge.

5. Between my initial research in 2007 and the completion of this project in early 2014, it was possible to observe a shift in the labor pool. While in 2007 most of the domestic workers I knew came from centrally located favelas, by 2014 they were all coming from more distant suburbs: the Baixada Fluminense, Niterói, São Gonçalo.

6. While reliable figures are impossible to obtain, Rocinha residents whom I asked estimated that less than 1 percent of the favela population is involved with crime or trafficking. With a total population of around 200,000, this means only about 2,000 people. Other residents said that they thought that there were only about 500 traffickers in the entire favela.

7. Colonial race relations were later importantly reenvisioned by early Brazilian social scientists, Gilberto Freyre ([1933] 1964) in particular. Drawing on nostalgic memories of his own upbringing as part of the elite planter class, Freyre idealizes racial mixing as harmonious, thereby erasing the coercion and power dynamics infused in slave/master relations. Freyre and his contemporaries cited the high degree of racial mixing in Brazil, in contrast to the more stringent models of racial segregation in the United States, as evidence of what came to be called Brazil's "racial democracy" (and which was later dubbed the myth of racial democracy by Freyre's critics). The idea of a racial democracy remains powerful in Brazil, where discrimination is widely attributed to class and economic status, not race, despite the obvious linkages between the two (Needell 1995).

8. Rio, like the other cities of the time, already had a sizable urban slave and free black population (Graham 1992; Fischer 2008).

9. Ramshackle tenements, called *cortiços,* were a precursor to the establishment of larger favelas. As they proliferated, they raised concern on the part of city officials and local leaders, who subsequently sought solutions to the overcrowding and building hazards they posed (Valladares 2008). Solutions were often less than humane. One of the most prominent cortiços, called the Cabeça de Porco (Pig's Head), was destroyed in the late 1800s, leaving thousands of people homeless. In the years that followed, an aggressive hygiene campaign was

waged against the tenements under the leadership of Osvaldo Cruz, Rio's public health minister in 1903–9. At Cruz's behest, new laws were passed, allowing for forced vaccination of the "dangerous classes" (Hochman 2009; Valladares 2008). Despite such draconian policies, the urban poor were far from passive victims of government attempts to control their places of residence or their bodies, and the "Vaccine Revolt," a large-scale protest in response to forced smallpox immunization, broke out across the city in November of 1904. The cortiços' representation as a blight on the otherwise modern city was also related to the imagined cultural excesses of residents. Early literature such as Azevedo's widely read fictional work "The Slum" (1898) described communal housing as the *zona franca* of excess and promiscuity while at the same time idealizing the sense of community present among the poor.

10. Considerable antimigrant sentiment marked the early years of government policy in Rio. One of the foremost planners suggested that the city should "control the entrance into Rio of individuals of low social conditions, and return individuals of this low condition to their home states of origin" (Burgos 1998: 27).

11. Though fear of the physical illness of favela residents is not nearly as prominent today as it was at the turn of the century, I heard numerous comments from middle- and upper-class cariocas (Rio residents) demonstrating that the fear of contracting diseases from the poor is still alive and well. In particular, such discourse centered on the health of nannies, who were widely believed to be potential carriers of tuberculosis.

12. Brazil was the only colony in the New World to host the royal court of its colonizing power. The Portuguese court, fleeing Napoleon, arrived in Rio in 1808 and remained until 1821. Once settled, they sought to remake the city in the image of Paris, building opera houses and theaters and wide avenues (Schultz 2001; Carvalho 1982). The concern with the project of modernity on the part of newly decolonized elites has played an important role in shaping early policy on the favela. Euclides da Cunha's seminal work, *Os sertões* (1902), signals the way in which modernizing urban projects were linked to spectacle and violence in the elite carioca imaginary of the period. Da Cunha's chronicle of the Bahian Canudos War reflected the tension between supposed rural backwardness and the forward-looking urban population of the nation's capital. Canudos was a millenarian religious community that, under the leadership of its charismatic leader, grew to over ten thousand people, challenging the planter economy as well as the hegemony of Catholicism. When the government sent troops to destroy the settlement, what was really at stake was how the new nation was going to deal with deviations from the modernity vision. Soldiers carried out a massive slaughter, even beheading the community leader, foreshadowing decades of spectacle and atrocity as accepted responses to challenges to Brazilian order and progress. It is no small irony that this early pivotal event gave the favela its name. Returning soldiers were given land in what would become the first

favelas, which they named "favella" after a plant that grew there. Furthermore, the rural = backward/urban = modern dichotomy established during this time is also especially important for understanding contemporary prejudice against places like Rocinha where rural migrants make up the core of the population and are doubly marginalized because of their favela residence and rural roots.

13. Living just a bit down the coast from the city's wealthiest areas and the growing beachfront leisure culture that would make Rio famous, Rocinha residents were well positioned to work in the service industry. They organized their own public transportation to and from the city, foreshadowing the immense favela-organized and favela-operated transportation system in place today, which includes hundreds of motorcycle taxis, private bus lines, and passenger vans carrying residents to every corner of Rio and surrounding areas. By the mid-twentieth century, Rocinha had grown into a small city in its own right.

14. Over time, a variety of policies were developed to solve the favela problem as it pertained to urban space: from the sterile and orderly "proletariat parks" constructed in the 1940s (Burgos 1998) to housing projects like City of God, which forcibly relocated residents to the dusty periphery of the city in the 1970s (Lins and Entrekin 2006). Although many *favelados* won hard-fought battles for rights to their land and homes and achieved some means of legal protection under the law (Fischer 2008), the specter of removal continues today, especially with the arrival of international events like the World Cup and the Olympics.

15. Subversives in this case were members of the upper and middle classes on the political left (Green 2003).

16. Even before this, we can see an exception centered on the exploitation of the indigenous population. In a classic example of what Taussig (1986, 1993) described as mimesis inherent to the colonial encounter, spectacular accounts of Tupi cannibalism served to dehumanize indigenous Brazilians and provided the rationale for the introduction of a European form of cannibalism: a colonial occupation aimed at extracting local resources while saving native souls and working native bodies to death in the process. Tupi cannibalism's ritualized delineation of social relationships and tribal hierarchies was replaced by a new social order, the colonial one, where devotion to the idols of the market and the wealth of whites was paramount (Wisniewski 2009; Madureira 2005).

17. While the idea of the exception is centered on its extraordinary nature, states of exception, like the violent conflicts they sow, are actually permanent paradigms of government, often moving seamlessly from one incarnation to another (Agamben 1998, 2005).

18. The idea of the narco-traffic-controlled favela as a "parallel state" or a "state within a state" has also come from social scientists seeking to explain the persistence of trafficker governance in favelas (see Valladares 2008) as well as from traffickers and from the state itself. In the favelas under their control, traffickers openly support the parallel state model through the development of a

vocabulary of statehood, where the kingpins are presidents, their soldiers generals, and so forth. See chapter 1.

19. It was the military government itself that enabled the emergence of Rio's narco-trafficking factions. The practice of imprisoning political prisoners and common criminals in the same cells led to the creation of the first organized gang, the Comando Vermelho (Red Command); the color pays homage to the communist leanings of the political prisoners who contributed to the gang's formation and early ideology. See chapter 1.

20. As Jensen and Rodgers (2009: 231) aptly note in the comparative case of Nicaraguan gangs, though gang members may be fighting against racism and marginalization in the general sense, they are not fighting *for* anything. The same might be said of Rocinha's traffickers.

21. While the narco-traffic had its roots in communist ideology, organized crime itself has undergone a neoliberal shift (see chapter 1), which has interesting global parallels. The U.S. gang scholar John Hagedorn notes that gangs in the United States changed in the 1970s. This shift (which we might think of as from "gangster" to "gangsta") was marked by a spike in violence. This rise, Hagedorn writes, was caused by "the adoption of economic functions by some urban gangs, the use of violence to regulate illicit commerce, the proliferation of firearms, the effect of prison on neighborhood gangs, and the effects of mainstream cultural values associated with money and success on gang youth with limited opportunities" (1998: 369–70). A similar shift can be observed in the fallout from the wave of neoliberal reforms in Rio in the early 1990s.

22. Whitehead explains, "In the light of not only encountering violence more frequently as part of ethnographic fieldwork, but also through more properly understanding the historical importance of colonialism and neocolonialism in establishing certain codes of violent practice, anthropology has now moved towards ideas that stress the centrality of bodily and emotive experiences of violence to the normal functioning of any given social order" (2007: 1–2).

23. In attempting to understand the interrelation of violence and culture, there has also been a tendency to understand war as constituting such a complete rupture in an existing social fabric that it gives way to radically new cultures of war, to radically different forms of sociality. Countering this reductionist tendency, Lubkemann compellingly argues for ethnographic engagement with "war as a social condition" (2008: 15) focused on the interrelation of human agency during periods of violence with a whole host of other cultural and historical experiences that are themselves important parts of war and violence.

24. Here I would like to emphasize that I use the term *war* to highlight the ongoing militarization present in the favela and in the larger city. This is in contrast to the way the term is used in two other contexts: to authorize the state of exception, which depends on it being a war for its continuance; and as a media market strategy to sell stories through sensationalizing language. In my usage,

militarization is a war because of its asymmetry, its ongoing nature, and its link to mediation and commodity regimes.

25. In moving from violence to war, following Riches (1986: 24), I define *war* as "violence that is subject to a certain level of organization." Whitehead and Finnström offer a similarly useful and more nuanced definition: "'War' is not an aggregation of violent acts that finally reaches a given threshold of carnage to become war rather than armed conflict, counterinsurgency, or peacekeeping, but is the invocation and creation of a particular political reality that engages allies, enemies, civilians and soldiers in a particular style of violent interaction" (2013: 7–8).

26. Marx explains, "The discovery of gold and silver in America, the extirpation, enslavement and entombment in mines of the aboriginal population, the beginning of the conquest and looting of the East Indies, the turning of Africa into a warren for the commercial hunting of black-skins, signaled the rosy dawn of the era of capitalist production" (1887: 527).

27. Neoliberalism has followed a particular trajectory in Brazil. The military period was characterized by an economic boom, principally through the adoption of aggressive state-led import substitution policies (Haggard 1990: 161–88; Evans 1995; Filho 2010), but the return to democracy was marked by slow growth and rampant inflation. President Fernando Henrique Cardoso, widely considered the father of Brazilian neoliberalism, implemented a wave of policies, including the widespread privatization of state-controlled industry. João Biehl explains that Cardoso, "worked towards state reform that would make Brazil viable in an inescapable economic globalization and that would allow alternative partnerships with civil society to maximize the public interest within the state" (2005: 21; cf. Cardoso 1998, 2005). The effects on the urban poor, however, were dramatic. Neoliberal reforms in Brazil, like elsewhere, deepened already present social fissures and economic and class disparities. Violence increased.

As Alexander Dent writes of the Brazilian case, "In its earlier phase, in the 1980s and early 1990s, neoliberalism's proponents sought to 'free' markets that were once been controlled by bureaucrats . . . and propagate an ethos of 'competition'" (2012: 29). The consequences of these policies were widely criticized (Wacquant 2003, 2008; Caldeira 2001, 2002; Goldstein 2003; Hecht 1998; Biehl 2005). In Rio, as elsewhere, the conventional neoliberalism led to the "rise of 'informal' economies," "an unequal distribution of incomes as well as urban space," and the "unevenness of 'development' by trickledown theory" (Dent 2012: 30). All these features had direct bearing on the rise of "organized crime" in places like Rocinha.

Neoliberalism, however, does not stay long in the classical version of privatization and deregulation, but, in what Jamie Peck aptly describes as its "zombie" tendencies, born-again neoliberalism finds new ways to govern people by constantly morphing into new modes of exploitation (Peck 2010). This has been the case in Brazil as elsewhere. Dent explains that "current practitioners of neoliberal doctrines including small and large businesses, and NGOs propounding entrepreneurial 'participation' and 'training' as antidotes to unemployment, have turned to newer tasks" (2012: 30). The Horatio Alger ideology described here is alive and well in Rio's favelas, where zombie neoliberalism has clearly shape-shifted, reimposing itself in the form of "fixes" for the woes it has created.

28. The drug trade and the commodification of favela violence could not happen without favela residents, whose labor generates capital for traffickers and capitalists while maintaining their own marginalization. Hence it is accumulation for some and dispossession for others.

29. Militarization and commodification as the "where" of war also expands the field of actors involved in favela conflict. Early anthropological work on violence identified three central subjects involved in any given violent act: perpetrators, victims, and witnesses (Riches 1986). But favela militarization challenges any simple divide between these categories, especially if one sees the capital and consumption as going hand in hand with violence. For example, traffickers and police are perpetrators of violence, but they are also victims of structural inequality. If state and societal neglect is a form of violence, then those who make (or fail to make) the decisions that allow for residents to remain impoverished are also perpetrators. Witnessing is also a form of entailment with violence: as bystanders fail to act in response to the suffering they observe they too participate in the reproduction of oppressive social relations. If we understand consumption as a form of participation in violence, the tourists who consume favela violence are also perpetrators. And what about you and me?

30. This is in contrast to structural violence, which is largely invisible or not recognized as violence per se.

31. Despite the fact that the vast majority of favela residents I know strictly obey the law and believe that doing so is their ticket to social inclusion, they are nonetheless constructed as a threat to public security.

32. These words mean "invading, cleaning, and pacifying."

33. Ironically, BOPE's power, and that of the police in general, is appropriated by traffickers for *their* uses. Chucky, for example, wore a vest with the police insignia on it, and it was common to see traffickers sporting the BOPE logo on ball caps or wearing BOPE uniforms, thereby producing another layer of spectacle.

34. The rise of "human difference" as a global commodity is not necessarily new in the Brazilian context. Indeed, we can observe predecessors of Favela, Inc. in the manner in which cannibalism became emblematic of the Tupi, or in how essentialized Africanisms have influenced the branding of Afro-Bahian ethnicity (Sansone 2003).

35. As I take up in more detail in chapter 4, these images are also consumed by those inside the favela.

36. "Poorism" or "slumming," as it was initially called, has a much longer history, dating to Victorian England. See chapter 4.

37. There are, however, a few problems with the classification of this group as middle class. The salary range for Class C remains extraordinarily low ($300–$1,000 R per month, or US$150–$500), especially in the context of Rio's rising cost of living (Pedroso 2012). Furthermore, the emergence of this "new class" reduces class status to pure economics. Many of those in Class C still live in favelas under the scarcely disputed control of organized crime. While favela residents now might be able to afford the new television they could not have dreamed of purchasing a decade ago, this does not mean that the social prejudice they suffer due to their residence in a favela has disappeared as a consequence of their (slightly) elevated consumer status and their classification as part of a new middle class.

38. The selective integration of certain strategic favelas by the state has occurred concurrently with a boom in "rights talk." Citizenship has become *the* clarion call. Certainly the changes in Brazil's urban landscape have created some on-the-ground improvements for favela residents. But, as I argue in chapter 5, these victories should be viewed within the larger movement of capital and the state as entangled with a web of rights, regulation, consumerism, and citizenship. The extension of "rights" to previously excluded favela residents is itself part of a spectacle of Brazilian modernity as the country prepares to host the world.

39. There are other excellent ethnographies that do this very well. See Goldstein 2003; Scheper-Hughes 1993; Perlman 2010; Penglase 2014. See also Lubkemann 2008: 10–12 for an insightful critique of the tendency in the anthropology of violence to focus on conflict, thereby obscuring other activities that inform wartime experience.

40. *Pagode* is a kind of samba. Like the baile funk, it not only refers to a genre of music, but also to a party where that music is played.

41. There are other scholars doing important ethnographic work on policing in Brazil. See French 2013; Vargas and Alves 2010; and Denyer Willis 2009, 2014.

42. While race is certainly an important component in defining favela experience, I do not take up this issue at length in this book. See Alves 2014; Sheriff 2001; Goldstein 2003; Telles 2006; Perry 2013; Vargas 2004, 2006, 2008; and Vargas and Alves 2010 for a discussion of race and violence in Brazil more broadly.

43. The other company owners, unfortunately, were not open to participation in this study. They attributed this to problematic exchanges with previous researchers. Nonetheless, I was able to interview several of the guides who worked for these companies.

CHAPTER 1

1. Beto is a pseudonym. I knew him by another nickname, and I still do not know his real name. I have attempted to keep his exact title vague here so as to

protect his identity, though he repeatedly insisted that he didn't care if people knew who he was.

2. Beto's desire to talk is indicative of the way in which anthropologists can themselves become part of the commodity world. Beto was acutely aware of his broader social invisibility despite his high public profile within the boundaries of the favela. Speaking to a foreign anthropologist was a form of legitimation, of vicarious travel, and of raising his status. He enjoyed the fact that I wanted to study him and learn about his perspective. In addition, I was commodified because of my youth and gender. While I recognized the relative advantages of this interpretation of me as a researcher, I was also cautious to always interview traffickers in the presence of their girlfriends or in informal public settings on the street or at the beco near my house. Beto's girlfriend, in particular, was especially instrumental in facilitating interviews. Coming from the upper middle class, Katia also wanted to talk about her parallel life with someone. Once I made it very clear to her that I had no romantic interest in any of the objects of her affection, she was eager for me to meet the traffickers she socialized with so that she could ask my opinion about them.

3. The neighboring favela was close enough to Rocinha that, although Beto was not technically from the community, he was not considered an outsider in the same way that other traffickers from across the city were. It was like he was "almost" from Rocinha. At later points in my fieldwork, with conflicts and rival gang skirmishes elsewhere in the city, Rocinha harbored other traffickers from the same overarching faction, the Amigos dos Amigos (ADA). ADA members who were not from the community itself were largely disliked by residents, who felt that they were rude and disrespectful as compared to local bandidos.

4. Around the same time I took a trip to the United States, and several of the same group asked me to bring back Obama election pins for them.

5. In this case, it is not so much that trafficking is honorable as it is that policing is considered dishonorable because of the well-known link between police and corruption.

6. By this is I mean, robbery, holdups, mugging, car theft, etc.

7. A direct citation of the article here is not possible, as it would compromise Beto's anonymity.

8. These kinds of privileges were linked to his status in the criminal underworld. Regular inmates and low-level traffickers cannot afford the bribe needed to get these amenities.

9. His freedom here indicates further entanglement between crime and the justice system.

10. I was therefore unable to speak with Beto after 2012.

11. I employ the term *trafficker state* to describe Rocinha's trafficking regime. There has been an ongoing debate among scholars about whether "state" is the right characterization (see Arias 2006: 3–8 for a good summary of the various

positions). With this term and with the presentation of ethnographic evidence surrounding its use in Rocinha, I seek to emphasize how the traffickers I interviewed purposely identify the narco-regime as a state and how they saw the evocation of the trappings of the state as a recourse to power and legitimation. The trafficker state is *not*, as I see it, a separate or parallel entity, distinct from the larger Brazilian one. As such, I intend the term to both delineate a particular aspect of the wider Brazilian state of which the favela and its traffickers are part and to reflect the terminology that arose in my ethnographic fieldwork.

Finally, the criminal world of Rocinha at the time of my research was highly organized, consolidated, and centralized. I see it as somewhat of an anomaly given that in many if not most other favelas in Rio, such consolidation is not the norm. In this way, I would caution against generalizing to other communities. Each place has its own history, trafficker-resident relationship, and hierarchy. Historical gang conventions make a difference as well. Thus, this chapter is about the trafficker state of Rocinha, an ADA-controlled favela, at a particular (and perhaps peculiar) moment in time. Nonetheless, traffickers' legitimizing tactics, their attempts to consolidate capital by imitating an imagined state, their claims to monopoly over the legitimate use of force, and their use of symbolic capital are certainly found elsewhere.

12. There are numerous cinematic accounts of the birth of the CV. See *Quase dois irmãos* (2004), and *400 contra 1* (2011).

13. These terms have been used since as descriptors for all favela residents, regardless of the fact that a very small proportion of any given favela population is involved with trafficking.

14. Today there are three main trafficking factions in Rio: the CV, the Terceiro Comando (TC), and the ADA.

15. The degree of tension and unrest between different narco-factions has a profound impact on the quality of favela life. In some places, conflict between groups is so pervasive that residents find themselves continuously caught in the crossfire, living in neighborhoods that have been nicknamed "Baghdad," "Gaza," or "Vietnam." In these war-torn areas, trafficker attempts to control public space extend beyond the landscape to include efforts to mark the bodies of residents as property of the gang. Juliana Farias (2009) describes how in the communities where she worked different factions had their own gang colors and associated clothing brands. Residents' awareness of these symbols was central to their quotidian security. They deliberately avoided wearing colors or brands associated with the faction enemy (or enemies), lest they be suspected of being an *alemão* (German, a local euphemism for "traitor").

16. A large portion of the narcotics that pass through Rocinha are headed for Europe (Gay 2009), but Brazil itself is actually the second largest consumer of cocaine in the world, after the United States. Cocaine from the Andes and mari-

juana from Uruguay and Paraguay likely travel along extralegal networks and transport systems that mirror the smuggling routes of other legal (but illicitly transported) goods (Nordstrom 2007), but given the impossibility of "following" this particular commodity chain, it is hard to say for certain. What is clear is that rank-and-file favela-based traffickers are not performing the actual work of international smuggling. Most don't even have passports.

Furthermore, despite the considerable profit that favela trafficking generates, most of the revenue from the drug economy goes elsewhere. Bosses and dealers might enjoy lavish lifestyles according to local standards, but their income pales in comparison to the kind of opulence made famous by Pablo Escobar. Favela traffickers, even those in key markets like Rocinha, are simply not in the same league as other global kingpins, like El Chapo, boss of the Mexican Sinaloa cartel, whose fortune recently landed him on *Forbes* magazine's "most wealthy" list (Beith 2010). Another notable distinction is that unlike the large, highly organized cartels of Mexico or Colombia, Brazilian trafficking is relatively small and more localized (Misse and Vargas 2010: 101).

17. Brazilian drug laws are highly contradictory and often unevenly applied. Though a 2006 law decriminalized personal use, concurrent legislation classifies drug crimes under a special code of "heinous crimes." The decision about what constitutes possession for personal use (with the offender being a "user") and what constitutes possession for distribution (with the offender being a "trafficker") is left to the discretion of the local police chief (*delegado*) in the jurisdiction where the arrest is made. Judges rarely challenge police classifications, which are certainly influenced by police perceptions of social class and places of residence of the detained. In Rio in particular, because drug trafficking is so widely perceived as the cause of "civil war," those accused of it (even if they have are arrested with minuscule amounts of drugs) are typically given maximum sentences. (See Lemgruber, Cano, and Musumeci 2013.)

18. Older residents say that it is only recently that consumption has become so public; it used to be more subtle, out of respect for elders and children.

19. Middle-class buyers who enter the favela also face the risk of being targeted by police. The few officers who patrolled the border of Rocinha were constantly stopping me (and most other gringos I knew) to search my purse and pockets for drugs. After being stopped three times in one day, I remarked on the efficiency of these cops to an English class I taught at one of the Rocinha NGOs. The entire room burst out laughing at my naïveté. "Those cops," they said, "are not trying to enforce the law! They think you look like a good person to get a bribe from! They want to find some drugs on you so they can get paid!" Dealers serving middle-class clientele are clearly better informed about the dangers of police and bribery than I was. The more typical scenario is that a favela-based middleman brings the drugs to an outside dealer who then distributes them through their social networks of consumers (Rafael 1998). Middle-class

dealers, operating outside the favela, are rarely targeted by law enforcement, despite their central role in perpetuating violence and drug abuse.

20. According to Beto, the role of *vapor* is one of the few that can be occupied by women.

21. There are no hard and fast rules about how many favelas one dono controls. In Rocinha, the dono controlled only Rocinha, but it is not uncommon in other parts of the city for one dono to control several small favelas.

22. The boss selects his fiel on the basis of long-standing friendship or familial ties. While the same boss governed Rocinha for the tenure of my fieldwork, two of his top confidants were killed in the course of a year.

23. Not all bosses were so kind. A dono who ruled in the late 1990s kept pet alligators to whom he allegedly fed the chopped-up body parts of his enemies. He was known for using his position to prey on young girls. One mother told me that he would wait at the foot of the stairs leading up to their house for her daughter to come home from school. She shuddered as she remembered: "Just talking about it makes my skin crawl. I was terrified that he would want to make her his girlfriend and that we would have no choice but to leave the *morro* [lit. "hill"; slang for favela] to get away." The sense of fear and powerlessness she expressed was echoed in numerous conversations I had with other residents who have traumatic memories of being on the wrong side of trafficker desire. A "professional" or "rational" boss was always preferred by residents.

24. Trafficker funerals are apparently no ordinary affair, though I never personally attended one. In discussing them one day, a nontrafficker friend broke into a comedic reenactment of what he had witnessed at a recent funeral. He threw himself repeatedly on the floor, pretending to be embracing the coffin of the deceased, "NOOOOO! How can you leave me all alone? You will never see your son grow . . . ! NOOOOO!" "First it's the mothers and aunts," he explained. "Then all the mistresses that are usually kept apart come converging on the coffin. Oh, you should see the cat fights!" Traffickers' wealth is presumably divided among these women as well as other family members, including children, when they are killed or imprisoned. It is also widely known that traffickers' money is laundered in legitimate businesses. Money is reportedly invested in ongoing legal enterprises (real estate, stores, transportation companies) the revenue from which both sustain traffickers' families after their death or allow them to maintain a certain lifestyle while incarcerated. These businesses are run by what are called *laranjas* (oranges) who are paid to administer them.

25. Donos maintain important connections inside the country's prisons, and historically entire favelas and factions have been run from prison cells over mobile phones (see Biondi 2010; *Quase dois irmãos* 2004; Gay 2005; Penglase 2008). The mere fact that prisoners are able to procure cell phones with relative ease is indicative of the symbiosis between prison officials and organized crime

within the penitentiary. I explore the role of the prison as a punitive apparatus that contributes to the proliferation of organized crime in the next chapter.

26. Politicians also play an important though unclear and understudied role in organized crime. Local political leadership, however, was widely regarded by residents to be co-opted by the traffic. The boss of Rocinha did just this during the elections that took place during my fieldwork. He picked the candidate he wanted for *vereador,* or local legislator, and prohibited all others from campaigning in the favela. This was not unique to Rocinha but happened in a number of other communities during the election season. This caused considerable uproar, and the military was called in to ensure that all candidates could campaign. They occupied Rocinha for several days during which various candidates visited and distributed thousands of flyers. Nonetheless, the boss's candidate won in a landslide. Traffickers' involvement with municipal and state politics is not aimed at enacting some form of change in favela policy in the broad sense but instead is limited to an attempt to place their own political representatives in local government so as to protect and advance their business interests.

27. It is important to consider the extent to which these "welfare" activities are truly about caring for or bettering the lives of residents or whether they are tactics for winning the local support necessary to continue to secure the drug market of the favela.

28. However, if residents encounter a problem with traffickers, they can't call on the police to protect them and are usually forced to flee the favela.

29. Wresting territory from the control of traffickers is the current objective of state strategy in favelas in the lead-up to the Olympics and the World Cup. In dozens of communities, traffickers are being expelled and occupying police forces— Unidades de Polícia Pacificadora (UPPs)—installed. See chapter 5 for a more complete treatment of this topic.

30. Beto's evocation of the word *worldwide* to signal the global nature of trafficking is a bit of an inflation. His participation (and probably that of his bosses) was probably mostly localized. Nonetheless, the drug trade that he referred to is an international enterprise.

31. A similar attitude toward crime as "work" is found in the Chicago housing projects; see Venkatesh 2008.

32. Furthermore, though there is a seeming paradox between trafficker appeals to statehood and corporate models of governance and the ongoing assertion of power through the use lavish forms of violence and death, these paradoxical modes of governance are also present in the construction of state legitimacy.

33. When traffickers said that the life of crime was one of the only options available to them, they were usually referring to the option to make a good, decent salary. The vast majority of favela residents are employed outside of the drug industry and earn less than traffickers (especially those in

higher positions) do. Beto frequently talked about how by twenty-five he made considerably more money than his mother, who worked three different jobs as a domestic servant.

34. The alienation that Beto described was even more acutely experienced by the dono. In early 2010, he unsuccessfully attempted to fake his death, hoping to take his fortune and simply disappear into retirement (in what seems to be a typical fantasy for "wanted" traffickers). This indicates deep disillusionment with his role at the helm of the business.

35. Boaventura Sousa Santos (1995) provides a cogent analysis of favela dispute resolution and parallel legal systems that predates the emergence of the narco-traffic. Writing of the 1970s favela in which he worked, he explains, "Because of the structural inaccessibility of the state legal system, and especially because of the illegal character of the favelas as urban settlements, the popular classes living in them devise adoptive strategies aimed at securing the minimal social ordering of community relations. One such strategy involves the creation of an internal legality, parallel to (and sometimes conflicting with) state official legality" (124).

36. In the case of Rocinha, this means that residents are prohibited from committing crimes in the entire Southern Zone of the city. The traffickers ensure that this rule is followed by controlling the fencing of stolen goods. Thieves are somewhat dependent on the structural organization of these traffic-controlled fences. Each neighborhood has its own. This allows traffickers to track the entrance of stolen goods into the community should they so require. So while petty crime is to some extent discouraged in specific forms, traffickers profit from its continued occurrence. As the government installs UPPs in strategic favelas, there has been an increase in incidents of assault, robbery, and other crimes in these areas. This is because the favela population is no longer prohibited from such acts by the traffic.

37. I did not witness this event.

38. In order for the law of the traffic to work, traffickers must also rely on residents to denounce other residents for crimes. I observed a number of people struggle with the way in which they were co-opted as active participants in the maintenance of trafficker-backed public order. In one case, a resident had had some things stolen from his apartment and was debating whether to report the incident to the boca. On the one hand, he argued, he didn't have any other options to get his stolen items back. "This is just how we do things, how we resolve things." On the other hand, he was reticent because he knew that denouncing someone to the traffic affirmed the right of the traffickers to enforce justice and to punish, and he couldn't control the kind of punishment the offender would receive, though in a flash of the black humor that Goldstein (2003) has chronicled as a coping mechanism in the charged terrain of the favela, he made a number of sarcastic remarks about how he would cut the person's head off him-

self for having stolen his iPhone. But the implications bothered him nonetheless, as he felt he would be implicated on a spiritual or ethical level if the offender were killed.

39. "Bare life" is a concept developed by Agamben (1998) to describe the state of being of people who are stripped of legal and citizen status as a result of the institution of a state of exception. If we consider the transgression of trafficker law by a resident to be a state of exception in minutiae, then the status of that resident becomes one of bare life, where they are punishable even by death under the trafficker system.

40. Once when hiking in the forest above the favela with a group of kids from the NGO that I worked with, we came upon a clearing with old tires scattered about. Immediately, the kids got extremely nervous and turned around. One stated that the place was called the crematorium, where traffickers burned the bodies of the people they had killed. In the post-pacification favela, police are reportedly using these same spaces to torture suspected traffickers.

41. Because of the public nature of punishment and the openness of who does what for the firm, the traffickers who administer punishment (like Beto did) are especially feared by residents. Beto felt victimized by this, claiming, "In the favela there is lots of prejudice against people of my 'class' [i.e., traffickers /punishers]."

42. When residents asked me to buy them goods abroad they were often the kinds of luxury items (e.g., $300 perfume) that I could not afford.

43. Even the use of the term *dono,* or owner, is suggestive of the nexus between violence and consumption. The dono "owns" the favela not only through his monopoly on violence but also by virtue of his role at the helm of a financial enterprise based on the dominance of territory and the labor of his company.

44. His use of "bling" in English here also connects this style to American hip-hop, which has been influential in Brazil, especially in favela culture.

45. For a cinematic representation of the figure of the patricinha, see *Quase dois irmãos* 2004. See also Gay 2005.

46. Patricinhas (or potential patricinhas) typically come to the favela to bailes funk and connect with trafficker boyfriends there. However, Katia and Beto met because his sister was a domestic servant in her house and knew that she liked a certain kind of man (dark skinned) that she couldn't find in her social circle.

47. See also Herschmann and Freire 2003; Palombini 2010; and Scruggs and Lippman 2012.

48. While beyond the scope of the current inquiry, proibidão has interesting parallels with Mexican *narcocorridos,* or drug ballads (Wald 2001).

49. For the working classes of the community, it is hard to sleep the night of the baile and hard to get up for work the next day.

50. In the months to come, his death greatly exacerbated the conflict between the two communities, as Rocinha, a giant in the world of interfavela warfare,

began to pour resources into the battle. Eventually, in fall 2009, just days after Rio was awarded the 2016 Olympic Games, the war escalated into the downing of a police helicopter.

CHAPTER 2

1. Such uniforms are typically purchased by traffickers from supply stores in the center of the city.

2. Several different types of fireworks were common in Rocinha. At first, the sound of any at all made me jump (and usually made people laugh at me), but after some time I learned to distinguish between the different meanings they connoted. Fireworks that came from only one part of the favela could be in celebration of the birthday of a trafficker or his children. The soccer fireworks were usually discernible because a collective cheer coming from thousands of homes where the game was being watched preceded them. However, fireworks that moved, that traveled from one neighborhood to another, were the kind that signaled danger.

3. This was the case in five out of six of the police actions that I witnessed as a resident of Rocinha during 2008–10.

4. Though there have been some changes in the style of policing in the post-pacification period, the underlying dynamics as I describe them here remain very much the same. See chapter 5 for a more detailed exploration of pacification's ruptures and continuities in the specific context of Rocinha. In addition, given the relatively small number of favelas that have been pacified—only 38 of the over 1,200 in the city as of January 2015—the policing conditions described here remain typical of favela-state interaction in the majority of poor communities in Rio.

5. Wacquant first developed his model of the penal state based on research in Chicago. He has since extended it to other places, Brazil included. In his writings on Brazil, he explains that like in other places, the penal state is rolled out to "respond to the disorders spawned by the deregulation of the economy, the desocialization of wage labor, and the relative and absolute immiseration of sections of the urban proletariat" (2008: 62). Brazilian neoliberalism, in his interpretation, amounts to a veritable "dictatorship over the poor," whose work is no longer needed by the capitalist system and whose only function is as subjects upon which the violence of the penal state can be worked out. The favela scholar Janice Perlman disputes the picture Wacquant paints. She highlights, in particular, two ways in which Brazil is different from the other cases he describes. Whereas the introduction of such reforms in other parts of the "developed world" has meant the destruction of the social safety net and the rollback of the welfare state, Brazil never really had a highly developed welfare state to roll back (Perlman 2009:

159). Furthermore, she contends, in the time since the implementation of the first wave of neoliberal policies under President Cardoso, the welfare state in Brazil has actually expanded. Huge successes have been won, as indicated by the growth of the middle class. Conditional cash transfers, under Lula's Bolsa Familia plan, for example, have been successful in reducing extreme poverty. Second, Perlman also sees the proliferation of Rio's informal economy as protecting the vulnerable groups Wacquant calls the "surplus population" (159). She contends that informal sectors allow for employment opportunities beyond the formal sector, thus keeping more residents afloat economically. While this might well be the case, recent policy shifts regarding formalization, which I discuss at length in chapter 5, are aimed precisely at stamping out informality, so as to bring the poor into the folds of the "official" economy.

6. These militias are self-composed and generate revenue in their mafia-like tactics of demanding protection fees. They are not "state supported" per se, but because of the political clout of many of the actors involved in them, they have not been targeted to the same extent as the narcotraffic. See Cano 2012 for an analysis of the evolution of state-militia relations over time. Estimates for 2012 put the total number of favelas occupied by the militia at 41 percent (BPSF 2013).

7. See www.diplomatique.org.br/editorial.php?edicao=71. Private security is also on the rise as the security demands of the World Cup and Olympic Games are opening up the space for large-scale international security initiatives that include not just bodies but electronic surveillance systems as well. This expansion of the security sector will likely be one of the legacies of the mega-events.

8. As a point of comparison, for the same year Mexico had a rate of 23.7, the United States 4.09, and the United Kingdom 1.0 (BPSF 2013).

9. In a 2003 study on the racial politics of Rio's military police, Ramos and Musumeci note that despite the predominance of black police, the police as a whole are still widely perceived as being "very" racist by 43 percent of the population, with 30 percent saying that the police are more racist than the rest of society (2005: 10). Sixty percent of those interviewed about police "stop and search" policies felt that they were stopped because of their physical appearance, with 40.1 percent saying that police targeted them because of the color of their skin. Other studies have shown that nonwhites are more than twice as likely to die in confrontations with police (BPSF 2013). The upshot is that both white and nonwhite police officers targeted nonwhite citizens, with these racial categories being especially complex and subjective in the Brazilian context. Police themselves are also victims of racial prejudice, and the idea that status is based solely on rank within the force and not related to skin color, makes the internal, institutionalized racism of the Military Police difficult to challenge (Ramos and Musumeci 2005: 11). On the question of race and policing in Brazil, see French 2013; Mitchell and Wood 1999; Smith 2013; Vargas 2004, 2006, 2008; Vargas and Alves 2010.

10. Since state governments are reluctant to turn over data on the number of police deaths, both in and out of service, we must rely on other estimates, such as those that measure rates based on incidents reported in the press. See, e.g., Roberta Trindade's blog at http://robertatrindade.com.br/.

11. Despite rhetoric to the contrary, this pattern of citizen inequality as it pertains to policing is not changing under pacification. See chapter 5.

12. Though exact figures are impossible to obtain, residents that I asked thought that about 1 percent of the population of Rocinha is involved with trafficking. As for the employment situation of the other 99 percent, the unavailability of employment statistics for favelas in general and the widespread practice of working in the informal economy make it difficult to know what percentage of the population is employed, where, and for what wage.

13. The famous Brazilian *jeitinho* contributes to the differential application of the law. The *jeito,* or *jeitinho* in its diminutive form, is an extralegal method of getting things done, ranging from failing to perform a legal duty (like writing a traffic ticket) to larger-scale types of corruption (Levine 1999: 403). The manipulation of a legal situation is largely dependent on the power the offender yields in regard to law enforcement. As Roberto DaMatta (1991) has emphasized, social status determines how police and other civil servants act when laws are broken. In particular, DaMatta, in his classic work, notes the use of the expression "Do you know who you are talking to?" (*você sabe com quem está falando?*), which is employed by the middle and upper classes to intimidate (usually) lower-class police in order to subvert the law. Cf. Jauregui 2013, 2014 on class status, law enforcement, and corruption in India.

14. *Playboy* is a slang term for young male members of the middle and upper classes. Jorge's observation of the uneven application of the law on the street also rings true for the administration of trafficker justice (see Arias and Rodrigues 2006). A former trafficker explained to me that the dono is far less likely to punish people from the upper echelons of favela society and would not dream of targeting a foreigner like me. She felt, however, that as someone who had been previously involved in crime, she was much more disposable given her lower-class status in Rocinha. She feared that her former colleagues could easily kill her: "Who would notice or care if I disappeared? Who would investigate? Nobody!"

15. Brazil does not have nearly enough public defenders to meet the needs of its growing prison population. UN testimony on the condition of Brazil's penal system recently stated, "The inadequacy of public defense is another major contributor to the large number of arbitrary imprisonments in Brazil. Public Defender's Offices are responsible for providing legal assistance to poor people, but they lack the structure to fulfill their mandate. In 2007, Brazil had 1.9 public defenders for every 100,000 inhabitants, a situation that has not improved significantly since then. It is important to emphasize that it is illegal in Brazil for lawyers to provide pro bono services to individuals" (www.conectas.org/en/actions/foreign-

policy/news/conectas-reports-situation-of-pre-trial-detainees-in-brazil-to-un).
See also Alves 2014 on the biases and shortcomings of the Brazilian criminal
justice system, particularly how it deals with black offenders.

16. See Linger 2003 on the "wild power" of the police and impunity as linked
to the military regime.

17. Though it has not enjoyed the same celebrity status as BOPE, ROTA has
been just as deadly. See Barcellos 1992; Caldeira 2002. BOPE is the Elite Special
Force of the Military Police. The Civil Police counterpart is the Coordenadoria de
Recursos Especiais (CORE).

18. Torture as a central police practice is evidenced by numerous reports in a
wide variety of contexts against multiple kinds of victims. Prison guards are
reported to regularly use torture (Fraga 2006). Police allegedly torture their own
recruits during training (see www.folha.uol.com.br/cotidiano/882713-promo
toria-denuncia-29-policiais-por-tortura-em-treinamento.shtml; http://g1.globo
.com/rio-de-janeiro/noticia/2013/11/pm-substitui-4-oficiais-apos-morte-de-recruta-
em-treinamento-no-rio.html). And allegations of police torture remain common
in Rio, even in the climate of police reform that has accompanied pacification.
See chapter 5 for a more detailed description of post-pacification torture
scandals.

19. Hinton (2006) notes, for example, that the two branches maintain entirely
separate criminal databases and communication systems.

20. Moonlighting in other security-related positions, called working *bico*,
falls into a legal gray zone, and there is little regulation of the practice, which has
become a commonplace, if understudied, one. See Brito et al.'s 2011 study on
working bico in Pará.

21. Interestingly, the data reveal that most victims of police extortion are
white, highly educated, and middle class, precisely not the demographic that
lives in the favela. This raises questions about who reports police abuse. I assume
that these figures do not account for favela residents' experiences given that
those in the favela most likely do not feel empowered to report or are afraid to
do so.

22. Paying off police is a regular activity on the part of traffickers. This was
included in Beto's self-described list of job activities, and Katia observed the payoffs on numerous occasions.

23. Traffickers feel that they have historically assumed the role of the police,
regulating resident behavior according to their own system of justice. The trafficker's role in maintaining social order perpetuates discourses of state abandonment while legitimating criminal rule by painting the drug boss as an altruistic
figure who protects favela residents. I found the success of trafficker-instituted
social order a source of pride for Rocinha residents from all walks of life, even
those who openly opposed the presence of the traffic more generally. Especially
at the beginning of my fieldwork, when people were eager to reassure me of my

safety as a novice favela resident, a day did not go by without someone telling me how safe I was because of the efficiency and power of trafficker law and order. Significantly, such claims regarding the safety of the favela were almost always made in contrast to the lawlessness and danger believed to be endemic to the larger city and/or natural to other favelas located in other parts of the city.

24. The criminal and ganglike activities of the police are reflected in the moniker "Comando Azul" (Blue Command), which is cited by Alvito in his 2001 study (in contrast to the Comando Vermelho, the trafficking faction). But perhaps the most extreme case of the use of police authority for extortion is embodied by the presence and growth of militias. See Cano and Duarte 2012.

25. As Whitehead and Finnström point out, what they call the technomodern and the magico-primitive are both integral components in the current landscape of global war. In particular, in the U.S. wars in Afghanistan and Iraq, drones, night vision goggles, and other forms of paraphernalia-enhanced conflict are in fact not all that different from supposedly "premodern" modalities of violence such as assault sorcery or witchcraft (2013: 1–25). How different are drones from invisible sorcery attacks really?

26. These quotations were taken from the original BOPE website: www .boperj.org. The original site has since been hacked and is no longer operating. The anthem appears in its entirety in Soares, Batista, and Pimentel 2006. The trafficker/BOPE contrast is well illustrated by the depiction of trafficker versus BOPE torture in the blockbuster film *Tropa de elite*, directed by José Padilha but developed in collaboration with former BOPE officers Batista and Pimentel, thus giving the production an air of authenticity and authority. In the film, traffickers are shown "necklacing" their victims in piles of burning tires, while BOPE uses the more civilized methods of drowning, suffocation, and forced sodomy to clean up the city. See chapter 4 for more on how BOPE is produced as an object of popular fascination.

27. The professionalization of atrocity is also employed by traffickers and is well documented in other literature on genocide. See Hinton 2002.

28. The Big Skull is simultaneously fetishized as a commercial good. Miniature skulls are a now a popular children's toy, inside and outside the favela. See chapter 4.

29. BOPE, however, is certainly not unique in this regard, as the spectacle of modernity as a quality of war today is also reflected in the use of smart bombs and touchless, and therefore supposedly more "humane," torture.

30. This remains an urban legend and doesn't gibe well with BOPE's focus on modernity and weaponry.

31. While I was unable to obtain permission to reprint the photos here, BOPE's new, professionally designed website features an extensive photo gallery of officers dressed as skulls and posing for a photographer. See www.bopeoficial .com/.

32. Sensational crime shows like *Cidade alerta,* in addition to the nightly news, use a rhetoric of war to describe the security situation in the city. *O Globo,* the city's largest newspaper (and part of the most powerful media syndicate in Brazil), regularly publishes stories under the heading "The War against the Traffic." Furthermore, use of the armed forces and tanks in recent pacification projects in several of the city's largest favelas made the image of the state at war even more explicit.

33. Trafficker intelligence aside, logistically speaking, it is difficult to mobilize the large numbers of police necessary to invade Rocinha without tipping off traffickers. One informant stated that BOPE did not conceal its activities well, especially given its natural penchant for drama and spectacle. He explained that prior to moving to a new headquarters in a more central area of the city, the Special Forces were located across a bridge in the city of Niterói. If they were heading to Rio to invade a favela, they had to cross the bridge, attracting attention and putting the traffickers on alert.

34. Interestingly, the comments do not include objections to BOPE. It is hard to say if that is because they are simply not posted or whether what appears on the page is censored by the squad's social media administrators.

35. Traffickers frequently stencil or carve the initials of their faction on their weapons. When I asked about this, I was told that the practice helps their police counterparts redirect the weapons to them in the event that they are confiscated and that it is also a tactic intended to annoy those in rival factions in the event that they end up with them, since they have to scrape the writing off in order to avoid looking at the name of their enemy every day.

36. Brazil has the fourth largest prison population in the world, a population that has doubled in size over the past decade.

37. The hypocrisy of differential incarceration has come to public attention as the participants (powerful politicians) in the infamous *mensalão* (lit., "big monthly payment") corruption scheme have recently been sentenced to jail (Romero 2013). Many are held in "luxury" facilities and have been awarded work release status. In one particularly illuminating case, one politician-prisoner is earning about US$9,000 a month in his work release job as a hotel manager, more than triple the salary of other managers at the establishment.

38. Prisoner segregation by faction was developed in the aftermath of bloody gang wars inside the country's prisons in 2004 (Biondi 2010).

CHAPTER 3

1. Leite (2000) calls this the shift from the *"cidade maravilhosa"* (marvelous city) to the *"cidade partida"* (divided city).

2. The Comaroffs describe Ethnicity, Inc. as the commodification of human identity and sale of ethnic and cultural difference. Ethnicity, Inc. is particularly

prevalent "in many desperately poor parts of the world" where "the attenuation of other modes of producing income has left the sale of cultural products, and of the simulacra of ethnicized selfhood, one of the only viable means of survival" (2009: 139). The ethnicity market follows already well-established paths of global structural inequality, and Ethnicity, Inc. works through existing mechanisms for the purchase and sale of any other commodity, "with money[,] . . . commensuration, the calculus of supply and demand, price, branding" (24). While the Comaroffs emphasize the novel nature of Ethnicity, Inc., it has a much longer history in Latin America and the Caribbean, where the "branding" of ethnic identity began during the colonial era. Just as ethnic soldiering created the "Carib" brand (Whitehead 1990) and cannibalism created the "Tupi" brand (Staden, Whitehead, and Harbsmeier 2008), so also is violence constitutive of the favela as a global brand.

3. At the time of his visit to Rio, Ja Rule's music was not especially popular in Brazil. Most people in the favela had never even heard of him. To remedy this lack of initial interest, in the month prior to his arrival several cars circulated daily throughout the favela playing his hit songs at top volume. An enthusiastic voice cheerfully declared his importance as an American hip-hop artist, the first of his ilk to visit Rocinha. By virtue of an intense branding campaign of his own, Ja Rule was soon the talk of the favela.

4. This has not happened, but the discourse of charitable generosity and the stated motivation of solidarity with the poor reflect the discourses of solidarity tourists that I discuss in chapter 4.

5. See Beatriz Jaguaribe's excellent work (2004) on how this manifests in the context of Brazil.

6. This is not to say that film produces the conditions for other media; rather, all of these representations circulate and influence one another.

7. In recent years, there has been a rise in the number of short films made by favela and periphery residents, a movement that has been dubbed *cinema da quebrada*. See *5× favela—agora por nós mesmos* (2010), *Bróder* (2011), *Curta Saraus* (2010), and *Nota de xorte* (2011). Unfortunately, these films have not yet become commercially successful and have a somewhat limited viewership.

8. Cacá Diegues, one of the founders of the Brazilian Cinema Nova movement (see Johnson and Stam 1995; Nagib 2003), has directed dozens of films, including many of the country's most well known and acclaimed productions. Influential in the national film industry, he is active in the international film community and currently serves on the jury at Cannes. The remake of *Orfeu*, like most of the films discussed here, was financed in part by Globo Films, the cinema branch of the TV giant Rede Globo, which has a veritable monopoly on Brazilian media. Globo was run by the media mogul Roberto Marinho until his death in 2003 and has been widely criticized for its right-wing stance, including its ties to the military dictatorship (Oliveira 2008). Also important in the Brazilian film industry

is the government entity, Embrafilme. The Brazilian government levies taxes on foreign films distributed in the country, principally U.S. films, and uses the levy to fund the national film industry. Embrafilme determines the distribution of these funds, and the majority of the members of the board are based in Rio, which may skew the national film industry toward directors and topics in the south of the country.

9. *City of God* was directed by Fernando Meirelles and codirected by Katia Lund, whose role has largely been omitted in the awards nominations and subsequent press regarding the film. Meirelles, who started in advertising and television, commissioned a script written by Bráulio Mantovani based on Lins's novel but had no contacts in the favelas. (Mantovani went on to write the scripts for the two *Elite Squad* movies.) That is where Lund came in. She had extensive experience working in these communities (she also arranged Michael Jackson's famous favela video; see below), and under her supervision, most of the film's cast was drawn from the now-famous theater group, Nós do Morro, based in the favela of Vidigal.

10. The *Elite Squad* films, as well as *Bus 174*, were directed by José Padilha (in the case of *Bus 174*, with Filipe Lacerda). Padilha is currently directing the U.S. remake of the film *Robocop*. In interviews, Padilha describes *Bus 174* and the *Elite Squad* films as a trilogy, aimed at revealing how media, police, and politicians, respectively, contribute to ongoing violence in Rio. All three of the Padilha films, feature writing or screen appearances by the former BOPE officer Rodrigo Pimental. *Elite Squad* also has the same screenwriter as *City of God*. In sum, this is a very small group of people producing films with the same teams and with similar aesthetics.

11. *Favela Rising* is the exception among the Brazilian-made films, as it was directed and produced by a North American duo. According to the director's statement on the film's website, Zimbalist was looking for a story about inspiration in the face of violence when his producer encountered the nonprofit organization Afro-Reggae in Rio. Despite important differences with the other films here, notably the inclusion of real people, progress, and hope in the face of adversity, as I discuss at more length below, *Favela Rising* reproduces many aspects of the favelas as a brand.

12. For example, prime-time programing was dominated by the enormously popular *novelas* (soap operas) of the period, infamous for their all-white casts and depiction of Brazil's high society (Jaguaribe 2005, 2007, 2009; Hamburger 2008).

13. See also Leite 2005 for an analysis of the favela as the new hinterland.

14. Even the nomenclature reflects the imagined unity of the population; in recent years, as the term *favela* became increasingly problematized as pejorative, the word *community* was introduced to replace it. And yet, even as the favela is extolled as a site of community, at other moments its dark alleyways are

envisioned by one U.S. filmmaker as sites of anonymity and danger. The off-the-grid favela is the perfect place for social misfits and freaks of nature to conceal themselves. In the opening sequence of *The Incredible Hulk,* Bruce Banner, a.k.a. the Hulk, does exactly that. In the perpetual twilight of the favela's thoroughfares, even an anomaly like the Hulk can go unnoticed, concealed amid the "natural" depravity of the terrain.

15. A full discussion of the connection between race and criminality as it pertains to violence (both real and fictitious) are topics I hope to explore in future work. On race in Brazil generally, see Sheriff 2001; Telles 2006; Vargas 2004. On film and race in Brazil, see Stam 1997.

16. *Elite Squad* also includes a graphic portrayal of microwaving.

17. Not only does the good trafficker/bad trafficker motif make for good dramatic tension in these films, it also reflects two extremes of the types of traffickers one encounters in the favela. Everyone knows who the Bennys and Lil Zes are and takes this into account when interacting with them.

18. The choice of the character's name here is not unintentional: Angelica's angelic qualities save Benny from his bad ones.

19. Brazilian Candomblé, a syncretic religion that combines elements of African, Indian, and Catholic practices, involves the veneration of a group of deities called orixá. While all orixá have both dark and light sides, Exu is among the more ambivalent of the pantheon and for this reason was historically associated with the Catholic figure of the devil. Interestingly, Lucinho, the villain in Orpheus, is consistently clad in the colors of Exu as well. The association being made here between favela residents and the low or "base" elements of Afro-Brazilian residents is also a blatant stereotype, and the film's unidimensional representation of the religions themselves would also likely be offensive to most religious practitioners.

20. It is important to note that ideas of childhood and appropriate childhood activities are culturally determined. Dowdney's work on the induction of children into the narco-trafficking factions points to the fact that ideas about what constitutes childhood are not fixed or universal. "Notions of childhood," he writes, "are judged not by age but by 'preparation' to do the job" of trafficking (2003: 130). See also Drybread 2014b.

21. See also Machado da Silva and Leite on the construction of the at-risk favela youth or what they call the *"criminoso em potencial"* (2007: 550).

22. The image of the good kid caught up in a life of crime also arises in the Fox animated film *Rio* (2011). While the film might be read as propaganda for a cleaned-up Olympic Rio and a return to a happy, exotic Brazil, the plot includes bird smugglers, whose hideout is located in the favela. The territory of the slum is thus reproduced as one of illegality and illicit activity. The kidnapped birds are set free, however, by a favela child, who realizes that the smugglers are wrong and eventually saves the feathered protagonists.

23. The American television series *The Wire,* based in Baltimore, shows the same practice.

24. See http://revistaseletronicas.pucrs.br/ojs/index.php/revistafamecos /article/viewFile/7542/5407 and www.achegas.net/numero/38/augusto_38.pdf.

25. *Modern Warfare 2* also prefigures the introduction of live war games in the favela, such as the paintball tours currently being introduced for tourists. See chapter 5.

26. See Angelini 2013 for an insightful analysis of favela-based role-playing games that address urban violence.

27. The imagined grittiness of the favela has been appropriated in similar fashion by the Favela Chic restaurant and club chain, with locations in Paris and London. "There is nothing slummy about Favela Chic," their website boasts, explaining that the use of the word *favela* is intended as an homage to the creative pastiche of favela residents in constructing their homes, a creativity that inspired the proprietors to give their French cuisine a Latin flair. The favela is cool but only when consumed in conjunction with more conventional symbols of affluence: expensive cocktails, well-known musical acts, and gourmet food. The favela's poverty is used to mark out other spaces of affluence and consumption.

28. http://odia.ig.com.br/noticia/rio-de-janeiro/2013-09-17/filho-de-amarildo-e-o-futuro-nas-passarelas.html.

CHAPTER 4

1. Though tourism is often associated with very recent trends in interconnectedness and globalization, as a cultural practice, tourism is in fact a descendant of colonial travel, where the bodies and customs of ethnic, racial, and cultural others were the subject of a largely male European and North American gaze (Campbell 1988; Pratt 1992; McClintock 1995).

2. Structural violence, also called the violence of the everyday, causes suffering through the effects of inequality, racism, sexism, and classism (see Scheper-Hughes 1993; Scheper-Hughes and Bourgois 2004; Farmer 2004). In that it takes violence as its central object, favela tourism is also connected to the emergence of what scholars call dark tourism (Lennon and Foley 2000), thanatourism (Rojek and Urry 1997; Seaton 1996; Stone and Sharpley 2008), or trauma tourism (Clark 2006). Dark tourism involves visiting sites associated with death and disaster, where violence is the main attraction. While dark tourism has more traditionally focused on tours to memorials or to places where violence is firmly located in the past, the concept is usefully extended to include the spectacle of "live" displays of violence, represented here by the bodies of favelados, the space of the favela itself, and tourist performances. See Kirshenblatt-Gimblett 1998 on the semiotics of live display in cultural tourism more generally.

3. The genesis of the favela tour is a matter of much dispute; several different companies claim to have started it.

4. The success of Rocinha tourism has led to the development of new markets in new favelas. This number has only increased in the intervening years, especially as the pacified favela has become a touristic object promoted by the government. At the time of this study (2008–10), Rocinha dominated the market.

5. For example, one hostel that I worked at took an R$10 commission from each tourist that was sent on a favela tour.

6. See the previous chapter for a genealogy of the expansion of the favela into an icon of Rio and Brazil more broadly.

7. At one point there were as many as eight major companies operating in Rocinha. There were also three smaller, resident-run companies that take small groups on tour. I discuss them separately below.

8. The drivers of vans and jeeps were sometimes from the community but earned relatively low wages. They have very limited interaction with tourists due to the language barrier.

9. In hundreds of tours over a two-year period, I met only three Brazilian tourists. The presence of these middle-class guides is the only evidence that tours are closing class gaps in Rio.

10. http://noticias.r7.com/rio-de-janeiro/noticias/renda-da-rocinha-e-quase-10-vezes-menor-que-a-de-bairro-nobre-vizinho-20601118.html.

11. Other tour guides frequented an artisan fair that was developed to accommodate tourist dollars. For a time, tour guides took a commission for sales there, though the practice stopped after clashes with the Resident's Association over the practice.

12. As I learned during my six-month residence in Dirty Clothes, neither of these contentions was true. Residents in the neighborhood were, however, stigmatized and marginalized by those living in more affluent neighborhoods of Rocinha.

13. "Asphalt" is distinguished from favela roads, which are typically not paved.

14. See chapter 5 on the connection between citizenship and consumer power.

15. I address the declining security situation of the post-pacification favela in more detail in chapter 5. In regard to tourism, it is important to note that while organized tours continue in Rocinha, tourists do not enjoy the same security as they did under trafficker rule. In 2013–14, I heard numerous reports of tourists being assaulted and robbed while on tour, and one tourist was accidentally shot by traffickers who allegedly mistook him for an undercover police officer. Despite these departures from the long-standing safety of the tours, owners and guides (Carlos in particular) continue to insist that the favela is safe for tourists.

16. I asked Beto this question, and he confirmed that no such arrangement existed.

17. In all of my conversations, with guides, tourists and residents, I never heard of a single instance of a tour member being robbed or assaulted until after pacification.

18. See chapter 1 for an extended discussion of Beto and his role in Rocinha's trafficking hierarchy.

19. In the year prior to my fieldwork one company was caught taking tourists to meet traffickers and was subsequently shut down by authorities.

20. As I have suggested in previous chapters, "peace" in the favela is a result of a balance of interlocking factors that make daily life livable. During times of extreme conflict, the tours are shut down. During the prolonged faction war of 2004 they were suspended for several months. The booming favela tourism industry is yet another reason for mutual accommodation between the state and the narco-state. It is likely that the presence of large numbers of tourists contributes to the patterned nature of police actions in Rocinha. I have no doubt that police take tourists into consideration when planning their favela invasions. To enter, guns ablaze, in the middle of the day would endanger international visitors and make for a potential political disaster. Police invasions almost always take place at dawn, well before tourists arrive.

21. The terminology I use—"adventure" and "solidarity" tours—reflects the varieties of niche tourism in market parlance.

22. The invocation of *Charlie's Angels* is but another example of how repertoire's of spectacular violence from the U.S. film industry are used as a metaphor through which to discuss a certain kind of "glamorous" violent behavior and set of aesthetics. See also the use of Rambo and Chucky by traffickers discussed in chapter 1.

23. Under Brazilian law, "apologizing" for the traffic is considered a crime. Apologizing is most commonly used in reference to funk music, where writing and performing music that praises narco-life is punishable under the law. However, one solidarity tour company owner told me that when he first founded his tours, he was accused by numerous public officials of "apologizing" for the traffic simply by explaining the "favela situation" to foreigners and identifying the state's role in it. The adventure tour described here goes far beyond "apologizing" given that it involves openly associating with the traffic, making business deals with traffickers, being involved in drug distribution to tourists, and so on. This tour's illegality makes advertising impossible, but one hosteler gives the phone number of the guide to new arrivals and to other travelers he meets.

24. Adventure tours such as these are part of an emerging leisure market in which tourists seek out ever more outrageous and perverse experiences. Refugee camp tourism, where tourists can live the life of a refugee for a day, or death penalty tours, where tourists eat their last meal and sit in an electric chair, are striking examples of the lengths to which tourists are going for thrills (Pelton 2003).

25. See chapter 1 for a more in-depth discussion of these factors.

26. This is a pseudonym but one that captures the sentiment of the real name.

27. Like the photos generated by adventure tourists, I imagine that these pictures find their way onto social media.

28. Consequently, many people actively work to hide their place of residence in social and business transactions that take place outside of the favela.

29. "Leadership" here includes some people from the Resident's Association as well as some nonprofit leaders and merchants.

30. For more on the role of the Resident's Association in favela governance, see Santos 1995; McCann 2014.

31. PAC, or Programa de Aceleração do Crescimento, is an initiative of the federal government introduced under Lula that develops infrastructure across the country. PAC favelas receive major renovations, including the building of roads, hospitals, community centers, and sports complexes, and they are accompanied by social projects and, often, pacifying police forces.

32. One guide said that he had heard that the drug boss didn't like the idea anyway, believing it would jeopardize the security of the favela.

33. Unless, of course, residents were able to address these concerns in their literature and tours.

34. The chicken-chasing tourist in the opening vignette provides additional evidence of the way in which tourists actively work to create experiences that match their expectations, even in the face of evidence that those expectations are incomplete.

35. I consistently resisted being placed in the role of culture broker, since I felt that it was not effective for my study of tour dynamics. This proved difficult when guides introduced me as a researcher and told tourists to ask me questions.

36. See chapter 1.

37. This is Brazil's national motto, akin to "In God We Trust," and is printed on the flag.

CHAPTER 5

1. For a discussion of the "official" goals of the program, see interview with Rio security secretary and pacification architect José Mariano Beltrame: www .csmonitor.com/World/Americas/Latin-America-Monitor/2011/1020/Rio-s-top-cop-talks-public-safety-policy-favela-pacification-program. It is also important to understand that pacification was made possible by a unique set of political alliances. A federal program called PRONASCI was launched in 2007 to combat violence by strengthening the connection between "citizenship" and "security." The program provided states with funding and awarded them the independence to use this funding to address their own security priorities. In Rio the elections

of 2008 produced a timely political alignment between leadership on city, state, and federal levels for the first time in decades. This allowed for relatively unprecedented political collaboration on the security front and enabled support for pacification from all three levels of government. As of 2014, however, shifting political tides have led to a disintegration of these alignments.

2. Batista has since lost most of his fortune and is no longer funding pacification.

3. The UPP and the larger project of pacification of which it is a part are not entirely novel. Rather, the practice of community policing, favela upgrading (e.g., Favela Bairro), and economic formalization has been present in Rio favelas (in incomplete and unsuccessful form) for decades now, with the most recent incarnation prior to the UPP being the Grupamento de Policiamento em Áreas Especiais (GPAE), implemented in several favelas in 1999 and the early 2000s. This program, however, did not enjoy the same funding or political support as the UPP and was short lived. The Olympic exception, as I see it, has been instrumental in solidifying political and financial support for favela intervention that had not been previously possible. The instrumentality of the UPP to Rio's drive to become an Olympic host city is clear from the inclusion of the first UPP captain of the first pacified favela, Dona Marta, on the Brazilian Olympic Committee (Carvalho 2013: 288).

4. Mexico 1968 is a classic example.

5. There were police patrols at the entrance to the favela adjacent to the highway, but these police were more of a symbolic presence, sentinels marking the transition of urban space, than active law enforcement agents. Residents said that they were on the traffickers' payroll.

6. See Savell 2014 on the use of the military in pacification.

7. According to a recent report by the Brazilian Public Security Forum (2013), the tension between the long-standing soldier ethos of the militarized police force and pacifications' softer community policing–dispute resolution rhetoric represents a central, though unresolved, challenge to pacification. UPP officers even complained about their uniforms, which were no longer the combat gear of other branches of the Military Police but instead shirt and slacks.

8. See Cavalcanti 2014: 209–11 for a description of the treatment of trafficker houses in the media post-pacification.

9. Institute of Public Safety data showed that in the first year of police occupation there was a 50 percent increase in violent deaths in Rocinha and a 74 percent increase in rape (Rousso 2012).

10. This kind of profiling has long been commonplace in various favelas across the city (Machado da Silva and Leite 2008). The practice, however, has been heightened in the pacified favelas as residents have more daily contact with police.

11. The mere fact that a former BOPE officer was acting as a UPP commander is problematic in that it undermines discourse about the UPP as a different kind of police with a different mission. Edilson himself reportedly self-identified as BOPE and in many of his official press photos appears seated at his desk, with a mug and pin prominently displaying the Elite Squad emblem. After the incident with Amarildo, a new commander was appointed, Major Priscilla Azevedo, who had been the commander of the first UPP installed in Rio, in Dona Marta, where she was supposedly liked and respected by residents. As Rocinha and other favelas continued to be hot spots for violence and traffickers openly attacked UPP units, leadership of the citywide UPP project was given to a BOPE commander, Luís Cláudio Laviano, in late 2014. The use of BOPE officers in UPP leadership roles suggests a move away from "proximity" and "peace" toward more hard-line tactics.

12. Beltrame, lecture at Oste Rio, October 22, 2013. Over one hundred of Rocinha's UPP officers requested reassignments in the aftermath of the scandal, citing low morale. The transfer requests coincided with a heating up of the above-mentioned faction war. By November 2013, residents were reporting daily gunfire between traffickers, even in broad daylight, and in some parts of the favela traffickers were successfully enforcing a curfew to keep residents off the streets after 7 p.m.

13. Margaret Day published a series of photographs of unidentified Rocinha residents holding up signs that expressed their feelings about life and security in the community before and after pacification, with almost everyone identifying the "before" as safer. See www.brasil247.com/pt/247/favela247/160507/Fotos-retratam-opiniões-sobre-UPP-na-Rocinha.htm.

14. In fact, in 2012, *Veja* published an investigative report with details on how traffickers were paying UPP officers generous bribes not to interfere with business taking place off the main road.

15. Faction changes in Rocinha have long been interpreted as possible only with police participation. One resident described it as the police taking over and then selling the favela back to the highest bidder among the factions.

16. There have been numerous reports of corruption inside the UPP, including in the favelas of Coroa, Fallet e Fogueteiro, Mangueira, and Santa Marta.

17. Later, PAC became known as PAC 1. An expansion of the program, known as PAC 2, is now under way.

18. This lack of access has considerable drawbacks for residents, especially for the sick, elderly, or disabled.

19. Who had "connections" here was decided by the Resident's Association, which was charged with distributing the new residences. As there are long-standing ties between the traffic and the association, many were reportedly given to traffickers. Because the apartments were also supposed to be given to people with physical handicaps who could not move around the rest of the favela,

there were widespread reports of people "faking" ailments in order to get priority.

20. See http://rioonwatch.org/?p=6690. It is worth noting here that the increase in rents undermines popular, romanticized conceptions of favelas as "communities." Residents raising rents and evicting other residents is a reminder that Rocinha is not composed of a monolithic group of people but rather a place with deep class divisions.

21. Recently, President Dilma Rousseff inaugurated PAC 2, a second set of upgrading projects. The centerpiece of the plan for Rocinha was a *teleférico*, or cable car, connecting the various parts of the community. The cable car was estimated to use almost 75 percent of the total available funds for the favela. In the wake of nationwide protests against government allocation of funds, residents mobilized against the project, asking for the budget to be reallocated to address sanitation issues. They have been partially successful in combating the project, which as of early 2013 was reduced in scale.

22. See Eduardo Paes's interview on this policy: http://globotv.globo.com /rede-globo/rjtv-1a-edicao/v/ eduardo-paes-fala-das-operacoes-choque-de-ordem/996243/.

23. Kelling and Wilson (1982) first wrote about Broken Windows theory: www .theatlantic.com/magazine/archive/1982/03/broken-windows/304465/. Former and current New York City police chief and Broken Windows proponent William Bratton is a frequent consultant in Brazil. See www.americasquarterly.org /node/1500 and www.huffingtonpost.com/christopher-sabatini/the-favelas-in-rio-de-jan_b_580750.html.

24. On the Shock of Order on the beach, see http://veja.abril.com.br/060110 /sol-mar-organizacao-p-078.shtml.

25. Some Brazil-based franchises predated the UPP. Bob's Burgers, for example, has been in the favela for more than a decade. High priced compared to other favela-based burger joints, Bob's was the restaurant of choice for the top brass of the traffic during my residence in Rocinha. Every time I ate there, I sat between groups of traffickers who were chowing down on burgers and fries with their huge piles of guns and knives on the table next to them.

On the opening of Casa Bahia's Rocinha store, see http://g1.globo.com /economia/negocios/noticia/2012/11/casas-bahia-inaugura-primeira-unidade-na-rocinha.html.

As pacification has opened the favela to big business in unprecedented fashion, corporate enterprise has also experienced its security woes. After one electronics chain store in Rocinha was held up at gunpoint during broad daylight, management brought in their own off-duty police and security guards, adding to the already complex constellation of armed muscle in the favela. This illustrates how the overlap between security and economic "progress" helps shape the security future of the pacified favela. Where residents' demands for safety can be more or less ignored given their still-marginal social position, the big businesses that want to operate in the favela are able to pay for security. The question that remains is whether the state itself will provide this service or whether it will be outsourced to the remaining traffickers, to parts of the pacification police, or to a militia.

26. This particular characterization comes from interviews conducted in 2009 with Beto, my chief trafficking informant and head of Rocinha security at the time. His justification of *gatos,* summarized above, is similar to what Dent describes as a discourse of "piracy as a critique of the injustice of the international market, thought to be ruled by large corporations at the expense of an Everyman" (2012: 32).

27. http://oglobo.globo.com/rio/rocinha-descobre-preco-da-regularizacao-3331304.

28. See also Leite, http://oglobo.globo.com/rio/rocinha-descobre-preco-da-regularizacao-3331304.

29. Similar to a U.S. Social Security card.

30. This shift from state dependence and welfare ideologies to self-reliance and individual responsibility ideologies is part of changing neoliberal regimes worldwide. See Dent 2012; Peck 2010. On the expansion of favela-based microfinance, see http://rioonwatch.org/?p=7542.

31. This figure is based on an estimate made by the U.S. Consulate that was released by Wikileaks. It is unclear if the author means that if *all* favelas in Rio were incorporated into the formal economy it would grow the economy by US$21 billion or whether this figure is for those that are part of the government's announced plan to pacify between 35 and 45 favelas across the city.

32. http://riotimesonline.com/brazil-news/rio-real-estate/sao-conrado-new-heights-in-rio/.

33. See Cavalcanti 2014 on what she calls the threshold effect, or the way in which real estate values in the favela and its surroundings operate.

EPILOGUE

1. The dump would be made famous internationally by the 2010 film *Wasteland* and closed by municipal authorities in June 2012.

2. I was talking about João, from the Rocinha NGO, who needed his foot amputated from advanced diabetes and would have to wait three months for a spot in the public hospital unless we could find enough money to pay for the procedure in a private facility. His leg was black from the knee down, covered in gangrene, and he could no longer get out of bed to open the doors of the NGO.

3. After all, favelas are among the most studied places in the world (McCann 2006; Valladares 2008). As McCann notes, "You've probably heard the one about

Eskimo demography: how many Eskimos in the typical igloo? Five—a mother, father, two kids, and an anthropologist. The same joke might be made about Rio's favelas, but it would vastly undercount the anthropologists, to say nothing of the sociologists, political scientists, and assorted external agents of nongovernmental organizations" (2006: 19).

4. Extreme is not synonymous with helpless. The dump is not a last stop, as Kathleen Millar's (2014) work on the agency of Gramacho's garbage pickers shows.

5. See, for example, Whitehead's (2009) comparison of Malinowskian models of ethnographic fieldwork with present-day Human Terrain Systems counterinsurgency methods.

6. Ethnography in the favela, as I learned, is ultimately an exchange. Though this reality was below the surface of our friendships and collaborations, people exchanged information for what they thought I had to offer—stories of the United States, English lessons, occasional monetary loans.

7. By that point I had a family and could not justify making choices that might endanger my children. Everyone I knew in the favela agreed with me, especially as violence escalated in late 2013 and my pregnant belly grew. As an old friend in Rocinha said, "Listen, you can't run anymore."

8. Other "modernity projects" include groundbreaking energy initiatives like the Belo Monte Hydroelectric Complex (however problematic from a human rights standpoint), Brazil's increased foreign investment in Cuba, and Dilma's hard-line stance against U.S. spying programs. See also Mitchell 2013 on modernity and Brazil's space program.

9. Estimates from August 2013 put the increase at 56 percent in pacified favelas (Andrade 2013).

10. See www.jb.com.br/rio/noticias/2014/01/28/mp-vai-investigar-se-cabral-negociou-upp-e-financiamento-da-odebrecht/. The accusation, which is currently being investigated by the police, is that the outgoing governor Sergio Cabral used the expansion of the UPPs to secure support for his chosen candidate, now governor-elect Luiz Fernando Pezão.

11. Since the beginning of 2014, Brazil's prisons have also been in a state of emergency from riots and gang-on-gang murder. The penal system has been criticized by almost every major human rights organization and the United Nations for the appalling conditions.

Bibliography

Abufarha, Nasser. 2009. *The Making of a Human Bomb: An Ethnography of Palestinian Resistance.* Durham, NC: Duke University Press.

Agamben, Giorgio. 1998. *Homo Sacer: Sovereign Power and Bare Life.* Translated by Daniel Heller-Roazen. Stanford: Stanford University Press.

———. 2002. "The State of Emergency." Lecture, Centre Roland-Barthes, Universite Paris VII, Denis-Diderot. Accessed May 10, 2011. www .generation-online.org/p/fpagambenschmitt.htm.

———. 2005. *State of Exception.* Translated by Kevin Attell. Chicago: University of Chicago Press.

Allen, Robertson. 2013. "Virtual Soldiers, Cognitive Laborers." In *Virtual War and Magical Death,* edited by Neil Whitehead and Sverker Finnstrom, 152–70. Durham, NC: Duke University Press.

Allison, Anne. 2009. "The Cool Brand, Affective Activism and Japanese Youth." *Theory, Culture & Society* 26 (2–3): 89–111.

Alves, Jaime Amparo. 2014. "On Mules and Bodies: Black Captivities in the Brazilian Racial Democracy." *Critical Sociology* (Online First): 1–20.

Alves, Maria Helena Moreira, and Philip Evanson. 2011. *Living in the Crossfire: Favela Residents, Drug Dealers, and Police Violence in Rio de Janeiro.* Philadelphia: Temple University Press.

Alvito, Marcos. 2001. *As cores de Acari: uma favela carioca.* Rio de Janeiro: Fundação Getúlio Vargas.

Andrade, Hanrrikson de. 2013."Desaparecimentos em favelas do Rio aumentam após início das UPPs." *UOL*, August 3. Accessed February 18, 2015. http://noticias.uol.com.br/cotidiano/ultimas-noticias/2013/08/03/desaparecimentos-aumentaram-em-favelas-do-rio-apos-inicio-das-upps.htm.

Angelini, Alessandro. 2013. "Model Favela: You and Second Nature in Rio de Janeiro." PhD diss., City University of New York.

Appadurai, Arjun. 1990. "Disjuncture and Difference in the Global Cultural Economy." *Theory, Culture & Society* 7 (2): 295–310.

Arendt, Hannah. 1970. *On Violence*. New York: Harcourt Brace Jovanovich.

Arias, Enrique Desmond. 2006. *Drugs and Democracy in Rio de Janeiro: Trafficking, Social Networks, and Public Security*. Chapel Hill: University of North Carolina Press.

Arias, Enrique Desmond, and Corinne Davis Rodrigues. 2006. "The Myth of Personal Security: Criminal Gangs, Dispute Resolution, and Identity in Rio de Janeiro's Favelas." *Latin American Politics and Society* 48 (4): 5–81.

Arias, Enrique Desmond, and Daniel Goldstein, eds. 2010. *Violent Democracies in Latin America*. Durham, NC: Duke University Press.

Asad, Talal. 2007. *On Suicide Bombing*. New York: Columbia University Press.

Athayde, Celso, and M. V. Bill. 2007. *Falcão, mulheres e o tráfico*. Rio de Janeiro: Objetiva.

Azevedo, Aluísio, and David Rosenthal. 2000. *The Slum: A Novel*. Oxford: Oxford University Press.

Bakhtin, M. M. 1968. *Rabelais and His World*. Cambridge, MA: MIT Press.

Barcellos, Caco. 1992. *Rota 66*. São Paulo: Globo.

———. 2003. *Abusado: o dono do morro Dona Marta*. Rio de Janeiro: Record.

Barnes, Nicholas. 2014. "Rio de Janeiro's BOPE and Police Pacification: Fear and Intimidation in Complexo da Maré." June 6, *Anthropoliteia*. http://anthropoliteia.net/2014/06/06/rio-de-janeiros-bope-and-police-pacification-fear-and-intimidation-in-complexo-da-mare/#comments.

Baudrillard, Jean. [1981] 1994. *Simulacra and Simulation*. Ann Arbor: University of Michigan Press.

Bava, Silvio Caccia. 2013. "Violência e controle social." *Le Monde diplomatique Brasil*, June 4. www.diplomatique.org.br/editorial.php?edicao=71.

Beith, Malcolm. 2010. "Forbes Ranking." Malcolm Beith's personal blog, March 10. http://malcolmbeith.blogspot.com.br/2010/03/forbes-ranking.html.

Benjamin, Walter. 1968. *Illuminations*. New York: Harcourt, Brace & World.

———. 1999. *The Arcades Project*. Cambridge, MA: Belknap Press.

Bentes, Ivana. 2002. "'Cidade de Deus' promove turismo no Inferno." *Estado de S. Paulo*, August 31. www.consciencia.net/2003/08/09/ivana.html.

———. 2003. "The Sertão and the Favela in Contemporary Brazilian Film." In *The New Brazilian Cinema*, edited by Lúcia Nagib, 121–37. London: I. B. Tauris.

Biehl, João. 2005. *Vita: Life in a Zone of Social Abandonment.* Berkeley: University of California Press.

Biondi, Karina. 2010. *Junto e misturado: uma etnografía do PCC.* São Paulo: Editora Terceiro Nome.

Boltanski, Luc. *Distant Suffering: Morality, Media, and Politics.* Cambridge: Cambridge University Press, 1999.

Boorstin, D. 1961. *The Image: A Guide to Pseudo-Events in America.* New York: Harper & Row.

Booyens, Irma. 2010. "Rethinking Township Tourism: Towards Responsible Tourism Development in South African Townships." *Development Southern Africa* 27 (2): 273–87.

Bourdieu, Pierre. 1984. *Distinction: A Social Critique of the Judgment of Taste.* Cambridge, MA: Harvard University Press.

Bourgois, Philippe I. 1995. *In Search of Respect: Selling Crack in El Barrio.* Cambridge: Cambridge University Press.

Bratton, William, and William Andrews. "Eight Steps to Reduce Crime." *America's Quarterly* (Spring 2010). www.americasquarterly.org/node /1500.

Brazilian Public Security Forum (BPSF). 2013. "Annual Report." www .forumseguranca.org.br.

Brito, Daniel Chaves de, Jaime Luiz Cunha de Souza, and Roseane Magalhães Lima. 2011. "Policiais e o 'bico': a formação de redes de trabalho paralelo de segurança." *Revista Brasileira de Segurança Pública* 5 (8): 156–71.

Brito, Guilherme. 2013. "PM substitui 4 oficiais após morte de recruta em treinamento no Rio." *G1*, November 19. Accessed February 10, 2014. http:// g1.globo.com/rio-de-janeiro/noticia/2013/11/pm-substitui-4-oficiais-apos-morte-de-recruta-em-treinamento-no-rio.html.

Bróder. 2010. Directed by Jeferson De. Rio de Janeiro: Globo Films.

Broudehoux, Annie. 2007. "Spectacular Beijing: The Conspicuous Construction of an Olympic Metropolis." *Journal of Urban Affairs* 29 (4): 383–99.

———. 2010. "Images of Power: Architectures of the Integrated Spectacle at the Beijing Olympics." *Journal of Architectural Education* 63 (2): 52–62.

Bruner, E. M. 1987. "Of Cannibals, Tourists, and Ethnographers." *Cultural Anthropology* 4 (4): 438–44.

Burgos, Marcelo Baumann. 1998. "Dos parques proletários ao favela-bairro: as políticas públicas nas favelas do Rio de Janeiro." In *Um século de favela,* edited by Alba Zaluar and Marcos Alvito, 25–60. Rio de Janeiro: Fundação Getúlio Vargas.

———. 2002. *A utopia da comunidade: Rio das Pedras, uma favela carioca.* Rio de Janeiro: PUC-Rio.

Bus 174/Ônibus 174. 2002. Directed by José Padilha and Felipe Lacerda. New York: Hart Sharp. DVD.

Butler, S. R. 2010. "Should I Stay or Should I Go? Negotiating Township Tours in Post-Apartheid South Africa." *Journal of Tourism and Cultural Change* 8 (1–2): 15–29.

Caldeira, Teresa Pires do Rio. 2001. *City of Walls: Crime, Segregation, and Citizenship in São Paulo.* Berkeley: University of California Press.

———. 2002. "The Paradox of Police Violence in Democratic Brazil." *Ethnography* 3 (3): 235–63.

———. 2006. "'I Came to Sabotage Your Reasoning!': Violence and Resignifications of Justice in Brazil." In *Law and Disorder in the Postcolony,* edited by Jean Comaroff and John L. Comaroff, 102–49. Chicago: University of Chicago Press.

Caldeira, Teresa Pires do Rio, and James Holston. 1999. "Democracy and Violence in Brazil." *Comparative Studies in Society & History* 41 (4): 691–730.

Campbell, Howard. 2009. *Drug War Zone: Frontline Dispatches from the Streets of El Paso and Juárez.* Austin: University of Texas Press.

Campbell, Mary B. 1988. *The Witness and the Other World: Exotic European Travel Writing, 400–1600.* Ithaca, NY: Cornell University Press.

Cândida, Simone. 2010. "Eike, Bradesco e Coca-Cola financiam UPPs no Rio." Conversaafiada.com.br, August 24. www.conversaafiada.com.br /brasil/2010/08/24/eike-bradesco-e-coca-cola-financiam-upps-no-rio/.

Cannibal Tours. 1987. Directed by Dennis O'Rourke. Australia: O'Rourke & Associates. Film.

Cano, Ignacio, and Thais Duarte. 2012. *No Sapatinho: a evolução das milícias no Rio de Janeiro (2008–2011).* Rio de Janeiro: Fundação Heinrich Böll.

Cano, Ignacio, and Carolina Loot. 2008. "Seis por meia dúzia? Um estudo exploratório do fenômeno das chamadas 'milícias' no Rio de Janeiro." In *Segurança, tráfico e milícias no Rio de Janeiro,* compiled by Justiça Global Brasil, 48–103. Rio de Janeiro: Fundação Heinrich Böll.

Cardoso, Fernando Henrique. 1998. "Notas sobre a Reforma do Estado." *Novos Estudos do CEBRAP* 50: 1–12.

———. 2005. *A arte da política: a história que vivi.* Rio de Janeiro: Record.

Carneiro, Luciane. 2012. "Nas favelas, das TVs ao cartão de crédito." *O Globo,* October 10. Accessed January 25, 2014. http://oglobo.globo.com/economia /nas-favelas-das-tvs-ao-cartao-de-credito-6694173#ixzz2b7qWL7tN.

Carvalho, José Murilo de. 1982. "Political Elites and State Building: The Case of Nineteenth-Century Brazil." *Comparative Studies in Society and History* 24 (3): 378–99.

Carvalho, Mônica Batista. 2013. "A política de pacificação de favelas e as contradições para produção de uma cidade segura." *O Social em Questão* 16 (1): 285–308.

"Casas Bahia inaugura primeira unidade na Rocinha." 2012. *G1*, November 6. Accessed January 25, 2014. http://g1.globo.com/economia/negocios /noticia/2012/11/casas-bahia-inaugura-primeira-unidade-na-rocinha.html.

Castells, Manuel. 2000. *The Information Age: Economy, Society and Culture.* Vol. 1 of *The Rise of the Network Society.* Cambridge, MA: Blackwell Press.

Cavalcanti Rocha dos Santos, Mariana. 2007. "Of Shacks, Houses, and Fortresses: An Ethnography of Favela Consolidation in Rio de Janeiro." PhD diss., University of Chicago.

———. 2013. "Á espera, em ruínas: urbanismo, estética e política no Rio de Janeiro da PACificação." *DILEMAS: Revista de Estudos de Conflito e Controle Social* 6: 191–228.

———. 2014. "Threshold Markets: The Production of Real Estate Value between the 'Favela' and the 'Pavement.'" In *Cities from Scratch: Poverty and Informality in Urban Latin America,* edited by Brodwyn Fischer, Bryan McCann, and Javier Auyero, 208–37. Durham, NC: Duke University Press.

Chambers Erve, ed. 1997. *Tourism and Culture: An Applied Perspective.* New York: State University of New York Press.

———. 1999. *Native Tours: The Anthropology of Travel and Tourism.* Prospect Heights, IL: Waveland.

Christino, Márcio. 2003. *Por dentro do crime: corrupção, tráfico, PCC.* São Paulo: Escrituras.

Cidade de Deus/City of God. 2003. Directed by Walter Salles, Kátia Lund, Fernando Meirelles, et al. São Paulo: O2 Filmes. DVD.

Cidade dos homens/City of Men. 2002–5. Directed by Fernando Meirelles and Kátia Lund, adapted by Bráulio Mantovani. Rede Globo.

Cidade dos homens/City of Men. 2007. Directed by Paulo Morelli. New York: Miramax Films. DVD.

Cinco vezes favela. 1962. Directed by Marcos Farias, Miguel Borges, Cacá Diegues, Joaquim Pedro de Andrade, and Leon Hirszman. Rio de Janeiro: Centro Popular de Cultura da UNE. Film.

5× favela—agora por nós mesmos. 2010. Directed by Manaíra Carneiro, Wagner Novais, Rodrigo Felha, Cacau Amaral, Luciano Vidigal, and Cadu Barcellos. Rio de Janeiro: Globo Films.

Civico, Aldo. 2012. "'We Are Illegal, but Not Illegitimate'": Modes of Policing in Medellin, Colombia." *PoLAR: Political and Legal Anthropology Review* 35 (1): 77–93.

Clark, Laurie B. 2006. "Placed and Displaced: Trauma Memorials." In *Performance and Place,* edited by Leslie Hill and Helen Paris, 129–38. New York: Palgrave Macmillan.

Cobb, Amanda. 1998. "This Is What It Means to Say Smoke Signals: Native American Cultural Sovereignty." In *Hollywood's Indian: The Portrayal of the*

Native American in Film, edited by Peter C. Rollins and John E. O'Connor, 206–28. Lexington, KY: University of Kentucky Press.

Coimbra, Cecília Maria Bouças. 2001. *Operação Rio: o mito das classes perigosas: um estudo sobre a violência urbana, a mídia impressa e os discursos de segurança pública*. Rio de Janeiro: Oficina do Autor.

Comaroff, Jean, and John L. Comaroff, eds. 2006. *Law and Disorder in the Postcolony*. Chicago: University of Chicago Press.

Comaroff, John L., and Jean Comaroff. 2009. *Ethnicity, Inc*. Chicago: University of Chicago Press.

Conklin, Beth A. 2001. *Consuming Grief: Compassionate Cannibalism in an Amazonian Society*. Austin: University of Texas Press.

Coronil, Fernando. 1997. *The Magical State: Nature, Money, and Modernity in Venezuela*. Chicago: University of Chicago Press.

Crank, John. 2004. *Understanding Police Culture*. Cincinnati: Anderson Publishing.

Cuiabá, Rodrigo Vargas de. 2011. "Promotoria denuncia 29 policiais por tortura em treinamento." *Folha de São Paulo*, March 1. Accessed February 10. www1 .folha.uol.com.br/cotidiano/2011/03/882713-promotoria-denuncia-29-policiais-por-tortura-em-treinamento.shtml.

Cunha, Euclides da. 2002 [1902]. *Os sertões: Campanha de Canudos*. São Paulo: Atelie Editorial.

Curta Saraus. 2010. Directed by David Alves da Silva. São Paulo: Arte na Periferia.

DaMatta, Roberto. 1991. *Carnivals, Rogues, and Heroes: An Interpretation of the Brazilian Dilemma*. Notre Dame, IN: University of Notre Dame Press.

Das, Veena, and Deborah Poole. 2004. *Anthropology in the Margins of the State*. Santa Fe, NM: School of American Research Press.

Davis, Mike. 1990. *City of Quartz: Excavating the Future in Los Angeles*. London: Verso.

———. 2002. *Dead Cities: And Other Tales*. New York: New Press.

———. 2006. *Planet of Slums*. London: Verso.

———. 2008. Foreword to *A World of Gangs: Armed Young Men and Gangsta Culture*, by John Hagedorn, xi–xvii. Minneapolis: University of Minnesota Press.

Debord, Guy. 1993. *The Society of the Spectacle*. New York: Zone Books.

Deleuze, Gilles, and Félix Guattari. 1986. *Nomadology: The War Machine*. New York: Semiotext(e).

Dent, Alexander. 2012. "Piracy, Circulatory Legitimacy, and Neoliberal Subjectivity in Brazil." *Cultural Anthropology* 27 (1): 28–49.

Denyer Willis, Graham. 2009. "Deadly Symbiosis? The PCC, the State and the Institutionalization of Violence in São Paulo." In *Youth Violence in Latin*

America, edited by Dennis Rodgers and Gareth A. Jones, 167–82. New York: Palgrave.

———. 2014a. "Antagonistic Authorities and the Civil Police in São Paulo, Brazil." *Latin American Research Review* 49 (1): 3–22.

———. 2014b. "The Gun Library." *Boston Review,* April 8. www.bostonreview.net/world/graham-denyer-willis-pcc-gun-library-sao-paulo-prisons-crime.

Diuana, Vilma, et al. 2008. "Saúde em prisões: representações e práticas dos agentes de segurança penitenciária no Rio de Janeiro, Brasil." *Caderno Saúde Pública* 24 (8): 1887–96.

Doherty, Gareth, and Moises Lino e Silva. 2011. "Formally Informal: Daily Life and the Shock of Order in a Brazilian Favela." *Built Environment* 37 (1): 30–41.

Dowdney, Luke. 2003. *Crianças do tráfico: um estudo de caso de crianças em violência armada organizada no Rio de Janeiro.* Rio de Janeiro: 7 Letras.

Drybread, Kristen. 2014a. "Preserving the Integrity of Brazilian Prisons through 'Intimate' Searches." Paper presented to American Anthropological Association, December 6.

———. 2014b. "Murder and the Making of Man-Subjects in a Brazilian Juvenile Prison." *American Anthropologist* 116 (4): 752–64.

Eco, Umberto. 1986. *Travels in Hyper Reality: Essays.* San Diego: Harcourt Brace Jovanovich.

Elite Squad. 2007. Directed by José Padilha, Luiz Eduardo Soares, André Batista, and Rodrigo Pimentel. London: Optimum. DVD.

Elite Squad 2—The Enemy Within. 2010. Directed by José Padilha, Braulio Mantovani, and Rodrigo Pimentel. Rio de Janeiro: Globo Films. DVD.

"Empresa de Eike interrompe injeção de R$20 milhões em UPPs no Rio." 2013. *G1,* August 10. Accessed November 15, 2013. http://g1.globo.com/rio-de-janeiro/noticia/2013/08/empresa-de-eike-interrompe-injecao-de-r-20-milhoes-em-upps-no-rio.html.

Evangelista, Helio de Araujo. 2003. *Rio de Janeiro: violência, jogo do bicho e narcotráfico segundo uma interpretação.* Rio de Janeiro: Revan.

Evans, Peter. 1995. *Embedded Autonomy: States and Industrial Transformation.* Princeton: Princeton University Press.

Farias, Juliana. 2009. "De asfixia: reflexões sobre a atuação do tráfico de drogas nas favelas cariocas." In *Vida sob cerco: violência e rotina nas favelas do Rio de Janeiro,* edited by Luiz Antonio Machado da Silva, 173–90. Rio de Janeiro: Nova Fronteira.

Farmer, Paul. 2004. "An Anthropology of Structural Violence." *Current Anthropology* 45 (3): 305–25.

Favela Rising. 2010. Directed by Jeff Zimbalist and Matt Mochary. Brazil: All Rise Films. DVD.

Feghali, Jandhira, and Julita Lemgruber. 2006. *Reflexões sobre a violência urbana: (in)segurança e (des)esperanças.* Rio de Janeiro: Mauad X.

Feltran, Gabriel de Santis. 2012. "Governo que produz crime, crime que produz governo: o dispositivo de gestão do homicídio em São Paulo (1992—2011)." *Revista Brasileira de Segurança Pública* 6 (2): 232–55.

Ferguson, R. Brian, and Neil L. Whitehead. 1992. *War in the Tribal Zone: Expanding States and Indigenous Warfare.* Sante Fe, NM: School of American Research Press.

Filho, Alfredo Saad. 2010. "Neoliberalism, Democracy, and Development Policy in Brazil." *Development and Society* 39 (1): 1–28.

"Filho de Amarildo e o futuro nas Passarelas." 2013. *O Dia*, September 17. http://odia.ig.com.br/noticia/rio-de-janeiro/2013-09-17/filho-de-amarildo-e-o-futuro-nas-passarelas.html.

Fischer, Brodwyn. 2008. *A Poverty of Rights: Citizenship and Inequality in Twentieth-Century Rio de Janeiro.* Stanford: Stanford University Press.

———. 2014. "A Century in the Present Tense: Crisis, Politics, and the Intellectual History of Brazil's Informal Cities." In *Cities from Scratch: Poverty and Informality in Urban Latin America*, edited by Brodwyn Fischer, Bryan McCann, and Javier Auyero, 9–67. Durham, NC: Duke University Press.

Flor, Katarine, and Gláucia Marinho. 2013. "A favela agora virou a alma do negócio." *Brasil de Fato*, January 8. www.brasildefato.com.br/node/11477#.UPKmc9ghu1Q.facebook.

Flying Down to Rio. 1993. Directed by Thornton Freeland. New York: RKO Radio Pictures. Film.

Fraga, Paulo Cesar Pontes. 2006. "Tortura contra pessoas acusadas de crimes no Rio de Janeiro: a funcionalidade da violência contra os illegalismos." *Teoria e Cultura* 1 (2): 61–82.

Freire, Aluizio. 2007. "Cabral defende aborto contra violência no Rio de Janeiro." *G1*, October 24. Accessed January 25, 2014. http://g1.globo.com/Noticias/Politica/0,,MUL155710–5601,00-CABRAL+DEFENDE+ABORTO+CONTRA+VIOLENCIA+NO+RIO+DE+JANEIRO.html.

Freire-Medeiros, Bianca. 2007a. "A favela e seus trânsitos turísticos." *Revista do Observatório de Inovação do Turismo* 2 (2): 1–13.

———. 2007b. "A favela que se vê e que se vende: reflexões polêmicas em torno de um destino turístico." *Revista Brasileira de Ciências Sociais* 22 (65): 61–72.

———. 2009. *Gringo na laje: produção, circulação e consumo da favela turística.* Rio de Janeiro: Fundação Getúlio Vargas.

———. 2010. "Turistas no Brasil: muitas polêmicas e algumas conclusões sobre duas narrativas audiovisuais recentes." *Arquitextos* 122.

———. 2013. *Touring Poverty.* New York: Routledge.

Freire-Medeiros, Bianca, and Palloma Menezes. 2009. "Fotografando e pobreza turística." *Revista Antropológicas* 20 (1–2): 173–98.

French, Jan Hoffman. 2013. "Rethinking Police Violence in Brazil: Unmasking the Public Secret of Race." *Latin American Politics and Society* 4 (55): 161–81.

Frenzel, Fabian, Ko Koens, and Malte Steinbrink, eds. 2012. *Slum Tourism: Poverty, Power and Ethics.* New York: Routledge.

Frischtak, Claudio, and Benjamin R. Mandel. 2012. "Crime, House Prices, and Inequality: The Effect of UPPs in Rio." *Federal Reserve Bank of New York Staff Reports,* no. 542. www.newyorkfed.org/research/staff_reports/sr542.pdf.

Freyre, Gilberto. [1933] 1964. *The Masters and the Slaves: A Study in the Development of Brazilian Civilization.* New York: Alfred Knopf.

Fry, Peter. 2000. "Politics, Nationality, and the Meanings of 'Race' in Brazil." *Daedalus* 129 (2): 83–118.

——. 2005–6. "Ciência social e poliítica 'racial' no Brasil." *Revista USP* 68 (December–February): 180–87.

Galeotti, Mark. 2002. *Russian and Post-Soviet Organized Crime.* Aldershot: Ashgate.

Gambetta, Diego. 1993. *The Sicilian Mafia: The Business of Private Protection.* Cambridge, MA: Harvard University Press.

Gay, Robert. 2005. *Lucia: Testimonies of a Brazilian Drug Dealer's Woman.* Philadelphia: Temple University Press.

——. 2009. "From Popular Movements to Drug Gangs to Militias: An Anatomy of Violence in Rio de Janeiro." In *Megacities: The Politics of Urban Exclusion and Violence in the Global South,* edited by Kees Koonings and Dirk Kruijt, 29–52. London: Zed Books.

Geertz, Clifford. 1980. *Negara: The Theatre State in Nineteenth-Century Bali.* Princeton: Princeton University Press.

Girard, René. 1996. "Mimesis and Violence." In *The Girard Reader,* edited by James G. Williams, 9–19. New York: Crossroads.

Goffman, Erving. 1959. *The Presentation of Self in Everyday Life.* Garden City, NY: Doubleday.

Goldstein, Daniel M. 2004. *The Spectacular City: Violence and Performance in Urban Bolivia.* Durham, NC: Duke University Press.

——. 2012. *Outlawed: Between Security and Rights in a Bolivian City.* Durham, NC: Duke University Press.

Goldstein, Donna M. 2003. *Laughter Out of Place: Race, Class, Violence, and Sexuality in a Rio Shantytown.* Berkeley: University of California Press.

Gootenberg, Paul. 2008. *Andean Cocaine: The Making of a Global Drug.* Chapel Hill: University of North Carolina Press.

Graham, Sandra Lauderdale. 1992. *House and Street: The Domestic World of Servants and Masters in Nineteenth-Century Rio de Janeiro.* Austin: University of Texas Press.

Graham, Stephen. 2010. *Cities under Siege: The New Military Urbanism.* London: Verso.

Green, James N. 2003. "Clerics, Exiles, and Academics: Opposition to the Brazilian Military Dictatorship in the United States, 1969–1974." *Latin American Politics and Society* 45 (1): 87–117.

Grillo, Carolina. 2008. "O 'morro' e a 'pista': um estudo comparado de dinâmicas do comércio ilegal de drogas." *DILEMAS: Revista de Estudos de Conflito e Controle Social* 1 (1): 127–48.

Grossman, Dave. 1995. *On Killing: The Psychological Cost of Learning to Kill in War and Society.* Boston: Little, Brown.

Guenther, Katja M. 2009. "The Politics of Names: Rethinking the Methodological and Ethical Significance of Naming People, Organizations, and Places." *Qualitative Research* 9 (4): 411–21.

Hagedorn, John. 1998. "Gang Violence in the Postindustrial Era." In *Youth Violence,* edited by Michael Tonry and Mark H. Moore, 364–420. Chicago: University of Chicago Press.

———. 2008. *A World of Gangs: Armed Young Men and Gangsta Culture.* Minneapolis: University of Minnesota Press.

Haggard, Stephan. 1990. *Pathways from the Periphery.* Ithaca, NY: Cornell University Press.

Halnon, Karen Bettez. 2002. "Poor Chic: The Rational Consumption of Poverty." *Current Sociology* 50 (4): 501–16.

Hamburger, E. I. 2008. "A desigualdade social brasileira no cinema recente: *Cidade de Deus.*" *Revista de Antropologia* 52: 70–88.

Hardt, Michael, and Antonio Negri. 2004. *Empire.* Cambridge, MA: Harvard University Press.

Harvey, David. 1987. "Flexible Accumulation through Urbanization: Reflections on 'Post-Modernism' in the American City." *Antipode* 19 (3): 260–86.

———. 2003. "The City as a Body Politic." In *Wounded Cities: Destruction and Reconstruction in a Globalized World,* edited by Jane Schneider and Ida Susser, 25–46. London: Berg.

———. 2009. *Social Justice and the City.* Athens: University of Georgia Press.

Hautzinger, Sarah. 2007. *Violence in the City of Women: Police and Batterers in Bahia, Brazil.* Berkeley: University of California Press.

Hearne, Dennis W. 2009. "Counter-Insurgency Doctrine Comes to Rio's Favelas." *Wikileaks,* September 30. http://wikileaks.org/cable/2009/09/09RIODEJANEIRO329.html.

Hecht, Tobias. 1998. *At Home in the Street: Street Children of Northeast Brazil.* Cambridge: Cambridge University Press.

Henriques, Ricardo, and Silvia Ramos. 2011 "UPPs social: ações sociais para a consolidação da pacificação." www.ie.ufrj.br/datacenterie/pdfs/seminarios/pesquisa/texto3008.pdf.

Herbert, Steven Kelly. 1997. *Policing Space: Territoriality and the Los Angeles Police Department.* Minneapolis: University of Minnesota Press.

Herschmann, M., and João Freire Filho. 2003. "Debatable Tastes! Rethinking Hierarchical Distinctions in Brazilian Music." *Journal of Latin American Cultural Studies* 12: 347–58.

Hinton, Alexander Laban, ed. 2002. *Annihilating Difference: The Anthropology of Genocide.* Berkeley: University of California Press.

———. 2006. *Why Did They Kill? Cambodia in the Shadow of Genocide.* Berkeley: University of California Press.

Hinton, Mercedes S. 2006. *The State on the Streets: Police and Politics in Argentina and Brazil.* Boulder, CO: Lynne Rienner.

Hochman, Gilberto. 2009. "Priority, Invisibility and Eradication: The History of Smallpox and the Brazilian Public Health Agenda." *Medical History* 53 (2): 229–52.

Hoffman, Danny. 2011. *The War Machines: Young Men and Violence in Sierra Leone and Liberia.* Durham, NC: Duke University Press.

Holloway, Thomas H. 1993. *Policing Rio de Janeiro: Repression and Resistance in a Nineteenth-Century City.* Stanford: Stanford University Press.

Holston, James. 1989. *The Modernist City: An Anthropological Critique of Brasília.* Chicago: University of Chicago Press.

———. 2008. *Insurgent Citizenship: Disjunctions of Democracy and Modernity in Brazil.* Princeton: Princeton University Press.

Huggins, Martha Knisely. 1991. *Vigilantism and the State in Modern Latin America: Essays on Extralegal Violence.* New York: Praeger.

Huggins, Martha Knisely, Mika Haritos-Fatouros, and Philip G. Zimbardo. 2002. *Violence Workers: Police Torturers and Murderers Reconstruct Brazilian Atrocities.* Berkeley: University of California Press.

The Hulk. 2003. Directed by Ang Lee. New York: Universal Pictures. DVD.

Hulme, Peter, and Tim Youngs. 2002. *The Cambridge Companion to Travel Writing.* Cambridge: Cambridge University Press.

Human Rights Watch. 2009. *Lethal Force: Police Violence and Public Security in Rio de Janeiro and São Paulo.* Accessed July 12, 2012. www.hrw.org/sites/default/files/reports/brazil1209webwcover.pdf.

Husain, Saima. 2007. *In War, Those Who Die Are Not Innocent ("Na guerra, quem morre não é innocente"): Human Rights Implementation, Policing, and Public Security Reform in Rio de Janeiro, Brazil.* Amsterdam: Rozenberg.

Hutnyk, John. 1996. *The Rumour of Calcutta: Tourism, Charity and the Poverty of Representation.* London: Zed Books.

Instituto de Segurança Pública (ISP). 2013. "Comparativo das incidências publicadas no diário oficial no Estado." http://arquivos.proderj.rj.gov.br/isp_imagens/Uploads/ResumoOut13.pdf.

International Bar Association Human Rights Institute Report. 2010. "One in Five: The Crisis in Brazil's Prisons and Criminal Justice System." February. www.ibanet.org/Article/Detail. aspx?ArticleUid=a080f05b-71c1-4bb6-a058-46cd1ad7b2ee.

Jaguaribe, Beatriz. 2004. "Favelas and the Aesthetics of Realism: Representations in Film and Literature." *Journal of Latin American Cultural Studies* 13 (3): 327–42.

———. 2005. "The Shock of the Real: Realist Aesthetics in the Media and Urban Experience." *Space and Culture* 8 (1): 66–82.

———. 2007. *O choque do real: estética, mídia e cultura*. Rio de Janeiro: Rocco.

———. 2009. "Hijacked by Realism." *Public Culture* 21 (2): 219–27.

———. 2011. *Rio de Janeiro: Urban Life through the Eyes of the City*. New York: Routledge.

Jaguaribe, Beatriz, and Kevin Hetherington. 2004. "Favela Tours: Indistinct and Mapless Representations of the Real in Rio de Janeiro." In *Tourism Mobilities: Places to Play, Places in Play*, edited by Mimi Sheller and John Urry, 155–66. London: Routledge.

Jauregui, Beatrice. 2013. "Beatings, Beacons, and Big Men: Police Disempowerment and Delegitimation in India." *Law and Social Inquiry* 38 (3): 643–69.

———. 2014. "Provisional Agency in India: *Jugaad* and Legitimation of Corruption." *American Ethnologist* 41 (1): 76–91.

Jensen, Steffen, and Dennis Rodgers. 2009. "Revolutionaries, Barbarians or War Machines? Gangs in Nicaragua and South Africa." *Socialist Register* 45: 220–38.

Johnson, Randal, and Robert Stam. 1995. *Brazilian Cinema*. New York: Columbia University Press.

Kant de Lima, Roberto. 1994. *A polícia da cidade do Rio de Janeiro: seus dilemas e paradoxos*. Rio de Janeiro: Polícia Militar do Estado do Rio de Janeiro.

Kelling, George, and James Wilson. 1982. "Broken Windows: The Police and Neighborhood." *The Atlantic*, March 1. www.theatlantic.com/magazine /archive/1982/03/broken-windows/304465/.

Kirshenblatt-Gimblett, Barbara. 1998. *Destination Culture: Tourism, Museums, and Heritage*. Berkeley: University of California Press.

Kleinman, Arthur, Veena Das, and Margaret M. Lock. 1997. *Social Suffering*. Berkeley: University of California Press.

Kleinman, Arthur, and Joan Kleinman. 1996. "The Appeal of Experience, the Dismay of Images: Cultural Appropriations of Suffering in Our Times." *Daedalus* 125 (1): 1–23.

Koonings, Kees, and Dirk Kruijt. 2002. *Political Armies: The Military and Nation Building in the Age of Democracy*. London: Zed Books.

———. 2004. *Armed Actors: Organized Violence and State Failure in Latin America*. London: Zed Books.

———. 2009. *Megacities: The Politics of Urban Exclusion and Violence in the Global South*. London: Zed Books.

Lago, Luciana Correa do. 2000. *Desigualdades e segregação na metrópole: o Rio de Janeiro em tempo de crise*. Rio de Janeiro: Revan.

Lancaster, John. 2007. "Next Stop, Squalor." *Smithsonian Magazine* 37, no. 12 (March): 96–105. www.smithsonianmag.com/peopleplaces/squalor .html#ixzz1N38gscR5.

Lawrence, Nate. 2013. "Microfinance in Rio: A Brief Overview." *Rio on Watch*, April 11. http://rioonwatch.org/?p=7542.

Leeds, Elizabeth. 1996. "Cocaine and Parallel Polities in the Brazilian Urban Periphery: Constraints on Local-Level Democratization." *Latin American Research Review* 31 (3): 47–83.

Leite, Márcia Pereira. 2000. "Entre o individualismo e a solidariedade: dilemas da política e da cidadania no Rio de Janeiro." *Revista Brasileira de Ciências Sociais* 15 (44): 43–90.

———. 2005. "Violência, insegurança e cidadania: reflexões a partir do Rio de Janeiro." In *Rugidos e sussurros: mais promessas do que ações*, edited by Lopes de Carvalho, 66–70. Rio do Janeiro: IBASE.

———. 2007. *Para além da metafora da guerra: violência, cidadania, religião e ação coletiva no Rio de Janeiro*. São Paulo: Attar.

Leite, Renata. 2011. "Rocinha descobre o preço da regularização." *O Globo*, November 26. Accessed January 25, 2014. http://oglobo.globo.com/rio /rocinha-descobre-preco-da-regularizacao-3331304.

Lemgruber, Julita, Leonarda Musumeci, Ignacio Cano, Ana Paula Miranda, and Sonia Travassos. 2003. *Quem vigia os vigias? Um estudo sobre controle externo da polícia no Brasil*. Rio de Janeiro: Record.

Lemgruber, Julita, Márcia Fernandes, Ignacio Cano, and Leonarda Musumeci. 2013. *Usos e abusos da prisâo provisória no Rio de Janeiro—avaliação do impacto da Lei 12.403/2011*. Rio de Janeiro: Associação pela Reforma Prisional, Centro de Estudos de Segurança e Cidadania, and Universidade Cândido Mendes.

Lennon, J. John, and Malcolm Foley. 2000. *Dark Tourism*. London: Continuum.

Levine, Robert M. 1999. "How Brazil Works." In *The Brazil Reader*, edited by Robert Levine and John Crocitti, 402–7. Durham, NC: Duke University Press.

Lima, William da Silva. 1991. *Quatrocentos contra um: uma história do Comando Vermelho*. Petrópolis, Brazil: Vozes.

Linger, Daniel. 2003. "Wild Power in Post-Military Brazil." In *Crime's Power: Anthropologists and the Ethnography of Crime*, edited by Philip C. Parnell and Stephanie C. Kane, 99–124. New York: Palgrave Macmillan.

Lins, Paulo. 1997. *Cidade de Deus*. London: Bloomsbury Publishing.

Lins, Paulo, and Alison Entrekin. 2006. *City of God*. Translated by Alison Entrekin. New York: Black Cat.

Livingstone, Grace. 2004. *Inside Colombia: Drugs, Democracy, and War*. New Brunswick, NJ: Rutgers University Press.

Lo-Bianco, Alessandro. 2013. "Rent Doubles in Alemão—417 Families Have 15 Days to Move Out." Translated by Rachel Fox. *Rio on Watch*, January 30. http://rioonwatch.org/?p=6690.

Logan, John R., and Harvey Luskin Molotch. 1987. *Urban Fortunes: The Political Economy of Place*. Berkeley: University of California Press.

Lorenz, Aaron. 2007. "The Pleasures of Violence: Irony and Post-Testimonial Discourse in *Cidade de Deus* by Paulo Lins." *Penn Working Papers* 2 (1).

Low, Setha M. 2003. *Behind the Gates: Life, Security, and the Pursuit of Happiness in Fortress America*. New York: Routledge.

Lubkemann, Stephen. 2008. *Culture in Chaos: An Anthropology of the Social Condition in War*. Chicago: University of Chicago Press.

Ludemir, Julio. 2004. *Sorria, você está na Rocinha*. Rio de Janeiro: Record.

MacAloon, John. 2006. "The Theory of Spectacle: Reviewing Olympic Ethnography." In *National Identity and Global Sporting Events: Culture, Politics, and Spectacle in the Olympics and the Football World Cup*, edited by Alan Tomlinson and Christopher Young, 15–40. New York: State University of New York Press.

MacCannell, Dean. 1976. *The Tourist*. New York: Schocken Books.

———. 1984. "Reconstructed Ethnicity Tourism and Cultural Identity in Third World Communities." *Annals of Tourism Research* 11 (3): 375–91.

———. 1992. *Empty Meeting Grounds: The Tourist Papers*. New York: Routledge.

Machado da Silva, Luiz Antonio, ed. 2008. *Vida sob cerco: violência e rotina nas favelas do Rio de Janeiro*. Rio de Janeiro: Nova Fronteira.

Machado da Silva, Luiz Antonio, and Márcia Pereira Leite. 2007. "Violência, crime e polícia: o que os favelados dizem quando falam desses temas?" *Sociedade e Estado* 22 (3): 545–91.

Madureira, Luís. 2005. *Cannibal Modernities: Postcoloniality and the Avant-Garde in Caribbean and Brazilian Literature*. Charlottesville: University of Virginia Press.

Manfred, Rolfes. 2010. "Poverty Tourism: Theoretical Reflections and Empirical Findings Regarding an Extraordinary Form of Tourism." *Geojournal* 75: 421–42.

Manning, Paul, and Ann Uplisashvili. 2007. "'Our Beer': Ethnographic Brands in Postsocialist Georgia." *American Anthropologist* 109 (4): 626–41.

Manning, Peter. 1980. "Violence and the Police Role." *Annals of the American Academy of Political and Social Science* 452: 135–44.

———. 2001. "Theorizing Policing: The Drama and Myth of Crime Control in the NYPD." *Theoretical Criminology* 5 (3): 315–44.

Marques, Ângela Cristina Salgueiro, and Simone Maria Rocha. 2010. "Representações fílmicas de uma instituição policial violenta: resquícios da ditadura militar em tropa de elite." *Revista FAMECOS* 17 (2): 49–58. http://revistaseletronicas.pucrs.br/ojs/index.php/revistafamecos/article/viewFile/7542/5407.

Marx, Karl. 1887. *Book One: The Process of Production of Capital.* Vol. 1 of *Capital: Critique of Political Economy.* Translated by Samuel Moore and Edward Aveling. Moscow: Progress Publishers. www.marxists.org/archive/marx/works/download/pdf/Capital-Volume-I.pdf.

Masco, Joseph. 2014. *Theatre of Operations: National Security Effect from the Cold War to the War on Terror.* Durham, NC: Duke University Press.

Mayne, Alan. 1993. *The Imagined Slum: Newspaper Representation in the Three Cities, 1870–1914.* Leicester: Leicester University Press.

McCann, Bryan. 2006. "The Political Evolution of Rio de Janeiro's Favelas: Recent Works." *Latin American Research Review* 41 (3): 149–63.

———. 2014. *Hard Times in the Marvelous City: From Dictatorship to Democracy in the Favelas of Rio de Janeiro.* Durham, NC: Duke University Press.

McClintock, Anne. 1995. *Imperial Leather: Race, Gender, and Sexuality in the Colonial Contest.* New York: Routledge.

Michaels, Julia. 2011. "Rio's Top Cop Talks Public Safety Policy, Favela Pacification Program." *Christian Science Monitor,* October 11. www.csmonitor.com/World/Americas/Latin-America-Monitor/2011/1020/Rio-s-top-cop-talks-public-safety-policy-favela-pacification-program.

Millar, Kathleen. 2014. "The Precarious Present: Wageless Labor and Disrupted Life in Rio de Janeiro, Brazil." *Cultural Anthropology* 29 (1): 32–53.

Misse, Michel. 1997. "As ligações perigosas: mercado informal ilegal, narcotráfico e violência no Rio." *Contemporaneidade e Educação* 1: 93–116.

———. 2006. *Estudos de sociologia do crime e da violência urbana.* Rio de Janeiro: Lumen Juris.

Misse, Michel, and Joana D. Vargas. 2010. "Drug Use and Trafficking in Rio de Janeiro." *Vibrant-Virtual Brazilian Anthropology* 7 (2): 88–108.

Mitchell, Michael, and Charles H. Wood. 1999. "Ironies of Citizenship in Brazil: Skin Color, Police Brutality, and the Change to Democracy in Brazil." *Social Forces* 77 (3): 1001–20.

Mitchell, Sean T. 2013. "Space, Sovereignty, Inequality: Interpreting the Explosion of Brazil's VLS Rocket." *Journal of Latin American and Caribbean Anthropology* 18 (3): 395–412.

"MP vai investigar se Cabral negociou UPP e financiamento da Odebrecht." 2014. *Jornal do Brasil,* January 28. www.jb.com.br/rio/noticias/2014/01/28/mp-vai-investigar-se-cabral-negociou-upp-e-financiamento-da-odebrecht/.

Murtola, Anna-Maria. 2014. "Experience, Commodfication, Biopolitics." *Critical Sociology* 40 (6): 835–54.

Nader, Laura. 1969. "Up the Anthropologist—Perspective Gained from Studying Up." In *Reinventing Anthropology*, edited by Dell Hymes, 284–311. New York: Pantheon.

Nagib, Lucia. 2003. *The New Brazilian Cinema*. London: I. B. Tauris.

Nash, Dennison. 1981. "Tourism as an Anthropological Subject." *Current Anthropology* 22 (5): 461–81.

———. 1989. "Tourism as a Form of Imperialism." In *Hosts and Guests: the Anthropology of Tourism*, edited by Valene L. Smith, 37–53. Philadelphia: Univeristy of Pennsylvania Press.

———. 1996. *Anthropology of Tourism*. New York: Pergamon.

Nash, Dennison, and Valene L. Smith. 1991. "Anthropology and Tourism." *Annals of Tourism Research* 18 (1): 12–25.

Needell, Jeffrey D. 1995. "Identity, Race, Gender, and Modernity in the Origins of Gilberto Freyre's Oeuvre." *American Historical Review* 100 (1): 51–77.

Neri, Marcelo. 2012. *A nova classe média*. Rio de Janeiro: Fundação Getúlio Vargas.

Nordstrom, Carolyn. 2000. "Shadows and Sovereigns." *Theory, Culture & Society* 17 (4): 35–54.

———. 2004. *Shadows of War: Violence, Power, and International Profiteering in the Twenty-First Century*. Berkeley: University of California Press.

———. 2007. *Global Outlaws: Crime, Money, and Power in the Contemporary World*. Berkeley: University of California Press.

Nordstrom, Carolyn, and Antonius C. G. M. Robben. 1995. *Fieldwork under Fire: Contemporary Studies of Violence and Survival*. Berkeley: University of California Press.

Nota de corte/Cutoff Score. 2011. Directed by Bruno Bralfperr. São Paulo: Instituto Criar de TV e Cinema. YouTube.

Notícias de uma guerra particular. 1999. Directed by Kátia Lund and João Moreira Salles. Brazil: VideoFilmes. DVD.

Odede, Kennedy. 2010. "Slumdog Tourism." *New York Times,* August 9.

O'Doughtery, Maureen. 2002. *Consumption Intensified: The Politics of Middle-Class Daily Life in Brazil*. Durham, NC: Duke University Press.

Oliveira, Augusto Cesar Freitas de. 2008. "O filme do ano: observações periféricas sobre *Tropa de Elite*." www.achegas.net 38. www.achegas.net/numero /38/augusto_38.pdf.

Oliveira, Nelson de, and Alberto Mussa. 2007. *Cenas da favela: as melhores histórias da periferia brasileira*. São Paulo: Geração Editorial.

"Operação policial na Rocinha apreende 1 ton de maconha e deixa ao menos três mortos." 2009. *UOL Notícias,* March 25. http://noticias.uol.com.br /cotidiano/2009/03/25/ult5772u3356.jhtm.

O'Reilly, Conor. 2015. "Branding the Brazilian Pacification Model: A Silver Bullet for the Planet of Slums?" In *Colonial Policing and the Transnational Legacy: The Global Dynamics of Policing across the Lusophone Community*, edited by Conor O'Reilly. Aldershot: Ashgate.

Orfeu. 1999. Directed by Carlos Diegues. New York: New Yorker Video, 2002. DVD.

Orfeu Negro/Black Orpheus. 1959. Directed by Marcel Camus. Irvington, NY: Lopert Pictures Corporation. Film.

Perry, Keisha-Khan Y. 2013. *Black Women against the Land Grab: The Fight for Racial Justice in Brazil.* Minneapolis: University of Minnesota Press.

Pacheco, Gabriela. 2011. "Renda da Rocinha é quase 10 vezes menor que a de bairro nobre vizinho." *R7*, November 20. Accessed January 25, 2014. http://noticias.r7.com/rio-de-janeiro/noticias/renda-da-rocinha-e-quase-10-vezes-menor-que-a-de-bairro-nobre-vizinho-20601118.html.

Paes, Eduardo. 2009. "Eduardo Paes fala das operações 'Choque de Ordem.'" *1ª Edição.* RJTV, April 6. http://globotv.globo.com/rede-globo/rjtv-1a-edicao/v/eduardo-paes-fala-das-operacoes-choque-de-ordem/996243/.

Paiva, Anabela, and Sílvia Ramos. 2005. "Mídia e violência: como os jornais retratam a violência e a segurança pública no Brasil." *Boletim Seguranca e Cidadania* 10 (December). www.ucamcesec.com.br/arquivos/publicacoes/boletim10.pdf.

Palombini, Carlos. 2010. "Notes on the Historiography of *Música Soul* and *Funk Carioca*." *Historia Actual Online* 23: 99–106.

Pandolfi, Dulce Chaves, and Mário Grynszpan. 2003. *A favela fala: depoimentos ao CPDOC.* Rio de Janeiro: Fundação Getúlio Vargas.

Parnell, Philip C., and Stephanie C. Kane. 2003. *Crime's Power: Anthropologists and the Ethnography of Crime.* New York: Palgrave Macmillan.

Peck, Jamie. 2010. *Constructions of Neoliberal Reason.* Oxford: Oxford University Press.

Pedrosa, Fernanda. 1990. *A violência que oculta a favela.* Porto Alegre: L&PM Editores.

Pedroso, Rodrigo. 2012. "Nova definição da classe média abrange 54% da população brasileira." *Valor Econômico*, May 29.

Pelton, Robert. 2003. *The World's Most Dangerous Places.* 5th ed. London: Harper.

Penglase, Ben. 2008. "The Bastard Child of the Dictatorship: The Comando Vermelho and the Birth of 'Narco-Culture' in Rio de Janeiro." *Luso-Brazilian Review* 45 (1): 118–45.

———. 2009. "States of Insecurity: Everyday Emergencies, Public Secrets, and Drug Trafficker Power in a Brazilian Favela." *PoLAR: Political and Legal Anthropology Review* 32 (1): 407–23.

———. 2010. "The Owner of the Hill: Masculinity and Drug-Trafficker Power in Rio de Janeiro, Brazil." *Journal of Latin American and Caribbean Anthropology* 15 (2): 317–37.

———. 2014. *Living with Insecurity in a Brazilian Favela: Urban Violence and Daily Life.* New Brunswick, NJ: Rutgers University Press.

Perlman, Janice E. 1975. "Rio's Favelas and the Myth of Marginality." *Politics & Society* 5 (2): 131–60.

———. 1976. *The Myth of Marginality: Urban Poverty and Politics in Rio de Janeiro.* Berkeley: University of California Press.

———. 2009. "Megacity's Violence and Its Consequences in Rio de Janeiro." In *Megacities: The Politics of Urban Exclusion and Violence in the Global South,* edited by Kees Koonings and Dirk Kruijt, 52–68. London: Zed Books.

———. 2010. *Favela: Four Decades of Living on the Edge in Rio de Janeiro.* Oxford: Oxford University Press.

Pinheiro, Paulo. 1991. "Police and Political Crisis: The Case of the Military Police." In *Vigilantism and the State in Modern Latin America: Essays on Extralegal Violence,* edited by Martha Knisely Huggins, 167–89. New York: Praeger.

Pinheiro-Machado, Rosana. 2014. "Etnografia do 'rolezinho.'" *Carta Capital,* January 15. www.cartacapital.com.br/sociedade/etnografia-do-201crolezinho201d-8104.html.

Platt, Damian, and Patrick Neate. 2008. *A cultura é a nossa arma: AfroReggae nas favelas do Rio.* Rio de Janeiro: Civilizacão Brasileira.

Pratt, Mary Louise. 1991. "Arts of the Contact Zone." *Profession* (1991): 33–40.

———. 1992. *Imperial Eyes: Travel Writing and Transculturation.* London: Routledge.

Price, David. 2013. "The Role of Culture in Wars Waged by Robots: Connecting Drones, Anthropology, and Human Terrain System's Prehistory." In *Virtual War and Magical Death,* edited by Neil Whitehead and Sverker Finnström, 46–64. Durham, NC: Duke University Press.

Quase dois irmãos. 2004. Directed by Lúcia Murat. Brazil: Taiga Films. DVD.

400 contra 1. 2010. Directed by Caco Souza. Rio de Janeiro: Globo Films. DVD.

Rafael, Antonio. 1998. *Um abraço para todos os amigos.* Rio de Janeiro: Eduff.

Rameriz, Maria Clemencia. 2010. "Maintaining Democracy in Colombia through Political Exclusion, States of Exception, Counterinsurgency, and Dirty War." In *Violent Democracies in Latin America,* edited by Enrique Desmond Arias and Daniel Goldstein, 84–107. Durham, NC: Duke University Press.

Ramos, Alcida Rita. 1998. *Indigenism: Ethnic Politics in Brazil.* Madison: University of Wisconsin Press.

Ramos, Sílvia. 2009. "Meninos do Rio: jovens, violência armada e polícia nas favelas cariocas." *Boletim Seguranca e Cidadania* 13 (December). www .unicef.org/brazil/pt/BoletimCESeCNo13MeninosdoRio.pdf.

Ramos, Sílvia, and Leonarda Musumeci. 2005. *Elemento suspeito: abordagem policial e discriminação na cidade do Rio de Janeiro.* Rio de Janeiro: Civilização Brasileira.

Ribeiro, João Ubaldo. 1994. *Sergeant Getúlio.* London: Deutsch.

Riches, David, ed. 1986. *The Anthropology of Violence.* Oxford: Blackwell.

Rio. 2011. Directed by Carlos Saldanha. Los Angeles: Twentieth Century Fox Animation. DVD.

Robb Larkins, Erika. 2011. "The Spectacular Favela: Narco-Trafficking, Policing, and the Commodification of Violence in Rio de Janeiro." PhD diss., University of Wisconsin, Madison.

———. 2013. "Performances of Police Legitimacy in Rio's Hyper Favela." *Law & Social Inquiry* 38 (3): 553–75.

Robben, Antonius C. G. M., ed. 2010. *Iraq at a Distance: What Anthropologists Can Teach Us about the War.* Philadelphia: University of Pennsylvania Press.

Rojek, Chris, and John Urry. 1997. *Touring Cultures: Transformations of Travel and Theory.* London: Routledge.

Rolnik, Raquel. 2013. "Olympic City Monopoly: It Would Be Comic If It Weren't So Tragic." Translated by Nate Lawrence. *Rio on Watch,* February 28. http:// rioonwatch.org/?p=7058.

Romero, Simon. 2013. "Despite Convictions, Brazil Corruption Case Drags On." *New York Times,* May 10.

Roth Gordon, Jennifer. 2009. "The Language That Came Down the Hill: Slang, Crime, and Citizenship in Rio de Janeiro." *American Anthropologist* 111 (1): 57–68.

Rousso, Bruno. 2012. "Rocinha: 1 ano após ocupação, homicídios, estupros e roubo a casas sobem até 100%." *R7,* November 13. Accessed February 13, 2014. http://noticias.r7.com/rio-de-janeiro/noticias/rocinha-1-ano-apos-ocupacao-homicidios-estupros-e-roubo-a-casas-sobem-ate-100–20121113. html.

Rozema, Ralph. 2011. "Forced Disappearance in an Era of Globalization: Biopolitics, Shadow Networks, and Imagined Worlds." *American Anthropologist* 113 (4): 582–93.

Sabatini, Christopher. 2010. "The Favelas in Rio de Janeiro: Pacify and Serve." *Huffington Post,* May 18. www.huffingtonpost.com/christopher-sabatini /the-favelas-in-rio-de-jan_b_580750.html.

Said, E. W. 1979. *Orientalism.* New York: Vintage Books.

Sansone, Livio. 2001. "The Localization of Global Funk in Bahia and in Rio." In *Brazilian Popular Music and Globalization,* edited by Charles A. Perrone and Christopher Dunn, 136–60. New York: Routledge.

———. 2003. *Blackness without Ethnicity: Constructing Race in Brazil*. New York: Palgrave Macmillan.

Santos, Boaventura Sousa. 1995. *Toward a New Common Sense: Law, Science and Politics in the Paradigmatic Transition*. New York: Routledge.

Savell, Stephanie. 2014. "The Brazilian Military, Public Security, and Rio de Janeiro's 'Pacification.'" *Anthropoliteia*, July 7. http://anthropoliteia.net /2014/07/07/the-brazilian-military-public-security-and-rio-de-janeiros -pacification/#more-2579.

Scheper-Hughes, Nancy. 1993. *Death without Weeping: The Violence of Everyday Life in Brazil*. Berkeley: University of California Press.

———. 1995a. "The Primacy of the Ethical: Propositions for a Militant Anthropology." *Current Anthropology* 36 (3): 409–40.

———. 1995b. "Who's the Killer? Popular Justice and Human Rights in a South African Squatter Camp." *Social Justice* 22 (3): 143–64.

———. 2000. "Ire in Ireland." *Ethnography* 1 (1): 117–40.

Scheper-Hughes, Nancy, and Phillipe Bourgois, eds. 2004. *Violence in War and Peace*. Malden, MA: Blackwell.

Schmitt, Carl. 1985. *Political Theology: Four Chapters on the Concept of Sovereignty*. Cambridge, MA: MIT Press.

Schneider, Jane C., and Peter T. Schneider. 2003. *Reversible Destiny: Mafia, Anti-Mafia, and the Struggle for Palermo*. Berkeley: University of California Press.

Schultz, Kirsten. 2001. *Tropical Versailles: Empire, Monarchy, and the Portuguese Royal Court in Rio de Janeiro, 1808–1821*. New York: Routledge.

Schwartz, Stuart B. 1986. *Sugar Plantations in the Formation of Brazilian Society: Bahia, 1550–1835*. Cambridge: Cambridge University Press.

Scott, Peter Dale, and Jonathan Marshall. 1991. *Cocaine Politics: Drugs, Armies, and the CIA in Central America*. Berkeley: University of California Press.

Scruggs, Gregory, and Alexandra Lippman. 2012. "From Funkification to Pacification." Norient.com, May 23. http://norient.com/en/academic/rio-funk-2012/.

Seaton, A. V. 1996. "Guided by the Dark: From Thanatopsis to Thanatourism." *International Journal of heritage Studies* 2 (4): 234–44.

Seltzer, Mark. 1998. *Serial Killers: Death and Life in America's Wound Culture*. New York: Routledge.

———. 2007. *True Crime: Observations on Violence and Modernity*. New York: Routledge.

Sheller, Mimi, and John Urry, eds. 2004. *Tourism Mobilities: Places to Play, Places in Play*. London: Routledge.

Sheriff, Robin E. 2001. *Dreaming Equality: Color, Race, and Racism in Urban Brazil*. New Brunswick, NJ: Rutgers University Press.

Siegel, James T. 1998. *A New Criminal Type in Jakarta: Counter-Revolution Today.* Durham, NC: Duke University Press.

Silva, Jailson de Souza e, and Jorge Luiz Barbosa. 2005. *Favela: alegria e dor na cidade.* Rio de Janeiro: Senac Rio.

Skidmore, Thomas E. 1974. *Black into White: Race and Nationality in Brazilian Thought.* New York: Oxford University Press.

———. 1988. *The Politics of Military Rule in Brazil, 1964–85.* New York: Oxford University Press.

———. 1999. *Brazil: Five Centuries of Change.* New York: Oxford University Press.

Sluka, Jeffrey A., ed. 1999. *Death Squad: The Anthropology of State Terror.* Philadelphia: University of Pennsylvania Press.

Smith, Christen. 2013. "Strange Fruit: Brazil, Necropolitics, and the Transnational Resonance of Torture and Death." *Souls: A Critical Journal of Black Politics, Culture, and Society* 15 (3): 177–98.

Smith, Neil. 1996. *The New Urban Frontier: Gentrification and the Revanchist City.* London: Routledge.

Sneed, Paul. 2003. "Machine Gun Voices: Bandits, Favelas, and Utopia in Brazilian Funk." PhD diss., University of Wisconsin, Madison.

Soares, Luiz Eduardo. 1996. *Violência e política no Rio de Janeiro.* Rio de Janeiro: ISER.

———. 2000. *Meu casaco de general: 500 dias no front da Segurança Pública do Rio de Janeiro.* São Paulo: Companhia das Letras.

Soares, Luiz Eduardo, André Batista, and Rodrigo Pimentel. 2006. *Elite da Tropa.* Rio de Janeiro: Objetiva.

———. 2008. *Elite Squad.* Translated by Clifford E. Landers. New York: Weinstein Books.

Staden, Hans, Neil L. Whitehead, and Michael Harbsmeier. 2008. *Hans Staden's True History: An Account of Cannibal Captivity in Brazil.* Durham, NC: Duke University Press.

Stam, Robert. 1997. *Tropical Multiculturalism: A Comparative History of Race in Brazilian Cinema and Culture.* Durham, NC: Duke University Press.

Stone, P. R., and R. Sharpley. 2008. "Consuming Dark Tourism: A Thanatological Perspective." *Annals of Tourism Research* 35 (2): 572–95.

Strathern, Andrew, Pamela J. Stewart, and Neil L. Whitehead. 2006. *Terror and Violence: Imagination and the Nonimaginable.* London: Pluto.

Stronza, Amanda. 2001. "Anthropology of Tourism: Forging New Ground for Ecotourism and Other Alternatives." *Annual Review of Anthropology* 30: 261–83.

Suttles, Gerald D. 1968. *The Social Order of the Slum: Ethnicity and Territory in the Inner City.* Chicago: University of Chicago Press.

Taussig, Michael T. 1986. *Shamanism, Colonialism, and the Wild Man: A Study in Terror and Healing.* Chicago: University of Chicago Press.

———. 1993. *Mimesis and Alterity: a Particular History of the Senses.* New York: Routledge.

———. 1997. *The Magic of the State.* New York: Routledge.

———. 2003. *Law in a Lawless Land: Diary of a Limpieza in Colombia.* Chicago: University of Chicago Press.

———. 2004. *My Cocaine Museum.* Chicago: University of Chicago Press.

Telles, Edward. 2006. *Race in Another America: The Significance of Skin Color in Brazil.* Princeton: Princeton University Press.

Tilly, Charles. 1985. "War Making and State Making as Organized Crime." In *Bringing the State Back In,* edited by Peter Evans, Dietrich Rueschemeyer, and Theda Skocpol, 169–91. Cambridge: Cambridge University Press.

Tithecott, Richard. 1997. *Of Men and Monsters: Jeffrey Dahmer and the Construction of the Serial Killer.* Madison: University of Wisconsin Press.

Updike, John. 1994. *Brazil.* New York: Knopf.

Urry, John. 1990. *The Tourist Gaze: Leisure and Travel in Contemporary Societies.* 2nd ed. London: Sage.

———. 1996. "Tourism, Culture and Social Inequality." In *The Sociology of Tourism: Theoretical and Empirical Investigations,* edited by Yiorgos Apostolopoulos, Stella Leivadi, and Andrew Yiannakis, 115–33. New York: Routledge.

U.S. Counterinsurgency Field Manual. 2006. Created by the Department of the Army, Washington, DC.

Vaisman, Carolina. 2010. "Sol, mar e organização: a Prefeitura do Rio promove um choque de ordem para acabar com a balbúrdia em que se transformaram as praias cariocas." *Veja,* January 6. http://veja.abril.com.br/060110/sol-mar-organizacao-p-078.shtml.

Valentin, Karen, and Lotte Meinert. 2009. "The Adult North and the Young South: Reflections on the Civilizing Mission of Children's Rights." *Anthropology Today* 25 (3): 23–28.

Valladares, Licia do Prado. 2003. *Pensando as favelas do Rio de Janeiro, 1906–2000: uma bibliografia analítica.* Rio de Janeiro: Relume Dumará.

———. 2008. *A invenção da favela—do mito de origem a favela.com.* Rio de Janeiro: Fundação Getúlio Vargas.

Vargas, João Costa. 2004. "Hyperconsciousness of Race and Its Negation: The Dialectic of White Supremacy in Brazil." *Identities: Global Studies in Culture and Power* 11(4): 443–70.

———. 2006. "When a Favela Dared to Become a Gated Condominium: The Politics of Race and Urban Space in Rio de Janeiro." *Latin American Perspectives* 33 (49): 49–81.

———. 2008. *Never Meant to Survive: Genocide and Utopias in Black Diaspora Communities*. London: Rowman & Littlefield.

Vargas, João Costa, and Jaime Amparo Alves. 2010. "Geographies of Death: An Intersectional Analysis of Police Lethality and the Racialized Regimes of Citizenship in São Paulo. *Ethnic and Racial Studies* 33 (4): 590–610.

Venkatesh, Sudhir Alladi. 2008. *Gang Leader for a Day: A Rogue Sociologist Takes to the Streets*. New York: Penguin Press.

Venkatesh, Sudhir Alladi, and Ronald Kassimir. 2007. *Youth, Globalization, and the Law*. Stanford: Stanford University Press.

Ventura, Zuenir. 2004. *Cidade partida*. São Paulo: Companhia das Letras. Film.

Vianna, Hermano. 1999. *The Mystery of Samba: Popular Music and National Identity in Brazil*. Chapel Hill: University of North Carolina Press.

Villarejo, Amy. 2006. "*Bus 174* and the Living Present." *Cinema Journal* 46 (1): 113–18.

Wacquant, Loïc J. D. 2001. *Os condenados da cidade*. Rio de Janeiro: Revan.

———. 2003. "Toward a Dictatorship over the Poor? Notes on the Penalization of Poverty in Brazil." *Punishment and Society* 5 (2): 197–205.

———. 2008. *Urban Outcasts: A Comparative Sociology of Advanced Marginality*. Cambridge: Polity.

———. 2010. "Class, Race, and Hyperincarceration in Revanchist America." *Daedalus* (Summer): 74–90.

———. 2012. "Three Steps to a Historical Anthropology of Actually Existing Neoliberalism." *Social Anthropology* 20 (1): 66–79.

Wald, Elijah. 2001. *Narcocorrido: un viaje al mundo de la música de las drogas, armas y guerrilleros*. New York: Rayo.

Weiner, Eric. 2008. "Tourism or Voyeurism." *New York Times*, March 9.

West, Harry G., and Todd Sanders. 2003. *Transparency and Conspiracy: Ethnographies of Suspicion in the New World Order*. Durham, NC: Duke University Press.

Whitehead, Neil. 1990. "Carib Ethnic Soldiering in Venezuela, the Guianas, and the Antilles, 1492–1820." *Ethnohistory* 37 (4): 357–85.

———. 2004. *Violence*. Santa Fe, NM: School of American Research Press.

———. 2007. "Violence and the Cultural Order." *Daedalus* (Winter): 40–50.

———. 2009. "Ethnography, Torture and the Human Terrain /Terror Systems." *Fast Capitalism* 5 (2). www.uta.edu/huma/agger/fastcapitalism/5_2 /Whitehead5_2.html.

———. 2011. "The Cannibal War Machine." *Counterpunch*, July 1–3. www .counterpunch.org/2011/07/01/the-cannibal-war-machine/.

Whitehead, Neil, and Sverker Finnström. 2013. *Virtual War and Magical Death: Technologies and Imaginaries for Terror and Killing*. Durham, NC: Duke University Press.

Winant, Howard. 1992. "Rethinking Race in Brazil." *Journal of Latin American Studies* 24 (1): 173–92.

Wisniewski, Kent W. 2009. "Brasilino's Changing World: An Ethnography of a Caboclo Community along the Middle Rio Negro in Barcelos, Amazonas, Brazil." PhD diss., University of Wisconsin.

Young, Malcolm. 1991. *An Inside Job: Policing and Police Culture in Britain.* Oxford: Oxford University Press.

Zaluar, Alba. 1981. *Condomínio do diabo.* Rio de Janeiro: Revan.

———. 2004. *Integração perversa: pobreza e tráfico de drogas.* Rio de Janeiro: Fundação Getúlio Vargas.

Zaluar, Alba, and Marcos Alvito. 1998. *Um século de favela.* Rio de Janeiro: Fundação Getúlio Vargas.

Zaluar, Alba, and Alexandre Ribeiro. 1995. "Drug Trade, Crime, and Policies of Repression in Brazil." *Dialectical Anthropology* 20: 95–108.

Zilly, Berthold. 1998. "A guerra como painel e espetáculo: a história encenada em os sertões." *História, Ciências, Saúde-Manguinhos* 5: 13–37.

Zirin, Dave. 2014. *Brazil's Dance with the Devil: The World Cup, the Olympics, and the Fight for Democracy.* Chicago: Haymarket Books.

Index

Page references in italics indicate illustrations.

structural violence
    poverty, lack of opportunity, racial discrimination

performance
embodiment
mystification
dark tourism / modernity's discontents
commodification
discourses